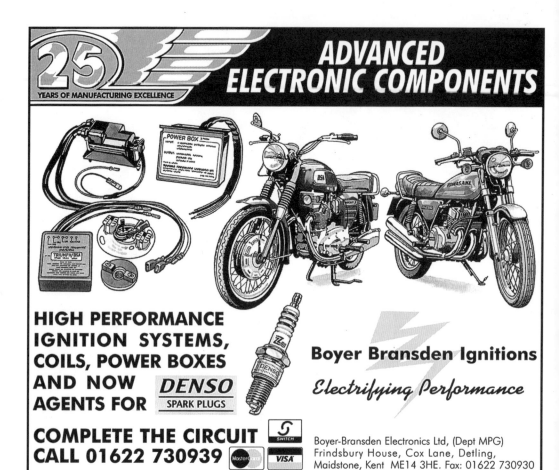

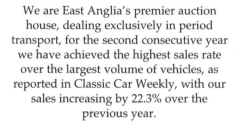

MILLER'S
Classic
Motorcycles
PRICE GUIDE

	DATE DUE	

MILLER'S CLASSIC MOTORCYCLES PRICE GUIDE 1999/2000

Created and designed by
Miller's
The Cellars, High Street,
Tenterden, Kent, TN30 6BN
Tel: 01580 766411

Consultant: Judith Miller

General Editor: Mick Walker

Editorial and Production Co-ordinator: Sue Boyd
Editorial Assistants: Jo Wood, Nancy Charles, Shirley Reeves
Production Assistants: Gillian Charles, Caroline Bugeja
Designer: Kari Reeves
Advert Designer: Simon Cook
Advertising Executive: Jill Jackson
Advertising Assistant: Melinda Williams
Indexer: Hilary Bird

Photographers: Ian Booth, Robin Saker, David Merewether

First published in Great Britain in 1998
by Miller's, a division of Mitchell Beazley,
imprints of Reed Consumer Books Limited
Michelin House, 81 Fulham Road
London SW3 6RB

© 1998 Reed Consumer Books Limited

A CIP catalogue record for this book is
available from the British Library

ISBN 1-84000-058-9

Illustrations and film output by CK Litho, Whitstable, Kent and
Perfect Image, Hurst Green, East Sussex
Colour origination by Pica Colour Separation Overseas Pte Ltd, Singapore
Printed and bound by Toppan Printing Co (HK) Ltd, China

Front cover illustrations:

1969 Triumph Tiger 100T, 490cc. **£2,000–2,500** *CROW*
A Speedway poster, c1932, 30 x 20in (76 x 50.5cm). **£200–250** *LE*
1958 Aprial Square 4 motorcycle with 1996 GP Jubilee sidecar. **£7,000–7,500** *CCR*
1960 Lambretta TV175 Series 2 scooter, 174cc. **£1,000–1,500** *MAY*
A transfer of a 1925–50s Scott motorcycles sign, 1998. **£3–4** *VMCC*
A BSA Dandy brochure, 1957, 10 x 7in (25.5 x 18cm). **£5–7** *DM*
c1937 Benelli Sport, 247cc, overhead camshaft. **£7,500–8,000** *AtMC*

MILLER'S
Classic
Motorcycles
PRICE GUIDE

Consultant
Judith Miller

General Editor
Mick Walker

1999-2000
Volume VI

CHRYSLER CORPORATION Presents... **Auction World Tour**

KRUSE INTERNATIONAL

SEPTEMBER 1998

2-8: AUBURN, IN - 28th year. 5,000 cars expected. "This is the world's largest vintage car auction." Kruse 800-968-4444. Held at Kruse Auction Park.

12: GREATER BOSTON, MA - 21st year. Held at the Topsfield Fairgrounds. Call Kruse 800-968-4444.

19: CHARLOTTE, NC - 21st year. Held at the Charlotte Motor Speedway. Call Kruse 800-968-4444.

25 & 26: DENVER, CO - 26th year. Auction rep: John Soneff (303)296-1688. Kruse 800-968-4444.

OCTOBER 1998

3: NEW ORLEANS, LA - 23rd Annual. Greater New Orleans Collector Car Auction. At Boomtown. Call Kruse 800-968-4444.

17 & 18 MIAMI, FL - Exotic and vintage car show and auction. Held at the Coconut Grove Convention Center. Local rep: Paul R. Alamo & Eddie Del Velle 305-883-7774. Kruse International 800-968-4444.

16, 17 & 18: BRANSON, MO - Collector Cars International presents the Branson Collector Car Auction. 400 cars expected. Celebrating a 15 year tradition of excellence. Call Jim or Kathy Cox at 800-335-3063.

23, 24 & 25: TORONTO, CANADA - RM Classic (905)206-1500

24 & 25: VOLO, IL - 26th year. Auction reps: Bill and Greg Grams (815)385-8408. Kruse 800-968-4444.

30, 31 & NOVEMBER 1: MICHIGAN INTERNATIONAL CLASSIC CAR SHOW - by RM Classic Car Productions (313)459-3311.

30 & 31: ATLANTA, GA - 24th year. Atlanta Collector Car Show and Auction. Gwinnett Civic Center. Call Kruse 800-968-4444.

31 & NOVEMBER 1: LAS VEGAS, NV - 24th year. "The Auction" at the Imperial Palace 3535 North Las Vegas Blvd. Call Don Williams at Black Hawk 925-736-0695. 168 car collection at No Reserve.

NOVEMBER 1998

7 & 8: BIRMINGHAM, ENGLAND - Annual NEC auction & classic car show. 50,000 attend, 400 cars, 1000 vendors. Be part of this event. Andrew Greenwood 011-44-484-660-622. Fax 011-44-484-660-623.

20, 21 & 22: DALLAS, TX - 26th year. Kruse/Leake Collector Car Auction, 400 cars, held indoors at Dallas Market Hall. Largest auction in Texas. Call Kruse 800-968-4444 or Leake 800-722-9942.

DECEMBER 1998

5 & 6: SARASOTA, FL - Cars and Music of Yesteryear's Museum Auction. Consignments accepted. Conducted at the former Bellm's Museum, with Martin Godbey. Kruse 800-968-4444 or 941-355-6500.

JANUARY 1999

8, 9 & 10: FT. LAUDERDALE, FL - 25th year. Local rep: Dave Rupp 561-533-7945. Kruse International 800-968-4444.

14-18: SCOTTSDALE, AZ - 28th year. One of the world's largest collector car auctions, over 1200 cars. Held at Kruse Auction Park West. Kruse 800-968-4444.

FEBRUARY 1999

6 & 7: GREATER FLORIDA GOLD COAST, FL - 18th year. Local rep: Donnie Gould 954-566-2209. Kruse 800-968-4444.

12, 13 & 14: ATLANTIC CITY, NJ - Atlantic City Classic Car Auction, G. Potter King, John Chiara 800-227-3868 or Kruse 800-968-4444.

19 & 20: PERRY, GA - One of the greatest auctions in the south. Held at the GA State Fairgrounds. Call Bill Bonbrake 912-956-2678. Kruse 800-968-4444.

26 & 27: OKLAHOMA CITY, OK - 15th year. Held at the Oklahoma State Fairgrounds, Int'l Trade Cntr. Auction rep: Rocky Santiago (405)843-6117. Kruse International 800-968-4444.

MARCH 1999

12, 13 & 14: TAMPA, FL - Collector car auction at the Tampa State Fairgrounds. Call Kruse International 800-968-4444. Auction rep: Dan Newcombe 813-449 1962.

20 & 21: FT. MYERS, FL - Collector car auction held at the Lee Convention Center. Auction rep: D. E. Foeller 941-643-2675. Call Kruse International 800-968-4444.

27 & 28: HOT SPRINGS, AR - 26th year. Collector car auction. Call Kruse International 800-968-4444.

APRIL 1999

9 & 10: CHARLOTTE, NC - Held at the Charlotte Motor Speedway. Call Kruse 800-968-4444.

10 & 11: LAS VEGAS, NV - 25th year. "The Auction" at the Imperial Palace 3535 North Las Vegas Blvd. Call Don Williams at Black Hawk 925-736-0695.

16 & 17: DENVER, CO - 27th year. Auction rep: John Soneff (030)296-1688. Kruse International 800-968-4444.

MAY 1999

APRIL 30, MAY 1 & 2: VOLO, IL - 27th year. Volo Auto Museum. New auction building and show car asphalt parking. Auction reps: Bill & Greg Grams (815)385-8408 or Kruse International 800-968-4444.

1 & 2: FORTH WORTH, TX - Call Kruse for more information 800-968-4444.

14, 15 & 16: AUBURN, IN - 8th year, Spring Motorfair - 1,000 cars. Held at the Kruse Auction Park in Auburn, In. 50 acres paved, 150,000 plus sq. ft. of storage under roof. Enter your car today. Kruse International 800-968-4444.

29: AUBURN, IN - 6th year. Vintage aircraft auction. Call Niles Walton for more information. 800-968-4444 ext. 247.

JUNE 1999

4, 5 & 6: TULSA, OK - 27th year. Largest indoor auction in the US. Leake Auto Auction. Call 800-722-9942 or Kruse International 800-968-4444.

26: NEW HAMSPHIRE INTERNTIONAL SPEEDWAY - 3rd year. Call Kruse International for details 800-968-4444.

SEPTEMBER 1999

18: CHARLOTTE, NC - 22nd year. Held at the Charlotte Motor Speedway. Call Kruse 800-968-4444.

OVER 250,000 COLLECTORS CARS AUCTIONED BRINGING MORE THAN $2.5 BILLION SINCE 1971
28th YEAR • 50 ANNUAL AUCTIONS

P.O. Box 190, Auburn, IN 46706 • 219-925-5600 • Fax: 219-925-5467
CALL 1-800-968-4444 FOR A FREE COLOR BROCHURE

CONTENTS

ACKNOWLEDGEMENTS

The publishers would like to acknowledge the great assistance given by our consultants:

Malcolm Barber
David Hawkins
81 Westside, London SW4 9AY
Tel: 0171 228 8000

Paul Atterton
Mike Jackson
Sotheby's 34–35 New Bond Street, London SW1A 2AA
Tel: 0171 493 8080

Kevin Jackson
Jackson Race Paints, The Willows, Pyecroft Road, Walpole St Peters, Wisbech, Cambs PE14 7PL Tel: 01945 780463

Steve Hockney
Cooper Mounts Farm, Benenden, Kent Tel: 01580 240481

Brian Verrall
Caffyns Row, High Street, Handcross, Nr Haywards Heath, West Sussex RH17 6BJ Tel: 01444 400678

We would like to extend our thanks to all auction houses, their press offices, and dealers who have assisted us in the production of this book, along with the organisers and press offices of the following events:

The International Classic Bike Show, Stafford
Louis Vuitton Classic

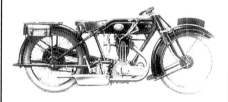

KEY TO ILLUSTRATIONS

*Each illustration and descriptive caption is accompanied by a letter code.
By referring to the following list of Auctioneers (denoted by *), Dealers (•), Clubs and
Museums (§) the source of any item may be immediately determined. Advertisers in
this year's directory are denoted by †.*

*Inclusion in this edition no way constitutes or implies a contract or binding offer on
the part of any of our contributors to supply or sell the goods illustrated, or similar
articles, at the prices stated. If you require a valuation for an item, it is advisable to
check whether the dealer or specialist will carry out this service and if there is a
charge. Please mention Miller's when making an enquiry. Having found a specialist
who will carry out your valuation it is best to send a photograph and description of
the item to the specialist together with a stamped addressed envelope for the reply.
A valuation by telephone is not possible. Most dealers are only too happy to help you
with your enquiry, however, they are very busy people and consideration of the above
points would be welcomed.*

AMOC § AJS & Matchless Owners' Club, Northants Classic Bike Centre, 25 Victoria Street, Irthlingborough, Northants NN9 5RG Tel: 01933 652155

AOM § Ariel Owners' Motor Cycle Club, Swindon Branch, 45 Wheeler Avenue, Swindon, Wiltshire SN2 6HQ

AT • † Andrew Tiernan, Vintage & Classic Motorcycles, Old Railway Station, Station Road, Framlingham, Nr Woodbridge, Suffolk IP13 9EE Tel: 01728 724321

ATF • A. T. Fletcher, (Enthusiast & Collector), Lancashire

AtMC • † Atlantic Motorcycles, 20 Station Road, Twyford, Berkshire RG10 9NT Tel: 0118 9342266

BC • Beaulieu Garage Ltd, Beaulieu, Hampshire S042 7YE Tel: 01590 612999

BKS * † Brooks (Auctioneers), 81 Westside, London SW4 9AY Tel: 0171 228 8000

BLM • † Bill Little Motorcycles, Oak Farm, Braydon, Swindon, Wiltshire SN5 0AG Tel: 01666 860577

BMM § Battlesbridge Motorcycle Museum, Muggeridge Farm, Maltings Road, Battlesbridge, Essex SS11 7RF Tel: 01268 769392/560866

BMW § BMW Club, c/o John Lawes (Vintage Secretary), Bowbury House, Kirk Langley, Ashbourne, Derbyshire DE6 4NJ Tel: 01332 824334

BOC § BSA Owners' Club, Rob Jones, 44 Froxfield Road, West Leigh, Havant, Hampshire PO9 5PW

BRIT * British Car Auctions Ltd, Classic & Historic Automobile Division, Auction Centre, Blackbushe Airport, Blackwater, Camberley, Surrey GU17 9LG Tel: 01252 878555

BTS § British Two Stroke Club, 5 Madden Close, Swanscombe, Kent DA16 0DH

C * Christie, Manson & Woods Ltd, 8 King Street, St James's, London SW1Y 6QT Tel: 0171 839 9060

CBX § CBX Riders Club (United Kingdom), 9 Trem y Mynydd, Abergele, Clwyd LL22 9YY Tel: 01745 827026

CCR • † Charnwood Classic Restorations, 107 Central Road, Hugglescote, Coalville, Leicestershire LE67 2FL

CGC * Cheffins Grain & Comins, 2 Clifton Road, Cambridge, Cambs CB2 4BW Tel: 01223 358721/213343

COEC § Cotton Owners' & Enthusiasts Club, Stan White, 62 Cook Street, Avonmouth, Bristol, Dorset BS11

CotC • † Cotswold Classics, Ullenwood Court, Leckhampton, Nr Cheltenham, Glos GL53 9QS Tel: 01242228622

COYS * Coys of Kensington, 2-4 Queens Gate Mews, London SW7 5QJ Tel: 0171 584 7444

CStC • † Cake Street Classics, Bellview, Cake Street, Laxfield, Nr Woodbridge, Suffolk IP13 8EW Tel: 01986 798504

DIF • Difazio Motorcycles, 25 Catherine Street, Frome, Somerset BA11 1DB Tel: 01373 462913

DM • Don Mitchell & Company, 132 Saffron Road, Wigston, Leicestershire LE18 4UP Tel: 0116 277 7669

DOT § Dot Owners' Club, c/o Chris Black, 115 Lincoln Avenue, Clayton, Newcastle-upon-Tyne, Tyne & Wear ST5 3AR

DSCM § Derbyshire and Staffordshire Classic Motorcycle Club, 51 Westwood Park, Newhall, Swadlincote, Derbyshire DE11 0R5 Tel: 01283 214542

DUC § Ducati Owners' Club, Martin Littlebury, 32 Lawrence Moorings, Sawbridgeworth, Herts CM21 9PE

GB • George Beale Motorcycles, White Heather, New Road, Peggs Green, Coleorton, Leicestershire LE67 8HL Tel: 01530 223611

GODE • Patrick Godet, Rue du Bel
Endroit, 76770 Le Houlme, France
Tel: 00 32 35 75 96 56

IICH * Hobbs & Chambers,
Chapel Walk Saleroom,
Chapel Walk, Cheltenham, Glos
GL50 3DS Tel: 01242 256363

HIST • Hi-Star Classics, 4 Park Lane
Herongate, Brentwood, Essex
CM13 3PJ Tel: 01277 812553

IMC § Indian Motorcycle Club,
c/o John Chatterton
(Membership Secretary),
183 Buxton Road, Newtown,
Disley, Stockport,
Cheshire SK12 3RA
Tel: 01663 747106 (after 6pm)

IMO § Italian Motorcycle Owners' Club,
Membership Secretary,
14 Rufford Close, Barton Seagrave,
Kettering, Northants NN15 6RF
Tel: 01536 726385

IVC • The Italian Vintage Company,
Lincolnshire Tel: 01673 842825

JCa • J. Cards, PO Box 12, Tetbury, Glos
GL8 8WB Tel: 01454 238600

JCZ § Jawa-CZ Owners' Club,
John Blackburn, 39 Bignor Road,
Sheffield, Yorkshire S6 IJD

LDM § London Douglas Motorcycle Club,
c/o Reg Holmes (Membership
Secretary), 48 Standish Avenue,
Stoke Lodge, Patchway, Bristol,
Glos BS12 6AG

LE • Laurence Edscer, The Old House,
The Square, Tisbury, Wiltshire
SP3 6JP Tel: 01747 871200

LEV § LE Velo Club Ltd, Kevin Parsons,
Chapel Mead, Blandford Hill,
Winterbourne, Whitechurch,
Blandford, Dorset DT11 0AB

LF * Lambert & Foster, 77 Commercial
Road, Paddock Wood, Kent
TN12 6DR Tel: 01892 832325

LSC § London Sidecar Club
Tel: 01923 229924

MAY •† Mayfair Motors, PO Box 66,
Lymington, Hampshire SO41 0XE
Tel: 01590 644476

MOC § Maico Owners' Club, c/o Phil
Hingston, 'No Elms', Goosey,
Faringdon, Oxfordshire SN7 8PA
Tel: 01367 710408

MVT § Military Vehicle Trust, 7 Carter
Fold, Mellor, Lancashire BB2 7ER
Tel: 01254 812894

NLM •† North Leicester Motorcycles,
Whitehill Road, Ellistown,
Leicestershire LE67 1EL
Tel: 01530 263381

OxM •† Oxney Motorcycles, Rolvenden,
Cranbrook, Kent TN17 4NP
Tel: 01797 270119

PA * Parkes Auctions Ltd, 2/4 Station
Road, Swavesey, Cambs CB4 5QJ
Tel: 01954 232332

PAN § Panther Owners' Club,
Graham & Julie Dibbins,
Oakdene, 22 Oak Street,
Netherton, West Midlands DY2 9LJ

PC Private Collection

PM •† Pollard's Motorcycles,
The Garage, Clarence Street,
Dinnington, Sheffield,
Yorkshire S25 7NA
Tel: 01909 563310

PS *† Palmer Snell, 65 Cheap Street,
Sherbourne, Dorset DT9 3BA
Tel: 01935 812218

PVE § Preston Vintage Enthusiasts,
Lancashire

REC § Rudge Enthusiasts Club Ltd,
c/o Colin Kirkwood,
41 Rectory Green, Beckenham,
Kent BR3 4HX
Tel: 0181 658 0494

RIM • Racing & Investment Motorcycles,
Warwickshire

RSS § Raleigh Safety Seven and Early
Reliant Owners' Club,
Mike Sleap, 17 Courtland Avenue,
Chingford, London E4 6DU
Tel: 0181 524 6310

S * Sotheby's, 34-35 New Bond Street,
London W1A 2AA
Tel: 0171 293 5000

SKC § Suzuki Kettle Club,
66 Provene Gardens,
Waltham Chase, Southampton,
Hampshire SO32 2LE

SOC § Suzuki Owners' Club,
PO Box 7, Egremont,
Cumbria CA22 2GE

SPU • Spurrier-Smith Antiques,
28, 39, 41 Church Street,
Ashbourne, Derbyshire DE6 1AJ
Tel: 01335 343669/342198

SUN § Sunbeam MCC, 18 Chieveley
Drive, Tunbridge Wells,
Kent TN2 5HQ
Tel: 01892 535671

Vel § Velocette Owners' Club,
Stuart Smith, 18 Hazel Road,
Rubery, Birmingham,
West Midlands B45 9DX

VER •† Verralls (Handcross) Ltd,
Caffyns Row,
High Street, Handcross,
Haywards Heath,
Sussex RH17 6BJ
Tel: 01444 400678

VICO •† Toni Vico, Reg. Tre Rivi 40 12040
Monteu Rodero (CN),
Piedmont, Italy
Tel: 00 39 173 90121

VJMC § Vintage Japanese Motorcycle
Club, PO Box 515, Dartford,
Kent DA1 3RE

VMCC § Vintage Motor Cycle Club,
Allen House,
Wetmore Road,
Burton-on-Trent, Staffordshire
DE14 1TR
Tel: 01283 540557

VMSC § Vintage Motor Scooter Club,
c/o Ian Harrop,
11 Ivanhoe Avenue,
Lowton St Lukes,
Nr Warrington,
Cheshire WA3 2HX

PAINTING YOUR CLASSIC MOTORCYCLE

If your motorcycle needs painting and you decide to do the work yourself, you must make sure that you are technically competent to complete the various tasks successfully. The best advice is that the more time you spend on preparation, the better the finish is likely to be.

Metal Components

Unless the original paintwork is sound, allowing you to paint over it, the first task is to remove the old finish. This is best achieved with Nitromors paint stripper, which can be washed off with water. Although you can use other, cheaper strippers, Nitromors will be more effective and, ultimately, will save you time and money. Whichever stripper you use, read the instructions carefully to ensure that it is compatible with the base metal.

Fibreglass and Plastics

After having been repaired as necessary, fibreglass panels should be rubbed down with 600 grade wet-and-dry paper to key any old paint and ensure a smooth surface. Rigid plastic tanks and panels should also be rubbed down with 600 grade paper.

Original Paintwork and Filler

Sound paintwork should be rubbed down with 600 grade wet-and-dry paper, as should any areas of filler. Always apply filler to bare metal, not old paintwork, as it may shrink.

Once you have stripped and prepared everything, you can proceed as follows:

Undercoat/Primer

An etch primer should be applied to bare metal and some fibreglass, but *not* plastics, followed by one of the following primers: two-pack (acrylic) or cellulose (open). On plastics, use a proprietary plastic primer, obtainable from a specialist paint distributor.
All the above should be rubbed down with 600 or 800 grade wet-and-dry paper before application of the top coat.

Top coat

There are several types of top coat: two-pack (polyester base coat metallic), two-pack (direct gloss) and cellulose (direct gloss). Remember, all metallics require a clear lacquer top coat. A non-metallic finish will be easier to apply, but will be more prone to fading than a metallic.

In many cases, coachlines and decals will need applying to complete the finish.

Health Warning

When working with paint materials, always follow the manufacturer's instructions. Also, good ventilation and the correct working temperature are vital, both for your health and for the quality of the finish.

Kevin Jackson – Jackson Race Paints

HOW TO USE THIS BOOK

It is our aim to make this Guide easy to use. Motorcycle marques are listed alphabetically and then chronologically. Autocycles, Dirt Bikes, Military Motorcycles, Monkey Bikes, Mopeds, Racing Bikes, Scooters, Sidecars and Specials are located after the marques, towards the end of the book. In the Memorabilia section objects are grouped by type. If you cannot find what you are looking for please consult the index which starts on page 174.

DOUGLAS 37

DOUGLAS (British 1906–57)

The Bristol-based Douglas Foundry took up motorcycle production in 1907 with a machine powered by a horizontally-opposed twin, and the company would keep faith with this engine layout until it ceased motorcycle production in 1957. Fore-and-aft installation made for a slim machine with a low centre of gravity, and the design's virtues were soon demonstrated in competition, Douglas machines taking first, second and fourth places in the 1912 Junior TT in the Isle of Man. Douglas were quick to realise the advantages of the countershaft gearbox, its 3-speed entries gaining the Team Prize in the 1914 Six Days Trial, a conspicuous success which resulted in the firm obtaining a wartime contract for the supply of military machines.

1914 Douglas 2¾hp, 348cc, fore-and-aft horizontally opposed twin cylinder engine, belt final drive.
£5,500–6,000 *BLM*

1912 Douglas Flat Twin 2¾hp, 348cc.
£6,500–7,000 *BKS*

r. **1919 Douglas 2¾hp Model V**, 348cc.
£4,600–5,000 *BKS*

Described in contemporary advertising as 'the business man's ideal mount possessed of that ease of control and turn of speed which is the making of a perfect touring machine'. The Douglas 2¾hp had, of course, been well proven in military service in WWI, its 348cc engine proving durable in adverse conditions and in the hands of novice riders.

Miller's Motorcycle Milestones

Douglas Model 2¾hp (*British 1913*)
Value £5,000–6,000
In 1906, 27-year-old William Douglas purchased the design of a flat-twin engine from the Fairey company. While Fairey ceased motorcycle production within the following two years, Douglas went on to become one of the top British manufacturers.

In the first part of the 20th century, horizontally-opposed engines were used by more than 50 motorcycle companies, including ABC, BMW, Puch and Zündapp. Douglas employed a longitudinal arrangement for his twin-cylinder powerplant. With the cylinders running fore-and-aft, it offered the advantages of being narrow (for excellent ground clearance) and of having a low centre of gravity. Soon, Douglas

began exploiting these virtues in competition, W. H. Bashall and E. Kickham coming first and second in the 1912 Junior (350cc) TT.

The 2¾hp model employed the same layout as Douglas's earlier design and the racing models. With a capacity of 348cc, the engine had a compression ratio of 4:1 and a maximum speed of 3,600rpm. This resulted in a power output of 6.5bhp, which was transmitted through a chain to a two- or three-speed gearbox of the company's own creation, then by belt to the rear wheel. A feature of all these early Douglas machines was the massive 'bacon slicer' external flywheel on the nearside of the machine.

Post-war, the 348cc Douglas engine was used by Freddie Dixon to gain his epic victory in the first ever sidecar TT in 1923.

r. **1957 Douglas Dragonfly**, 348cc.
£2,600–3,000 *BKS*

The Dragonfly arrived in 1955 and featured a revised engine with stronger crank case, single carburettor, and updated electrics and ignition. The duplex frame employed a conventional swinging arm with Girling dampers in place of the preceding torsion bar arrangement, while the Radiadraulic front fork gave way to an Earles-type leading link set-up.

Marque Introduction
provides an overview of the marque including factory changes and in some instances the history of a particular model. Introductions change from year to year and not every section will begin with an introduction.

Caption
provides a brief description of the motorcycle or item, and could include comments on its history, mileage, any restoration work carried out and current condition.

Source Code
refers to the 'Key to Illustrations' on page 7 which lists the details of where the item was photographed, and whether it is from a dealer, club or auction house. Advertisers are also indicated on this page.

Price Guide
these are worked out by a team of trade and auction house experts, and are based on actual prices realised. Remember that Miller's is a PRICE GUIDE not a PRICE LIST and prices are affected by many variables such as location, condition, desirability and so on. Don't forget that if you are selling it is quite likely you will be offered less than the price range. Price ranges for items sold at auction include the buyer's premium.

Italicised Footnote
covers relevant additional information about a motorcycle's restoration and/or racing history, designer, racing drivers and special events in which it may have participated.

Miller's Motorcycle Milestones
– a new special feature this year – highlights important historic motorcycle events and the effect they have had on the motorcycle industry.

FOREWORD

I am pleased to have been asked to provide the foreword for the sixth edition of *Miller's Classic Motorcycles Price Guide*.

I started as an apprentice mechanic in my father's garage in the mid-1950s and observed machines being used as daily transport which now command such interest among preservationists. The interest they generate today would have been difficult to foresee then. One of the earliest career memories I have of a road-going bike is winning the Thruxton 500 mile race in 1958 with Mike Hailwood, on a well-prepared Triumph T110.

Having moved after quite a successful road-racing career into the traction engine world for several years, I have rejoined the competition side of motorcycling this year as a sponsor at classic motorcycle races with a 350cc Manx Norton.

In other areas of preservation with which I am involved there are no written guidelines as to prices for sales and purchases of vehicles. With the increase in popularity of motorcycle restoration, the availability of a comprehensive reference work of detailed illustrations and price ranges is a bonus for all motorcycle enthusiasts. *Miller's Classic Motorcycles Price Guide* can help to avoid the pitfalls of over-priced and non-authentic machinery in today's marketplace.

Browsing through this guide makes me realise how fortunate I am to have owned and raced some of the fine examples shown, such as Triumphs, Nortons, Velocettes, Rudges etc. They are still as popular with today's motorcycling fraternity as they were in their heyday.

Dan Shorey.

THE MOTORCYCLE MARKET

Traditionally, the motorcycle auction held at the International Classic Bike Show at Stafford in April is considered to be the barometer of the classic bike market for the coming year, not only in Europe – where the show is probably the largest and most important – but internationally as well. This is still the case and, with Brooks, Palmer Snell and Sotheby's virtually the only auctioneers now selling motorcycles on a regular basis, there are few, if any, other areas in which reliable market trends can be gauged.

Over the years it has been apparent that the motorcycle market is less susceptible to fluctuations in worldwide market conditions than other areas of the classic vehicle field. During the past twelve months, the strong pound sterling (encouraged by high interest rates in the UK) has had an adverse affect on car values at auction and overseas buyers have been conspicuously fewer than in previous years. The latter situation also prevailed at the Brooks auction at Stafford, but did not prevent the sale from being a resounding success, with a record total value of £655,600 (the largest motorcycle sale ever held in Europe) and the greatest volume of machines on offer with nearly 700 lots.

As in previous years, the quality of the entry largely dictated the level of interest in any sale, whoever the auctioneer and wherever the venue, and in this respect the well-proven areas of interest are the same now as they have been in the past.

Single owner collections, particularly in those cases where the owner has or had a high profile and where a deceased estate is involved, continue to a attract attention because buyers know that the machines were previously unbuyable and the sale presents the only opportunity for them to own them before they disappear into another collection.

At Stafford, for example, a 1914 Pello and a 1903 Minerva brought £4,715 and £3,910 respectively, whilst a 1925 Norton Model 18 brought £10,135. Another deceased estate, where the owner had been a well-known VMCC member produced £6,037 for a 1912 Bradbury and £6,900 for a partly-restored Norton ES2 of 1928 (three times the pre-sale estimate). Certainly 'flat tanker' early machines – particularly four-stroke types – are doing better now and this reflects a strong home market in traditional British bikes, particularly pre-war ones.

Competition machines with a known provenance and with direct connections with well-known sporting figures, have always commanded high prices, the exception being the more recent and very expensive Japanese racing machines with which the average collector can neither identify nor, indeed, afford. A 1928 Sunbeam 493cc Works TT90 believed to be one of the team bikes from the 1928 Senior TT which secured the Team Prize that year recorded the highest price of the day at Brooks' Stafford sale at £16,675, whilst a landmark machine in the development of two-stroke racing – a Works 1965 MZ RE 125 Racer – realised a high £15,870. It was indelibly linked to works rider Derek Woodman to whom it had been handed over in 1965 – the year in which he consistently finished in the top six places in major Grand Prix events and other important races. Sotheby's sold a 1956 Norton Manx with competition history in the Slazenger team and with World Championship history for a high £20,700 last November. Coys sold the ex-Mike Hailwood Honda 350cc works racer last November for £169,000 – surely a world record?

Originality continues to be an important factor in determining prices, as does rarity, particularly when this is combined with scarcity. This was demonstrated by a highly original 1917 Harley-Davidson Model F at Stafford, in one owner's hands from 1933 until 1995 when it brought £11,500, whilst what is believed to be the only 1931 Model V Harley-Davidson running in the UK made £12,650. A probably unique 1902 Clarendon in extremely original condition sold for £8,395 at Sotheby's and a rare 1919 Matchless Model H combination sold in the same sale for £7,475.

Particularly desirable competition machines built up in recent years from original parts have also done well, a replica 1931 Douglas 500cc TT machine built up in 1995 selling at Brooks for £11,270 and a Norton JAP 'EWS' 500cc V-twin built by ex-Brooklands rider Frank Williams of Saltdean in the early 1960s bringing £7,935 at Sotheby's last November. Another Norton JAP 'Thor' with racing sidecar from the same source also brought £8,798 at Sotheby's.

Nostalgia can also, however, play a large part in determining why one particular machine will perform better at auction than another similar at a different venue, and the 1955 Vincent Black Knight 998cc sold by Brooks is a prime example. It was sold some 28 years ago by a Mr Richard Lonsdale for £160. A desire to own it once again prompted the same gentleman, bidding on the telephone at Stafford, to re-acquire it for £10,925. There is still a hard core of discerning collectors worldwide. Strong enough to ensure a strong defensive home market in certain sectors, although interest in post-war British singles is not quite as strong as it was.

Generally, sales continue to be dominated by British machines, although Japanese, Continental and American makes appear to be on the increase. With the modern British motor-cycle market experiencing a revival and the Triumph works fully employed, whilst Japan is going through a difficult economic period, trends away from British bikes in the past may well be reversed in the future, but Continental bikes still do well – witness the 1972 MV Agusta 750SS sold by Brooks for £13,225.

I continue to have the greatest confidence in the future of the market.

Malcolm Barber

ABC (British 1913–22)

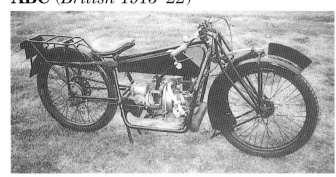

l. **1921 ABC,** 398cc, overhead-valve flat-twin, detachable heads, aluminium pistons, ball-bearing crankshaft, roller-bearing big ends, transverse bevel shaft to chain final drive, fitted semi-TT handlebars.
£2,600–3,000 *BKS*

Manufactured by the Sopwith Aviation & Engineering Co, the ABC motorcycle owed much to aircraft technology and the rapid advances made in that field during WWI.

AERMACCHI (Italian 1950–78)

1962 Aermacchi Ala Verde, 246cc, overhead valves, unit construction, 4-speed gearbox, full-width hubs, Dell'Orto carburettor, concours condition.
£2,000–2,300 *PC*

The American manufacturer Harley Davidson bought a half share in the Aermacchi motorcycle operation in 1960. Thereafter, the majority of production was destined for the USA, where the Ala Verde was sold as the Sprint. This is the European version.

1971 Aermacchi 350TV, 344cc, overhead valves, horizontal single cylinder, 5-speed gearbox, running, requires restoration.
£600–800 *BKS*

The 350TV was one of the final Aermacchi models to be built before Harley-Davidson took over complete control of the Italian Varese factory.

AJS (*British 1909–66*)

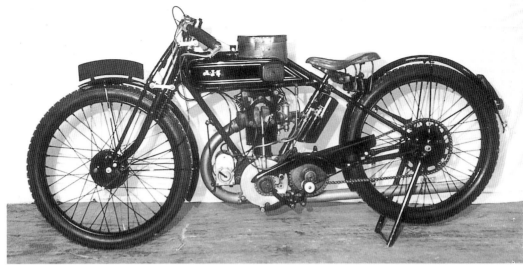

1923 AJS B3 Big Port, 349cc, overhead valves, single cylinder, matching frame/engine numbers, later gearbox, restored, very good condition.
£5,200–5,800 *BKS*

After victory in the 1920 Junior TT, and both Junior and Senior events in 1921, the overhead-valve AJS made its production debut in November 1922, delighting clubmen everywhere with its 'racer on the road' performance. Destined to achieve countless successes in the hands of privateers, the 350 AJS – later known as the 'Big Port' – changed only in detail before being superseded by a much revised model for 1929.

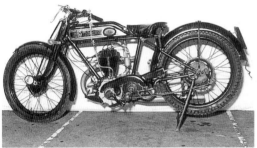

1928 AJS K4, 347cc, sidevalve, single cylinder.
£2,200–2,500 *PS*

This particular machine was one of the last 'flat tank' models to be built.

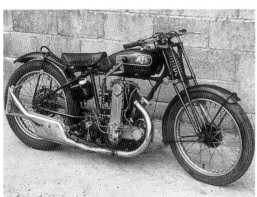

1929 AJS M7, 349cc, overhead camshaft, single cylinder, original, dry-stored, unrestored, requires recommissioning.
£5,200–5,500 *BKS*

AJS revamped their machines for 1929, the traditional 'flat tank' in black with gold lining being replaced by a more rounded saddle tank with magenta panels. New forks with triangulated tubular blades were fitted, but otherwise little changed mechanically.

AJS

One of Britain's 'top ten' marques, AJS's roots go back to 1910 and Wolverhampton, where Albert John Stevens and other members of his family constructed their first motorcycle – a 298cc, 2hp, sidevalve machine. Other singles and V-twins followed, and AJS became one of the first companies to offer overhead-valve models in their catalogue.

Racing was encouraged at Brooklands and elsewhere, and there were frequent factory entries in the TT, together with an attempt on the land-speed record. Eventually, however, financial problems forced the Stevens brothers to sell out to the Collier family in London, who ran Matchless.

AJS survived as a marque in its own right, however, alongside Matchless. Racing continued with the evolution of the R-Series camshaft engine under the auspices of the renamed Associated Motor Cycles (AMC) Limited, who added Sunbeam to the inventory in 1937, although that marque was subsequently sold to BSA.

AMC provided thousands of 350 'Matchie' singles to the War Department, and the same machine formed the basis of the civilian range – in 350 and 500cc versions – under both Matchless and AJS banners. On the competition side, AJS ran full teams in all the major trials and scrambles; Rod Coleman deservedly won the 350 World Championship on a 7R in 1953.

The most charismatic of all 'Ajays' was the 500cc 'Porcupine' twin, of which fewer than 10 works-only examples were made. Top race honours invariably eluded AJS with this fine sounding, but fragile, purpose-built racer. That said, in 1949, Les Graham won the first ever 500cc world title on a Porcupine.

AMC acquired James, Francis-Barnett and Norton during the 1950s, but lost commercial direction and went into receivership, whereupon they were purchased by Manganese Bronze Holdings in 1966. AJS survived this episode as a Villiers-powered, two-stroke scrambler, gaining two British championships before finally fading from the market in 1974.

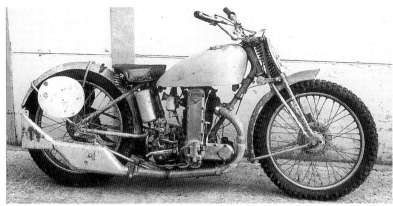

l. **1930 AJS R7,** 346cc, overhead camshaft, single cylinder, 3-speed gearbox, nickel-plated frame, unrestored, sound condition.
£5,000–5,200 *BKS*

Although not listed in the catalogue for 1930, AJS's two overhead-camshaft models, the 346cc R7 and 495cc R10, were available to special order.

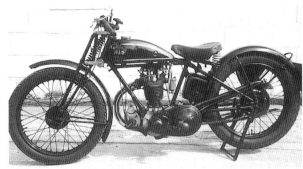

Make the most of Miller's
Condition is absolutely vital when assessing the value of a Classic Motorcycle. Top class bikes on the whole appreciate much more than less perfect examples. However a rare, desirable machine may command a high price even when in need of restoration.

l. **1931 AJS Big Port,** 349cc.
£2,850–3,250 *AT*

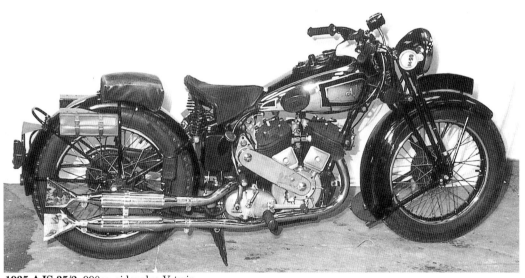

1935 AJS 35/2, 990cc, sidevalve V-twin.
£4,800–5,200 *BKS*

The early 1930s saw the ownership of AJS pass from the Stevens family in Wolverhampton to the Collier brothers, manufacturers of the Matchless motorcycle, in Plumstead. The company continued to offer a range of machines, from a 250cc overhead-valve sports model to the de luxe, 990cc, sidevalve, V-twin touring model, which was ideal for sidecar work. Road testing a 990cc model of 1933, The Motor Cycle *said: 'It looks comfortable and is comfortable . . . it looks fast and it is fast.'*

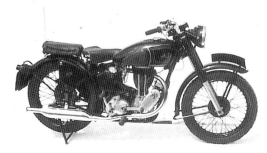

1946 AJS 16M, 348cc, overhead valves, single cylinder, pillion pad, black livery.
£1,600–1,900 *BLM*

1952 AJS 16MS, 348cc, overhead valves, single cylinder, older restoration.
£1,500–1,800 *CotC*

1954 AJS Model 20, 498cc, overhead valves, twin cylinders, foot-change 4-speed gearbox, 'jam pot' rear suspension units, original condition.
£2,200–2,400 *CStC*

1955 AJS Model 18S, 498cc, overhead valves, single cylinder, forward-mounted magneto, 'jam pot' rear suspension units, full-width brakes, concours condition.
£2,800–3,300 *BLM*

1959 AJS Model 18S, 498cc, AMC gearbox, Girling rear units, full-width hubs, improved alloy primary chain case, original specification.
£2,200–2,600 *BLM*

1956 AJS Model 16MS, 348cc, overhead valves, single cylinder, original, sound condition throughout.
£1,300–1,500 *PS*

1960 AJS Model 20, 498cc, completely restored, new seat and mudguards, black livery, concours condition.
£3,000–3,500 *BKS*

The AJS Model 20 was arguably one of the best looking machines of its era, being offered on the home market from 1949 to 1961. It was powered by an efficient twin-cylinder, 498cc, overhead-valve engine, which it shared with the Matchless G9. An increase in compression ratio to 8:1, in 1959, resulted in improved performance.

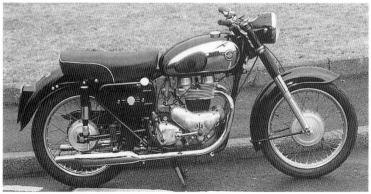

l. **1962 AJS Model 31,** 646cc.
£2,500–2,800 *PM*

The 646cc Model 31 replaced the 593cc Model 30 at the end of 1958.

ALLON (*British 1914–24*)

1919 Allon Two-Stroke, 292cc, Senspray carburettor, Fellows Baby magneto, 2-speed belt drive, completely restored.
£2,000–2,200 *BKS*

The first 292cc Allon, built by Alldays & Onions, appeared in September 1914, but all production was suspended until 1919 upon the outbreak of WWI. The machine was a well designed two-stroke, and was unusual in that one half of the crankcase was cast integral with the cylinder. It had a sloping top tube to accommodate a wedge-shaped petrol tank, which was an advanced design feature for the day. This particular machine was found derelict in a hedge near Glasgow and came into the possession of a member of the Allday family, whose father and grandfather had been involved in producing the original Allon motorcycle.

AMBASSADOR (*British 1947–64*)

l. **1950 Ambassador Popular,** 197cc, Villiers 6E 2-stroke engine, 3-speed gearbox, unrestored.
£550–600 *MAY*

Ambassadors were built in the pleasant outer London suburb of Ascot, the factory being founded by Kaye Don, a former Brooklands racing motorcyclist. The machines were equipped with Villiers two-stroke engines.

1959 Ambassador Popular, 173cc, Villiers 2L engine, requires restoration.
£320–350 *BKS*

ARIEL (*British 1902–70*)

1923 Ariel Sports, 3½hp, sidevalve engine,
3-speed gearbox, enclosed-chain primary drive,
belt drive to rear wheel.
£3,600–4,000 *BKS*

1925 Ariel Sports, completely restored,
one of only 2 known to exist.
£4,000–4,500 *PVE*

*Introduced for 1922, Ariel's Sports Model retained
the firm's familiar 3½hp sidevalve engine with its
widely-spaced valves, but contrived to be 45lb lighter
than its predecessor at 235lb. Although its 8hp
contemporary enjoyed the benefits of expanding
drum brakes, the Sports kept faith with bicycle front
and belt-rim rear stoppers. Essentially veteran in
concept, the 3½hp remained in production until 1925,
when the new Val Page-designed singles took over.*

r. **1933 Ariel 4F/600,** 601cc, overhead
camshaft, 4 cylinders, hand gear-change.
£9,000+ *AtMC*

 # Miller's
Motorcycle Milestones

Ariel Red Hunter 498cc (*British 1932*)
Value £2,000–4,000
The design of the range of Ariel singles was laid
down by Val Page in 1925, when he first joined
the Selly Oak, Birmingham, company. For the
1927 model year, Page moved the magneto
behind the engine, driving it by chain from the
camshaft, and so set a trend that continued for
three decades. The first Ariel Red Hunter
appeared for 1932, under the code VH32. It was
a tuned version of the four-overhead-valve, 498cc
(86.4 x 85mm), vertical-cylinder VG and was set-
off by red tank panels and wheel rim centres. It
also sported a specially tuned engine, racing
carburettor and competition magneto. The 'H' in
the prefix stood for Hunter.
  During the same year, Ariel ran into financial
trouble and was saved by Jack Sangster. The
company was reorganised, resulting in the work-
force, plant and range being slimmed down. Val
Page moved to Triumph and was replaced by
Edward Turner.
  After Turner's reorganisation, the 500 Red
Hunter was joined by a 346cc (72 x 85mm)
version, known as the NH. The one significant

change for 1935 was that the engine dimensions
of the VH 500 became long-stroke (81.8 x
95mm). Also listed were competition versions of
the Red Hunter series, which had single-port
heads, no lighting equipment, sump guards,
special lightweight mudguards and competition
tyres.
  At the end of 1936, the company became Ariel
Motors, and it retained that name for the rest of
its life.
  In many ways, the Red Hunter was to Ariel
what the Gold Star was to BSA. As early as
1933, Len Heath had won the Scottish Six Day
Trial on one of the Selly Oak singles. This was
followed in 1938 by a second famous victory in
the event, Heath being runner-up on another
Red Hunter.
  After WWII, the Red Hunter became one of the
company's best-selling machines. It gained yet
more success in competition as well: not only in
trials, but also in scrambles and road-racing events.
  Perhaps the most famous of all Red Hunters
was Sammy Miller's works 500 trials mount,
GOV 132. He used it to win countless events
right through to the mid-1960s.

Don't Forget!
*If in doubt please refer to
the 'How to Use' section at
the beginning of this book.*

r. **1938 Ariel Red Hunter,** 348cc,
twin-port, overhead-valve, single-
cylinder engine, completely restored.
£3,500–3,800 *AT*

1938 Ariel 4F/600, 599cc, non-original all-black finish, one owner from new.
£3,300–3,600 *BKS*

This particular motorcycle was supplied by Kings of Oxford on 10 November 1938, having been ordered at the Oxford Motor Show. Although the larger 995cc overhead-valve model had been launched in 1937, the 600 continued in production alongside the newcomer for several months.

1942 Ariel W/NG, 346cc, overhead valves, ex-army machine, restored for civilian use.
£1,300–1,700 *PM*

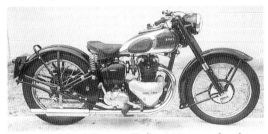

1949 Ariel Red Hunter Twin, 499cc, overhead-valve, parallel twin, iron head and cylinders.
£3,000–3,500 *BLM*

The first Ariel twin was publicised in late 1946, but it was November 1947 before full details were released. Two Models were announced: the KG500 de luxe and the KH Red Hunter. The latter was the more sporting of the two.

1949 Ariel VG, 499cc, overhead valves, single cylinder, 4-speed foot-operated gearbox.
£3,000–3,300 *VER*

The VG had seen few changes since 1945, apart from tele-scopic front forks having replaced the original girder type.

1947 Ariel VB, 598cc, sidevalve, single cylinder, solo or sidecar use, restored, excellent condition.
£2,000–2,300 *CotC*

1952 Ariel 4G Mk1, 995cc, overhead valves, four cylinders, completely restored.
£4,300–4,600 *AT*

Built from 1949 until 1953, the MkI 4G had twin exhaust pipes rather than the four pipes fitted to later models.

r. **1954 Ariel VH Red Hunter,** 499cc, overhead valves, single cylinder, 26bhp at 6,000rpm.
£2,500–3,000 *BLM*

Swinging-arm rear suspension appeared on the VH model for the first time in 1954.

1953 Ariel VH, 499cc, overhead valves, single cylinder, telescopic front forks, plunger rear suspension.
£1,900–2,200 *AT*

1954 Ariel Fieldmaster, overhead valves, parallel twin cylinders, restored.
£2,000–2,500 *AOM*

The Fieldmaster and its 650 Huntmaster brother were introduced in 1954, being based on a new duplex frame. The larger model featured a BSA A10-derived engine.

1955 Ariel LH Colt, 198cc, overhead-valves, single cylinder, telescopic front forks, plunger rear suspension, requires restoration.
£300–400 *AT*

The Colt was built from 1954 until 1959, essentially being a copy of the BSA C11G.

1955 Ariel Huntmaster, 646cc, overhead-valves, parallel-twin-cylinder engine, 35bhp at 5,750rpm.
£3,000–3,500 *BLM*

Detail changes, rather than radical alterations, were made to the Huntmaster for 1955; it was the last year of single-sided brakes on this model.

l. **1957 Ariel FH Huntmaster,** 646cc, non-standard paintwork and front mudguard.
£1,250–1,500 *PM*

The final version of the FH Huntmaster was built from 1957 to 1959.

1957 Ariel NH Red Hunter, 346cc, overhead valves, single cylinder, 4-speed gearbox, telescopic front forks, swinging-arm rear suspension, headlamp nacelle, fitted with earlier cylinder head.
£1,700–1,900 *BLM*

1956 Ariel Red Hunter VH, 499cc, overhead valves, single cylinder, aluminium head, telescopic forks, swinging-arm rear suspension.
£2,000–2,500 *AOM*

1958 Ariel VH Red Hunter, 499cc, restored 1995, fitted with rebuilt earlier 'iron' engine, non-standard alloy wheel rims, maroon livery.
£1,300–1,500 *BKS*

Nineteen-fifty-eight was a significant year for the Ariel company. The new Leader twin-cylinder two-stroke was announced in July, and although it was not broadcast at the time, this presaged the end of four-stroke motorcycle production at Selly Oak.

1960 Ariel Arrow, 247cc, twin-cylinder, piston-port, 2-stroke engine, alloy cylinder heads, iron barrels.
£600–800 *BKS*

Shorn of the Leader's bodywork, the Arrow was introduced for the 1960 season; it was discontinued in 1964.

1961 Ariel Super Sports, 247cc, completely restored.
£1,200–1,400 *BKS*

The Super Sports – later known as the Golden Arrow because of its distinctive colour scheme – was introduced by Ariel in 1961 to broaden the appeal of their two-stroke twin. It had a larger carburettor, a higher compression ratio, dropped handlebars and a flyscreen, all of which helped produce a capable sporting model.

BENELLI (*Italian 1911–*)

1974 Benelli 2C, 231cc, iron barrels, Marzocchi 32mm forks, double-sided Grimeca front brake, 'slashed' end cone silencers, original, completely restored, concours condition.
£1,400–1,600 *IMO*

1973 Benelli 650 Tornado, 643cc, overhead valves, unit construction, wet-sump lubrication, 5-speed gearbox, non-standard seat, requires restoration.
£550–600 *OxM*

The Benelli 650 Tornado is the Italian equivalent of the Triumph Bonneville and Yamaha XS650.

r. **1980 Benelli 654 Turismo,** 603.94cc, chain-driven, single overhead camshaft, 4 Dell'Orto carburettors, 5-speed gearbox, cast alloy wheels, triple Brembo disc brakes, good condition.
£1,400–1,600 *IVC*

The 654 Turismo and Sport were not really 650s, rather 600s. They were built during the De Tomaso era as Italian alternatives to the Honda four-cylinder models.

1984 Benelli 304, 231cc, single overhead camshaft, 4 cylinders.
£1,200–1,400 *IVC*

Essentially a revamped 254, the 304 was launched in 1983, but did not capture the unique style of the original. There was also a 125 twin with similar styling.

r. **1985 Benelli 900 Sei,** 905.9cc, only 600km since new, excellent condition.
£4,400–4,800 *BKS*

Introduced in 1980 as a replacement for Benelli's 750cc six, the 900 Sei featured a considerably revised engine and restyled cycle parts. The increase in capacity was achieved by enlarging the bore to 60mm, and increasing the stroke to 53.4mm, producing a displacement of 905.9cc. Power output was 80bhp at 8,400rpm.

BIANCHI (*Italian 1897–1967*)

1958 Bianchi 125T, 124cc, single-cylinder, piston-port, 2-stroke engine, unit construction, alloy head, iron cylinder, 4-speed gearbox, requires restoration.
£400–450 *MAY*

l. **1959 Bianchi Tonale,** 174.73cc, chain-driven, single overhead camshaft, unit construction, 4-speed gearbox, full-width hubs, telescopic front forks, swinging-arm rear suspension.
£550–650 *BKS*

Arguably the best known of Bianchi's post-war products, the Tonale was powered by an overhead-camshaft, 175cc engine. Initially, two forms were available: the standard touring version and a 14.5bhp sports model, which was intended to compete in the increasingly popular production races, such as the Giro d'Italia. In this form, the machine was equipped with Ace-bars, a flyscreen and racing seat.

BMW (*German 1923–*)

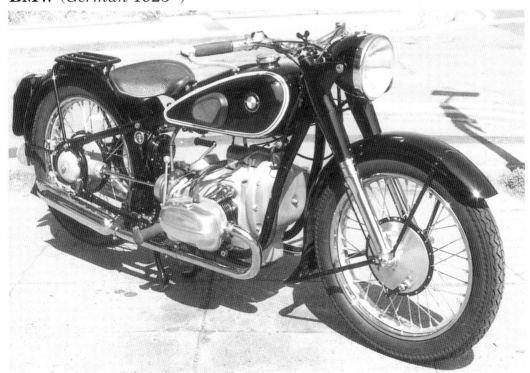

c1937 BMW R5, 494cc, overhead-valve, flat-twin engine, 24bhp at 5,800rpm, concours condition.
£8,000+ *AtMC*

The R5 was built in 1936 and 1937, with a total of 2,652 machines being produced. Most British journalists of the era rated it as a near perfect motorcycle, with a quality of ride, reliability, quietness and oil-tightness unknown on contemporary British machines. It was truly a 'Rolls-Royce' among pre-war bikes.

1952 BMW R25/2, 247cc, overhead valves, single cylinder, original.
£1,000–1,300 CotC

Detail improvements led to the R25 becoming the R25/2 during 1951. The new model could be recognised by the different pinstriping scheme and its bolted-on front mudguard stay, as opposed to a riveted item. A redesigned seat spring, similar to the R51 and R67 twins, was also used.

1962 BMW R50S, 494cc, overhead valves, 35bhp at 7,650rpm, shaft drive, Earles forks, non-standard carrier/top box, otherwise original, requires restoration.
£1,200–1,400 S

The R50S was sold between 1960 and 1962, with a total of 1,634 being produced.

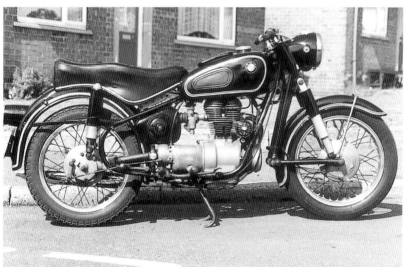

l. **1962 BMW R27,** 247cc, overhead valves, single cylinder, 18bhp at 7,400rpm, fitted with optional Denfeld dual seat.
£1,800–2,000 PM

The R27 was the last of BMW's singles line (until the F650 Funduro of the 1990s). It is difficult to distinguish the R27 from its predecessor, the R26, the major differences being the lack of a top bolt mount on the engine block and attachment bosses welded to the machine's frame on each side of the generator cover.

Miller's
Motorcycle Milestones

BMW R90S 898cc (German 1973–76).
Value £3,000–4,000.
The press called it 'Germany's sexiest superbike', which is an apt description of what is probably BMW's best-loved street bike of the post-war era.

The R90S was launched in a blaze of publicity on 2 October 1973, at the Paris show. This setting was fortunate, as it was there, 50 years before, that BMW had presented its very first motorcycle, the Max Friz-designed R32.

Paris also marked the arrival of the stroke-6 range, of which the R90S was the glamour model, the machine that hurled BMW to the very top in the superbike stakes.

Technically, the R90S used an 898cc (90 x 70.6mm) version of the famous BMW flat-twin engine and, as with all stroke-6 series models, saw a switch from a four-speed to a five-speed gearbox.

Compared to the standard R90, the 'S' variant put out an additional 7bhp (67 instead of 60). Weighing 200kg (441lb) dry, it could top 125mph.

But it was in its styling that the R90S really represented a major milestone in BMW's history. It featured a dual racing-style seat, fairing cowl,

twin hydraulically-operated front disc brakes, and an exquisite airbrushed custom paint job in smoked silver-grey (later also in orange) for the bodywork. The last meant that no two machines were ever absolutely identical. The small fairing not only provided a surprising degree of protection for the rider, but also housed a volt meter and electric clock. For the first time, BMW had employed a stylist for one of its machines, Hans Muth.

During its three-year lifespan (production ended in 1976), there were almost no changes, and the success of the R90S led BMW to build the fully-faired R100RS, which was a bestseller for well over a decade.

The R90S also proved popular at sports production racing events: it gained victories in the Isle of Man TT and at Daytona. America's BMW importers at the time, the New York-based Butler & Smith Co, even went as far as constructing a one-off racer based on the roadster.

Today, the machines that survive are eagerly sought by collectors, as they represent the nearest BMW have come to building a real sports bike.

1976 BMW R90S, 898cc, overhead-valve, 4-stroke, flat-twin, 67bhp at 7,000rpm, concours condition.
£5,000–6,000 *BMW*

1978 BMW R60/7, 599cc, overhead-valve, flat-twin, 40bhp at 6,400rpm, matching BMW panniers and crashbars, good original condition.
£2,500–3,000 *BMW*

Produced between 1976 and 1980, the R60/7 proved an efficient workhorse, with 11,163 examples being built.

r. **1986 BMW R65,** 649cc, overhead-valve, flat-twin, 48bhp at 7,250rpm, panniers, screen, heated handlebar grips.
£1,850–2,000 *LF*

The only difference between the R65 and the R80 of the same era was the former's short-stroke (82 x 61.5mm) engine with smaller valves and carburettors. In all, 8,258 examples were built between 1983 and 1993, when it was discontinued.

1978 BMW R100RS, 980cc, overhead-valve, flat-twin engine, 70bhp at 7,250rpm, twin Bing CV 40mm carburettors, completely reconditioned.
£6,750–7,000 *DIF*

The wind tunnel-developed RS fairing (by Pininfarina) not only provided excellent weather protection, but also allowed a top speed of around 125mph. It was soon copied by many other manufacturers. A total of 33,648 R100RS models were constructed between 1976 and 1984.

1984 BMW R80, 798cc, overhead-valve, flat-twin, 50bhp at 6,500rpm, monolever swinging-arm rear suspension (developed from R80G/S).
£1,500–1,750 *PC*

The wheels and forks from the K-Series appeared on the R80 twin of 1984.

l. **1987 BMW K75,** 740cc, double overhead camshafts, 3 cylinders, fuel injection, 75bhp at 8,500rpm, monolever rear suspension, Brembo brakes.
£2,500–2,700 *PC*

The unfaired K75 was added to the BMW range for 1987. It was finished in black with orange-red seat and pinstriping.

BROUGH-SUPERIOR (*British 1919–39*)

1924 Brough-Superior SS80, 998cc, sidevalve V-twin engine by J. A. Prestwich (JAP), completely original, extremely valuable early example.
£16,000–18,000 *VER*

1933 Brough-Superior 11-50, 1096cc, optional Monarch bottom-link front fork.
£7,250–7,500 *BKS*

Launched in 1933, the 1096cc 11-50 was the largest Brough-Superior to enter series production. Powered by a sidevalve V-twin of unusual 60° configuration, supplied exclusively to the Nottingham factory by J. A. Prestwich, it was conceived as a long-legged, effortless tourer and could exceed 90mph in solo form, or pull a heavy sidecar at up to 75mph. Production continued until 1939, by which time the 11-50 was the only JAP-powered machine in the Brough-Superior range. This particular machine was supplied new to the West Riding Constabulary.

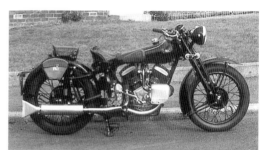

1935 Brough-Superior 11-50, 1096cc, twin carburettors, single float chamber.
£8,000–9,000 *PM*

1935 Brough-Superior 11-50, 1096cc, JAP sidevalve V-twin engine, completely restored 15 years ago, excellent condition.
£8,500–9,500 *CotC*

1939 Brough-Superior 11-50, 1096cc, JAP sidevalve V-twin engine, Norton gearbox, plunger rear suspension.
£7,000–10,000 *BLM*

BSA (*British 1906–7, late 1970s–*)

1912 BSA, 999cc, caliper rear brake, original condition, running order.
£7,500–8,500 *VER*

1924 BSA, 770cc, V-twin, front-mounted magneto, chain final drive, caliper brakes.
£5,000–5,500 *VER*

1926 BSA L26, 349cc, single-cylinder, sidevalve, 4-stroke engine, separate gearbox with hand-change, chain driven.
£3,000–3,500 *BKS*

Originally a munitions manufacturer, BSA began making bicycles in the late 1880s, but it was not until 1910 that the factory built its first motorcycle. Based at Small Heath in Birmingham, the company subsequently became one of the largest producers of motorcycles, exporting their products worldwide.

1929 BSA Model B29 De Luxe, 249cc, 3-speed gearbox with hand-change, saddle tank, non-standard mudguards and rear carrier, magneto internals missing, non-runner, requires restoration.
£900–1,000 *BKS*

1927 BSA 'Round Tank', 2¼hp.
£3,000–3,500 *BKS*

When BSA introduced their famous 'Round Tank' model in 1924, they hit upon a formula that was to endure for many years. Although the details changed, the design premise remained constant – to provide the purchaser with a reliable machine of good quality at reasonable cost as an alternative to public transport.

Don't Forget!
If in doubt please refer to the 'How to Use' section at the beginning of this book.

1930 BSA B30-4, 249cc, overhead valves, twin ports, single cylinder, restored to original specification, very good condition.
£2,000–2,200 *CotC*

1930 BSA Sloper, 493cc, overhead-valve, twin-port, single-cylinder engine, Brooklands cans, chrome tank, pillion pad, completely restored.
£4,000–5,000 *AT*

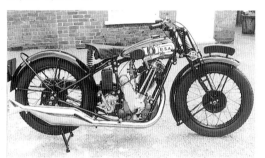

1931 BSA Sloper, 493cc, twin-port, cylinder head, 3-speed gearbox, hand-change, good condition.
£2,200–2,400 *VER*

1934 BSA Sloper, overhead-valve engine, original condition.
£3,500–4,000 *AT*

This particular model was only produced for one year.

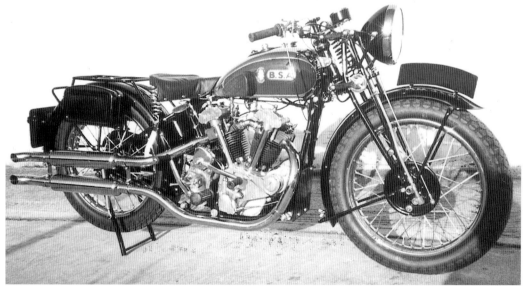

1934 BSA J34-11, 499cc, overhead-valve, V-twin, single carburettor between cylinders, front-mounted mag/dyno, dry sump, restored to show condition.
£10,000–12,000 *AT*

This motorcycle had originally been designed for the War Office, but later it was modified for civilian use.

r. **1936 BSA B1,** 249cc, sidevalve, single cylinder, would benefit from restoration.
£750–1,000 *AT*

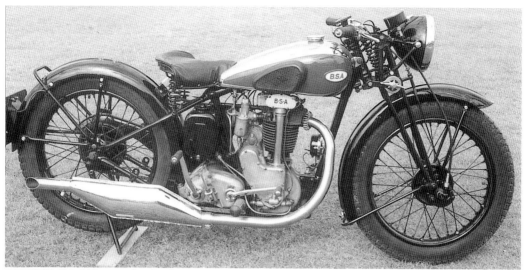

1936 BSA R4, 348cc, overhead-valve, single-port engine, excellent condition.
£3,200–3,750 *AT*

The engine of the R4 was developed by effectively halving a larger V-twin. It was only built for one year and is very rare.

1936 BSA R20 Blue Star, 348cc, overhead valves, twin ports, single cylinder, front-mounted mag/dyno, oil tank cast into front of crankcase, 4-speed foot-change gearbox, high-level exhaust, good original condition.
£2,500–2,800 *CotC*

1937 BSA M23 Empire Star, 496cc, overhead valves, partially restored, requires recommissioning.
£1,800–2,000 *BKS*

The man responsible for engineering the Empire Star series was Val Page, previously with Triumph, and before that, Ariel. The 1937 Empire Star proved an important machine to the future of the BSA competition range, for it was in that year, on 30 June, at Brooklands that a works-prepared 500cc Empire Star appeared on the starting grid, ridden by the great Wal Handley. Running on an alcohol mixture, this machine won the race at just over 102mph and, in the process, completed the fastest lap. At that time, the BMCRC awarded a Gold Star badge to any rider who topped 100mph during their meetings, and as a direct result of Handley's achievement, the first BSA Gold Star appeared in 1938.

1936 BSA B3 Empire Star, 249cc, overhead valves, single cylinder, 4-speed foot-change gearbox.
£1,800–2,000 *PM*

In 1936 many changes were made to BSA machines, while the Empire Star models were introduced to mark the Royal Silver Jubilee of the previous year.

Miller's
Motorcycle Milestones

BSA A7 Twin 495cc (*British 1946*)
Value £2,000–3,000
Almost every British manufacturer was affected by Edward Turner's Triumph Speed Twin, which appeared during the late 1930s. Like others, BSA responded in kind and commissioned its own version. Having finally selected a Val Page design from a number of prototypes constructed during the war years, the company launched its own twin in September 1946. Although it was outlined by Page, the actual task of putting the machine into production was the responsibility of Herbert Perkins.

The BSA twin featured a single camshaft. This was gear-driven and located at the rear of the crankcases, a pushrod tunnel being cast into the cylinder block. It gave the model a distinctive identity, which remained until the marque's final days, even being included on the unit-construction versions that began to appear in 1962.

Although the A7 and its brothers were not the most powerful, or even the best looking, of the British vertical twins, they were the most reliable, oil-tight and smoothest running. BSA's technical squad was quick to appreciate that it was preferable to have the pistons rising and falling together, since this provided a firing stroke for every rotation of the crankshaft. The original 1946 A7 displaced 495cc (62 x 82mm), giving a claimed maximum output of 26bhp at 6,000rpm.

In October 1949, a sports version made its debut at the Earl's Court show, being listed as the A7 Star Twin. With a higher compression ratio and twin carburettors, it had an increased power output of 31bhp (at the same rpm). The original A7 had a rigid frame, the Star Twin plunger rear suspension.

Herbert 'Bert' Hopwood joined BSA in 1949 and was given the task of enlarging the 500 A7's capacity to satisfy the sidecar enthusiast and also the export market. The result was the 646cc (70 x 84mm) A10 Golden Flash, which arrived the following year.

Probably the A7's most famous epic occurred in the 1952 ISDT, when a trio of the Small Heath twins won the coveted Maudes Trophy.

The A7/10 was also copied as the basis for the Meguro (later Kawasaki) 650 twin, which was still being built into the 1970s. One of Japan's very first large-capacity models to be exported, its British origins were proof that BSA had built a machine that was envied around the world.

1938 BSA Y13, 748cc, restored.
£9,500–10,500 *AT*

Produced from 1936 to 1938, the Y13 V-twin featured overhead valves and a foot-operated gearbox. It was developed from the smaller, 499cc J12 model.

1939 BSA M20, 493cc, sidevalve, single-cylinder engine, same ownership 1967–97, recently restored.
£500–600 *BKS*

Introduced prior to WWII, BSA's 493cc sidevalve M20 is now most commonly seen in its wartime military guise. However, the M20 proved popular, both before and after the war, in the civilian market, particularly as a sidecar tug.

l. **1937 BSA B21,** 249cc, overhead valves, hand gear-change, fully restored.
£2,150–2,400 *AT*

The B21 was built from 1937 until 1939. Together with the sidevalve B20 and B22 Empire Star, it shared the same bore and stroke measurements of 63 x 80mm. These machines also had a common, light alloy crankcase, with timing gears on the offside to drive the rear-mounted mag/dyno, and dry-sump lubrication.

l. **1946 BSA M20,** 496cc, sidevalve, single-cylinder engine, foot-change gearbox.
£1,500–1,700 *CotC*

1949 BSA A7, 497cc, overhead-valve, parallel twin, very good original condition.
£2,100–2,600 *CotC*

By 1949, BSA were getting into their post-war stride, introducing a host of new models and improved features for the existing range. Foremost among the latter was the option of plunger rear suspension for the twin and B-Series singles.

1947 BSA A7, 497cc, overhead valve, 360° vertical twin, one-piece iron cylinder block, one-piece iron head, 66 x 72.6mm bore and stroke, rigid frame, telescopic forks, fitted with later dual seat, requires restoration.
£1,500–1,800 *OxM*

1947 BSA B31, 348cc, overhead valves, single cylinder, 4-speed foot-change gearbox, rigid frame, non-standard silencer, requires restoration.
£1,000–1,100 *OxM*

1948 BSA B37, 348cc, overhead valves, single cylinder, rigid frame, first registered 1948, but built in 1947.
£1,300–1,500 *S*

BSA's policy of producing good quality machines at reasonable cost helped ensure their supremacy in the marketplace, and by the 1930s they were able to advertise that 'one in four is a BSA'. The company built some memorable models between the wars, including the 250 sidevalve 'Round Tank', various overhead-valve slopers, the J-Series V-twins and the first of the 'Goldies'. After WWII, BSA retained a share of the market by offering something for everyone, but poor management, a lack of product development and increasing competition from the Far East finally caused the collapse of the famous firm in 1971. Today, however, BSA seem to be in the ascendant again, with the release of a Gold-Star-influenced single and the prospect of a new Bantam.

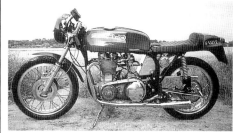

1950 BSA B33, 499cc, overhead valves, twin cylinders, 85 x 88mm bore and stroke, plunger rear suspension, dual seat, requires restoration.
£1,100–1,200 *OxM*

1951 BSA C11G, 249cc, overhead valves, telescopic forks, plunger rear suspension, unrestored condition.
£450–550 *BMM*

1951 BSA D1 Bantam, 123cc, 52 x 58mm bore and stroke.
£550–650 *AT*

In June 1948, one of BSA's biggest ever sales successes was launched. Known as the Bantam, it was a single-cylinder, piston-port, two-stroke and was based on the German DKW RT125.

1953 BSA Star Twin, 497cc, overhead-valve engine, 4-speed gearbox, plunger rear suspension.
£2,000–2,300 *PS*

This particular machine was supplied to the BSA factory rider Fred Rist who, a year earlier, had ridden as a member of the works-supported Maudes Trophy Team on a similar bike, gaining a Gold Medal in the 1952 ISDT.

r. **1954 BSA CB32,** 348cc, overhead-valve, pre-unit, single-cylinder engine, 4-speed, close-ratio RRT2 gearbox, clip-on handlebars, alloy wheel rims, unrestored, partially dismantled.
£2,300–2,500 *BKS*

1954 BSA B31, 348cc, overhead valves, single cylinder, swinging-arm frame.
£1,800–2,000 *BKS*

The B31 was a soft version of BSA's well-loved B-Series, pre-unit, overhead-valve single. It was an excellent workhorse, being a comfortable machine for commuter use and touring.

1954 BSA C10L, 249cc, sidevalve single-cylinder engine, alternator electrics, 3-speed gearbox.
£900–1,000 *PM*

1955 BSA DB34 Gold Star, 499cc, fully restored, converted to DBD specification.
£8,300–9,000 *BKS*

Introduced for the 1955 model season, the DB34 Gold Star essentially established the model's final form, the only major difference between it and the later DBD34 being the replacement of the standard carburettor with a 1½in GP instrument on the DBD. The new model was offered in Clubman, scrambles, trials and touring forms, although the Clubman variant is best remembered.

1955 BSA DB32 Gold Star Clubman, 348cc, Amal TT carburettor, RRT2 gearbox, light alloy fuel tank, aluminium wheel rims.
£5,200–5,600 *BKS*

c1956 BSA CB32 Gold Star, 348cc, US specification, export fuel tank, high handlebars, good condition.
£5,500–6,000 *BLM*

1956 BSA B31, 348cc, overhead valves, single cylinder, completely restored, excellent condition.
£1,500–1,750 *CotC*

For 1956, the B31 retained its 1945-type B-Series engine with few changes, but was given a new frame, tank, seat and wheels. The last came courtesy of the Ariel marque and had 7in diam, light alloy hubs.

1958 BSA A7 Shooting Star, 497cc, original unrestored condition.
£1,600–1,800 *PC*

The A7 Shooting Star and its bigger brother, the A10 Road Rocket, were the sports models of BSA's mid-1950s twins range. The former had a quicker 0–60mph time than the Gold Star, and an unusual metallic Mist Green finish on the tank (chrome panels), mudguards and side covers. It continued in production until the 1961 model year. This particular machine appeared in the TV series The Darling Buds of May.

r. **1959 BSA A10,** 646cc, overhead-valve, parallel twin, older restoration, virtually standard except for rear shock absorbers, very good condition.
£2,000–2,500 *CotC*

1957 BSA D3 Bantam Major, 148cc, piston-port, single-cylinder, 2-stroke, 3-speed gearbox, swinging-arm frame.
£600–650 *PM*

1958 BSA B31, 348cc, overhead valves, single cylinder.
£1,600–1,800 *PS*

New for 1958 were cast iron brake hubs (also used on the twins), a headlamp nacelle and a few other minor changes.

1959 BSA A7, 497cc, overhead valve, parallel pre-unit twin, iron barrels, alloy heads, completely restored, engine rebuilt to A7 Shooting Star specification.
£2,200–2,400 *PS*

1960 BSA DBD34 Gold Star Clubman, 499cc, overhead valves, single cylinder, alloy head and barrel, Amal GP carburettor, RRT2 gearbox, 190mm front brake, concours condition.
£8,000+ *PC*

r. **1961 BSA B40 Star,** 343cc.
£700–1,000 *BLM*

The B40 was introduced for 1961. It was similar to the C15, but there was no separate pushrod tube. It had 18in wheels and a 7in front brake.

1961 BSA A10 Super Rocket,
646cc, overhead-valve, pre-unit twin,
non-standard headlamp, matching
speedometer and tachometer.
£2,000–2,200 *BKS*

*Introduced in 1958, the Super Rocket
replaced the Road Rocket as BSA's
premier twin, offering more performance
thanks to a power output of 43bhp
compared to the latter's 40bhp. This was
achieved by increasing the compression
ratio and refining the engine's breathing.*

r. **1962 BSA C15 Star,** 247cc, overhead
valves, unit construction, single cylinder.
£900–1,100 *BLM*

*The C15 is the most popular of the
smaller BSAs because it is compact, has
a cobby appearance, and is easy use.
Spare parts are also widely available.*

1962 BSA A65, 650cc, overhead valves, twin cylinders, good original condition.
£2,200–2,400 *CotC*

1965 BSA A65 Lighting Café Racer, 654cc, overhead valves, twin cylinders, swept-back pipes, rear-sets, clubmans bars, alloy rims, race-type fuel tank and seat, later twin-leading-shoe front brake.
£2,750–3,250 *BLM*

l. **1965 BSA SS80,** 247cc, restored. **£1,200–1,400** *MAY*

The SS80 was a sports version of the C15 tourer. A major change occurred to all unit singles for 1965, when the points were repositioned in the timing cover. At the same time, the clutch mechanism was changed to rack-and-pinion.

1968 BSA A65 Thunderbolt, 654cc. **£1,500–1,700** *PS*

The single-carburettor Thunderbolt was one of BSA's best unit twins, being much easier to keep in tune than the twin-carburettor variants.

1968 BSA D14 Bantam, 172cc, single-cylinder,
2-stroke, 61.5 x 58mm bore and stroke, 4-speed
gearbox, older restoration, very good condition.
£400–600 *CotC*

*The BSA Bantam was only built in D14 form for
one year.*

1968 BSA D14/4S Bantam Sports,
173cc, fair condition.
£550–650 *BMM*

*The 1968 Bantam Sports, with four-speed gearbox,
was fitted with a larger-diameter exhaust pipe and
had a higher compression ratio than standard.*

Make the most of Miller's

*Condition is absolutely vital when assessing
the value of a Classic Motorcycle. Top class
bikes on the whole appreciate much more
than less perfect examples. However a rare,
desirable machine may command a high
price even when in need of restoration.*

1969 BSA B25, 247cc, overhead valves,
single cylinder.
£700–800 *MAY*

1971 BSA B25T Victor, 247cc, US East Coast
export model, high-level exhaust, alloy tank,
white frame.
£1,500–1,600 *BOC*

l. **1970 BSA Firebird,**
654cc, overhead valves,
unit construction, high-
level exhaust pipe on
nearside, converted to
touring trim.
£3,000–3,500 *PM*

*The Firebird street
scrambler was initially
intended for the
American market.*

CALTHORPE (*British 1911–39*)

c1914 Calthorpe Junior, 249cc, inlet-over-exhaust single, belt final drive.
£4,500–5,000 *AtMC*

1921 Calthorpe, 249cc, JAP engine.
£1,600–1,800 *BKS*

The Calthorpe marque was founded by George Hands, production taking place between 1911 and 1939, during which period the company suffered various financial problems. In the 1920s, the machines were fitted with a variety of proprietary engines, including Villiers, Blackburne and JAP.

1936 Calthorpe Competition, 348cc, overhead valves.
£3,850–4,000 *VER*

In 1936, the Calthorpe 348 and 494cc engines were fitted with new heads and barrels, which provided total enclosure of the valve gear.

CLARENDON (*British 1901–11*)

1902 Clarendon Motorcycle, 2.25hp, restored in the 1970s, history from before WWII, original and largely complete.
£8,500–9,500 *S*

The first Clarendon motorcycle appeared in 1902 and, in addition to their own 3hp engines, the company utilised engines made by Scout, Birch, Hamilton, Whitley and Coronet. Robust design and excellent finish were the hallmarks of the marque. This particular machine is thought to be the only Clarendon to survive.

COTTON (*British 1919–80*)

c1935 Cotton 25J, 500cc, overhead-valve, twin-port JAP engine, high-level dual exhaust system, rigid frame.
£4,500–5,000 *AtMC*

The 25J was one of the more sporting Cottons of its era, and its styling is typical of the Gloucester marque in the 1930s.

r. **1965 Cotton Continental,** 249cc, Villiers 4T, twin-cylinder, 2-stroke engine, 17bhp at 6,000rpm.
£1,500–2,000 *COEC*

CZ (*Czechoslovakian 1932–*)

l. **1965 CZ Trail,** 249cc, piston-port, single-cylinder, 2-stroke, finished in orange and cream, high-level exhaust system, only 1,170 miles from new.
£900–1,000 *BKS*

Although best known in the UK for their economical road bikes, the Czech CZ company were at the forefront of off-road competition during the 1960s, and were among the first to market trail machines, utilising the experience gained in ISDT competition. That competition heritage was reflected in the machines' better than normal build quality when compared to the road models.

r. **1977 CZ Enduro,** 250cc.
£400–500 *PC*

The Enduro was based on the all-conquering CZ motocross machine of the late 1960s and early 1970s. It was also offered with a 175cc engine.

DKW (*German 1919–81*)

1954 DKW RT250S, 244cc, single-cylinder 2-stroke, 70 x 64mm bore and stroke, 4-speed gearbox.
£1,200–1,800   *PC*

The RT250 single came on to the market in 1952. Essentially, it was an enlarged RT200 with a more modern appearance. Later, the model was sold as the RT250VS, denoting Earles-type front forks in place of the original telescopic types shown here.

1951 DKW RT200, 191cc, single-cylinder, piston-port 2-stroke.
£1,000–1,400   *PC*

Based on the very successful RT125, the RT200 of 1951 was basically a larger-engined version of the smaller bike, but with detail improvements to components such as the frame and front forks. The RT125 also gained telescopic front forks from January 1951. The major difference between the RT125 and the RT200 was that the former only had a three-speed gearbox, while the latter had a four-speed.

Miller's Motorcycle Milestones

DKW 122cc RT125 (*German 1939*)
Value £800–1,900
Together with BMW and NSU, DKW were equally responsible for the rapid growth of the German motorcycle industry during the first half of the 20th century.

The story of this great marque really began with the birth, on 30 July 1898, of Jorgen Skafte Rasmussen in Nakskow, Denmark. The young Rasmussen left for Germany in 1904, moving to Zschopau, 20 kilometres south of Chemnitz in Saxony, in 1907.

Rasmussen established DKW (*Das Kleine Wünder*, meaning 'the little miracle') in 1919. The fledgling company's first full year of trading was 1920. A major milestone came in 1921, with the Hugo Ruppe-designed 122cc auxiliary engine. This could be attached to a conventional pedal cycle and used to drive the rear wheel by a belt. By mid-1922, 25,000 of these miniature engines had been sold, the 2-stroke motor gaining an excellent reputation for reliability.

From then on expansion was rapid, the sales of DKW motorcycles powering ahead. By 1928, the company had become the largest motorcycle producer in the world.

In 1929, DKW merged with Audi, Horch and Wanderer to form a new enterprise called Auto Union AG. In 1934, instead of pistons with

deflectors, the Schnürle patented system of inverted scavenging with pistons was first employed by the firm.

By the mid-1930s, DKW was building some of the fastest 250cc racing motorcycles in the world, using supercharged, double-piston twin-cylinder engines. In 1939, the company not only had the largest racing department, with around 150 technicians, but more significantly was set to launch its most famous model, the RT125. This lightweight motorcycle, designed by Hermann Weber, was not only an instant hit with the German army, but also proved ideal for a vast number of other tasks.

The RT125 was powered by a unit-construction, 122.2cc (52 x 58mm), piston-port two-stroke engine fitted with a three-speed gearbox. Not only was it produced in huge numbers during WWII, but it also became the most copied motorcycle of all time. The British BSA Bantam, American Harley-Davidson Hummer, Soviet Moska and even the original Yamaha YA1 (Red Dragon) were all influenced by the DKW design.

Post-war, DKW's Zschopau plant found itself in the Russian sector when Germany was partitioned. It went on to make motorcycles for the Warsaw Pact countries, first under the IFA name, later MZ. DKW itself relocated to Ingolstadt in the west, so the RT125 was built on both sides of the Iron Curtain!

DMW (*British 1945–71*)

l. **1951 DMW Deluxe,** 197cc, Villiers 6E engine, plunger frame, under-seat toolbox.
£1,000–1,500   *DSCM*

DMW stood for Dawson's Motors, Wolverhampton.

DOUGLAS (*British 1906–57*)

1911 Douglas Flat Twin 2¾hp, 348cc.
£5,500–6,500 *VER*

*The original Douglas engine was a fore-and-aft,
horizontally-opposed twin, which was mounted in
little more than an extended pedal cycle frame.*

1914 Douglas Model 2¾hp, 348cc.
£4,000–4,500 *LDM*

The Douglas Lady's Model is now extremely rare.

1916 Douglas WD Two-Speed, 348cc,
horizontally-opposed, air-cooled, twin-cylinder
engine, belt final drive, single rear brake.
£1,800–2,000 *C*

*Douglas motorcycles began to emerge from the
Bristol factory set up by William Douglas in 1907.
By 1912, they had progressed enough to be a force
to be reckoned with in the Isle of Man TT races
and many other competitions. By virtue of its
pioneering engine layout, the Douglas ran more
smoothly than many of its competitors, and
demand for it was brisk. The company soon
became a major British manufacturer, producing
over 12,000 motorcycles before the end of 1914.
Robust, lively and easily maintained, the Douglas
was a logical choice for use by British Army
despatch riders during WWI. The War Office
placed very large orders, and Douglas built over
25,000 machines before the Armistice in 1918. For
several years after the war, there was a strong
market in overhauled ex-WD motorcycles, this
particular machine being one of them.*

  **Miller's
Motorcycle Milestones**

Douglas Model 2¾hp (*British 1913*)
Value £5,000–6,000
The history of the Douglas marque began in
1906, when 27-year-old William Douglas
purchased the design of a flat-twin engine from
the Fairey company. While Fairey ceased
motorcycle production within the following two
years, Douglas went on to become one of the top
British manufacturers.

In the first part of the 20th century,
horizontally-opposed engines were used by
more than 50 motorcycle companies, including
ABC, BMW, Puch and Zündapp. Douglas
employed a longitudinal arrangement for his
twin-cylinder powerplant. With the cylinders
running fore-and-aft, it offered the advantages
of being narrow (for excellent ground clearance)
and of having a low centre of gravity. Soon,
Douglas began exploiting these virtues in
competition, W. H. Bashall and E. Kickham
coming first and second in the 1912 Junior
(350cc) TT.

The 2¾hp model employed the same layout as
Douglas's earlier design and the racing models.
With a capacity of 348cc, the engine had a
compression ratio of 4:1 and a maximum speed
of 3,600rpm. This resulted in a power output of
6.5bhp, which was transmitted through a chain
to a two- or three-speed gearbox of the
company's own creation, then by belt to the rear
wheel. A feature of all these early Douglas
machines was the massive 'bacon slicer' external
flywheel on the nearside of the machine.

The 2¾hp Douglas was equipped with brakes on
both wheels (an advanced feature for the time),
the front operating on the wheel rim, the rear by
means of a pulley. Thanks to its good stability,
light weight (172lb) and a maximum speed of
almost 50mph, the 2¾hp Douglas became one of
Britain's most popular bikes, a trend that
continued in military service during WWI.

Post-war, the 348cc Douglas engine was used
by Freddie Dixon to gain his epic victory in the
first ever sidecar TT in 1923.

r. **1926 Douglas EW,** 348cc.
£5,000–5,500 *BKS*

*During 1925, Freddie Dixon joined Cyril
Pullin and Rex Judd at the Douglas
factory, where they shared a common
interest in racing machines. It was
Pullin who was responsible for the
creation of an entirely new 350cc model,
which was called the EW. This machine
made its debut at the 1925 Olympia
show, creating unprecedented interest.
It was priced very competitively at
£42.10s.0d, and proved to be very
reliable. Before long, it began to be used
in competition, notably in trials.*

l. **1950 Douglas MkV,** 348cc, overhead-valve, horizontally-opposed twin.
£2,500–2,700 *CotC*

Douglas began post-war production in 1947 with, not surprisingly, a flat twin, but unlike the vast majority of previous models, the new T35's engine was mounted across the frame. Even the earliest Douglas flat twins had been of unit construction, but the newcomer displayed even greater innovation, having swinging-arm rear suspension controlled by torsion bars, and a leading-link Radiadraulic front fork assembly. After a series of frame breakages on prototype machines had been cured and further development work carried out to increase engine output, the revised version was dubbed the MkIII. Subsequently, this was replaced by the MkIV in 1949, followed by the MkV for the 1950 season.

1951 Douglas 90 Plus, 348cc, fitted with Feridax dual seat and rear luggage carrier from new.
£5,000–5,300 *BKS*

In 1949, Douglas introduced their new 80 Plus and 90 Plus models, both being 350cc sporting twins. The higher model number signified higher engine performance, the 90 Plus having a compression ratio of 8.25.1 to give 28bhp. The engine was specially prepared at the factory and had heavily-finned cylinder heads and barrels to enhance cooling to cope with the extra power output. The enhanced performance also required improved braking and, accordingly, new 9in brakes were fitted, cooling fins being incorporated in the front hub to dissipate heat. The new machine was finished in a splendid gold livery – retained throughout its production life – and caused great interest.

1957 Douglas Dragonfly, 348cc.
£1,400–1,600 *BKS*

Introduced at the 1954 Motorcycle Show, the Dragonfly recorded a top speed of just over 70mph when tested by The Motor Cycle in 1955. The machine featured an all-welded frame with Earles-type front forks and pivoted-fork rear suspension, which provided fine handling characteristics. Its fixed headlamp and cowling, which blended into the lines of the large 5½ gallon fuel tank, endowed the Dragonfly with a distinctive style.

DUCATI (*Italian 1946–*)

1958 Ducati 175TS, 174cc, bevel-driven overhead camshaft, single cylinder, 62 x 57.8mm bore and stroke, unit construction, 4-speed gearbox, restored to concours condition, fitted with non-standard Ducati clip-ons, tachometer and extended bellmouth for Dell'Orto UBF carburettor.
£2,800–3,000 *PC*

The 175TS is now extremely rare.

1958 Ducati 175 Sport, 174.5cc, bevel-driven overhead camshaft, single cylinder, unit construction, wet-sump lubrication, 14bhp at 8,000rpm, 4-speed gearbox, geared primary drive, restored to original specification, rare tyre pump on nearside front downtube.
£2,700–3,100 *DUC*

The 175 Sport was produced between 1958 and 1961.

r. **1966 Ducati Monza,** 248cc, modified to café racer style, racing tank and seat, alloy wheel rims.
£1,350–1,500 *PS*

1966 Ducati 100 Cadet, 98cc, single-cylinder 2-stroke, fan-cooled, 4-speed foot-change gearbox, telescopic forks, swinging-arm frame, completely restored to concours condition.
£1,100–1,200 *DUC*

l. **1972 Ducati 750GT,** 748cc, 90° V-twin valve-spring engine, 80 x 74.4mm bore and stroke, Canadian import, optional Scarab twin-disc conversion, stainless steel mudguards, leading-axle forks, Conti silencers, concours condition.
£2,800–3,800 *PC*

Making its debut in prototype form in 1970, the 750GT entered production, albeit on a limited basis, in 1971. It was Ducati's first production V-twin.

1973 Ducati 250 Mk 3, 248cc, single overhead camshaft, single cylinder, 5-speed gearbox, Italian import, touring trim, unmodified matching speedometer and tachometer.
£1,600–1,800 *PC*

1973 Ducati 250 Mk 3, 248cc, overhead camshaft, single cylinder, 5-speed gearbox, correct Borrani alloy rims, Silentium silencer and chrome Aprilia headlamp, non-standard Marzocchi rear shock absorbers from an earlier model, missing gold lines on fuel tank.
£2,200–2,400 *DUC*

Miller's
Motorcycle Milestones

Ducati 748cc 750SS (*Italian 1974*)
Value £6,000–10,000
V-twin engines have been around since the very dawn of motorcycling, but have rarely been seen in the L-shaped configuration chosen by Ducati's chief designer, Ing. Fabio Taglioni, when he created the 750GT prototype in 1970. This despite the layout's inherent advantages of smooth running, excellent cooling and a low centre of gravity. In part, this may have been due to the need to accommodate the horizontal cylinder within the frame, which could easily lead to an over-long wheelbase and poor handling.

However, as Moto Guzzi and Aermacchi singles had so ably demonstrated, a horizontal engine was not necessarily a disadvantage, and Taglioni partially solved the problem of length by placing the front cylinder between the two front downtubes of the frame. The result was a package that handled extraordinarily well, and what originally set out to capture the grand touring market quickly became a sportster and racer *par excellence*.

One of the biggest racing upsets of all time occurred at the Imola 200 on 23 April 1972, when Paul Smart and Bruno Spaggiari finished a stunning 1–2, riding specially-prepared Desmo versions of the Ducati 750 V-twin. They defeated the cream of the big league – Honda, Suzuki, Kawasaki, Moto Guzzi, Triumph, BSA and MV Agusta, the last with the great Giacomo Agostini aboard.

Ducati subsequently cashed in by offering replicas of the Imola machines, known as the 750SS (Supersport). Eventually, 450 examples were constructed during 1973–74.

The engines of these machines shared the 747.95cc (80 x 74.4mm) capacity of the 750GT touring model, but embodied a number of improvements to aid performance. In addition to the Desmodromic valve gear, the compression ratio was increased, and there were double-webbed connecting rods for extra strength, special camshafts and 40mm (instead of 32mm) Dell'Orto carburettors.

In SS form, the engine would rev to 8,800rpm and drove through the standard 5-speed gearbox in unit with the engine. Primary drive comprised the usual gears. For riders who wanted even more performance, there was a kit to transform the bike into a full Formula 750 racer.

After the original 750SS came the 900SS (and a new 750SS) in 1975. These, however, were built in far larger numbers, and their engines featured square instead of round outer casings.

1974 Ducati 750SS, 748cc, completely original except for missing 'Desmo' decal on fuel tank.
£9,000+ *PC*

Based on Paul Smart's 1972 Imola 200 race winner, the 750SS is as near to being a pukka racing motorcycle as any road-legal machine can be. To many, it is the definitive Ducati V-twin of the 1970s. It was the first production Ducati V-twin to feature Desmo heads and triple disc brakes, and was only listed in 1973 and 1974. For 1973, the 750SS had leading-axle forks, while the 1974 model had a central axle. Only 450 were built.

1974 Ducati 239, 239cc, single overhead camshaft, single cylinder, 5-speed gearbox, touring trim with conventional handlebars, correct Lafranconi silencer.
£1,900–2,000 *PC*

The engine capacity of this model was created to beat French tax laws. This particular machine was imported to the UK in 1974.

Don't Forget!

If in doubt please refer to the 'How to Use' section at the beginning of this book.

l. **1974 Ducati 750 Sport,** 748cc, overhead-camshaft 90° V-twin, 32mm Dell'Orto carburettors with accelerator pumps.
£4,000–4,200 *BKS*

This particular machine was one of the last 750 Sport models produced. Notable features included central-axle forks (usually with Brembo brake equipment), forward-mounted clip-ons, square black plastic CEV switchgear and polished outer engine covers.

1977 Ducati GTL, chain-driven single overhead camshaft, parallel twin cylinders, 5-speed gearbox, electric starter and kickstarter, wire-spoke wheels with Borrani rims, dual Brembo disc front brakes, drum rear brake, seamed Lafranconi silencers, stainless steel mudguards, original specification.
£1,800–2,000 *BLM*

This particular bike is an American export version of Ducati's parallel twin. It was styled by the automobile stylist Giogetto Giugiaro of Italdesign Studio, Milan, who also penned the similar 'square style' 860GT Ducati of the same era.

1978 Ducati Darmah SD, 864cc, 90° V-twin engine, bevel-driven overhead camshafts, Desmo valve operation, unit construction, wet-sump lubrication, 5-speed gearbox, non-standard paintwork, mechanically sound.
£1,500–1,700 *BKS*

The Darmah – named after a fabled tiger in a well-known children's book – was one of Ducati's most stylish models. It was the work of Italjet owner Leopoldo Tartarini who, since he had ridden around the world on a Ducati 175 in 1958, had long been associated with the Bologna marque.

1979 Ducati 350GTV, 349cc, non-standard silencers and headlamp brackets.
£1,200–1,400 *MAY*

Developed from the 350/500 Sport Desmo parallel twin, the GTV had an uprated valve-spring GTL engine in a Sport Desmo chassis. Alterations included the fitting of a dual seat, conventional handlebars and ND Desmo clocks.

r. **1980 Ducati 900SS,** 864cc, Desmodromic 90° V-twin engine, bevel-driven single overhead camshaft, 40mm Dell'Orto pumper carburettors, 5-speed gearbox, Conti silencers, Goldline Brembo brakes, black and gold finish.
£4,000–4,500 *PC*

1980 Ducati Vento, 340cc, single overhead camshaft, single cylinder, valve-spring head, 76 x 75mm bore and stroke, 29bhp at 8,000rpm, 5-speed gearbox, 12 volt electrics, cast alloy wheels, triple Brembo disc brakes.
£1,500–1,700 *PC*

This particular bike was built under licence in the Spanish (Barcelona) Mototrans factory. It had the same dimensions as Italian Ducati 350 singles.

r. **1980 Ducati Darmah Sport,** 864cc, 90° V-twin engine, bevel-driven camshaft, 5-speed gearbox in unit with engine, non-standard fairing, front mudguard and fork gaiters, Campagnolo wheels, remote-reservoir Marzocchi shock absorbers, Conti silencers.
£2,500–2,900 *PC*

This particular machine is a Mk 2 version with revised seat and non-standard fairing.

1981 Ducati 600SL Pantah, 583cc, Desmo 90° V-twin, belt-driven overhead camshafts, 80 x 58mm bore and stroke, original except for mirrors and black on middle of seat hump, restrictive standard Conti or Silentium 2-into-1-into-2 exhaust replaced by Conti 2-into-1 system.
£2,300–2,600 *IVC*

1983 Ducati 900 Mike Hailwood Replica, 864cc.
£4,500+ *PC*

From 1983, the Ducati 900 series of 90°, bevel-driven, overhead-camshaft V-twins benefited from the introduction of a new three-dog gearbox.

1985 Ducati Mille NCR, 973cc, Desmo V-twin, bevel-driven valve gear, NCR bodywork, optional 2-into-1 exhaust.
£5,000+ *DUC*

The engine of this model was based on the late-1984 864cc unit with round engine casings and hydraulic clutch. However, its capacity was increased to 973cc (88 x 80mm bore and stroke), and it was fitted with plain big-end bearings and a higher-output oil pump.

1985 Ducati Mille Replica, 973cc, Desmo V-twin, 5-speed 3-dog gearbox, hydraulic clutch, plain-bearing big-ends, round outer covers, optional factory 2-into-1 exhaust, concours condition.
£5,800–6,000 *PC*

Very few of the Mille models were built.

1991 Ducati 851 Strada, 851cc, Desmo V-twin, double overhead camshafts, 4 valves per cylinder, 92 x 64mm bore and stroke, Weber/Marelli fuel injection.
£4,000+ *VICO*

Introduced in 1988, the 851 was restyled for 1989. Changes included 17in instead of 16in wheels, red body parts, and white frame and wheels. Then, for the 1990 model year, Ducati introduced the twin-seat version shown here, which was produced until the end of 1992, being superseded by the 888 model.

DUNELT (*British 1919–56*)

l. **1928 Dunelt Flat Tank,** 249cc, single-cylinder 2-stroke engine.
£3,400–3,800 *SPU*

Dunelt motorcycles won the Maudes Trophy in 1929 and 1930, but before that the marque was best known for a range of 2-strokes, headed by the 500cc model with its double-diameter piston. The machines were built in Birmingham, although the firm – Dunford & Elliott – were steel makers in Sheffield, who had entered the motorcycle industry in 1919. From the end of the 1920s, they began to fit Sturmey-Archer four-stroke engines to their machines, among them the 348cc Montlhéry and 495cc Majestic.

l. **1950 AJS Model 16M,** 348cc.
£1,300–1,500 *BKS*

AJS and Matchless motorcycles were among the first machines to become available with pivoted-fork rear suspension, which was introduced on to the home market in 1949. However, there were many riders who preferred a rigid rear end, which resulted in machines thus equipped being offered for road use until 1955.

r. **1936 Ariel 4F/600,** 601cc, concours condition.
£9,000+ *AOM*

The original Ariel Square Four was designed by Edward Turner, and the production model was first shown at Olympia in late 1930. That was a 500, still with overhead camshaft. The 600 debuted two years later.

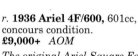

l. **1948 Ariel VH Red Hunter,** 499cc (81.8 x 95mm) long-stroke overhead-valve single, restored to near original condition.
£3,500–4,000 *AOM*

At the end of the war, Ariel immediately began production of their civilian models, which included the famous Red Hunter. At first this had a rigid frame, then plunger and finally swinging-arm rear suspension.

r. **1953 Ariel 4G MkII,** 995cc, overhead valves, 4 cylinders, 4 separate exhaust pipes, 34.5bhp at 5,400rpm, telescopic front forks, plunger rear suspension, fully restored, excellent condition.
£3,500–3,750 *CotC*

The four-pipe Square Four MkII was introduced in 1953 with revised cylinder head and block, plus separate manifolds.

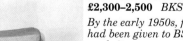

l. **1955 Ariel Model NH,** 346cc.
£2,300–2,500 *BKS*

By the early 1950s, financial control of Ariel had been given to BSA although the factory made its own way without the fact being brought to public attention at the time. There can be no doubt that Ariel produced soundly-engineered and well thoughout single cylinder motorcycles, and of these the 346cc Model NH was the mainstay in the medium-weight range. These machines were powered by a single-cylinder, air-cooled overhead valve engine with a separate gearbox, electric lighting and dual seat as standard.

l. **1956 Ariel Huntmaster,** 646cc, overhead-valve twin, 4-speed foot-change gearbox, standard except siamesed exhaust.
£2,500–3,000 *AOM*

Making its debut in prototype form during 1944, the Ariel twin was the work of Val Page. It was first publicised in 1946 at a Brands Hatch grass meeting.

1958 Ariel 4G MkII, 995cc, 150 miles since full restoration, oil pump replaced with a Morgo unit, Norton cartridge oil filter, excellent condition.
£5,750–6,000 *S*

This late-model MkII would have been produced in the final months of the factory's existence and, partly thanks to its SU carburettor, was arguably the most docile of all the fours from Selly Oak.

r. **1985 Benelli 654 Sport Series II,** 603.94cc, capable of over 120mph, original, excellent condition.
£1,800–2,200 *IVC*

l. **1981 Benelli 254,** 231cc, chain-driven single overhead camshaft, 44 x 38mm bore and stroke, 5-speed gearbox, cast alloy wheels, disc front brake, drum rear, 4-into-2 exhaust, concours condition.
£2,200–2,800 *IMO*

The four-cylinder 250 Benelli roadster appeared in 1976 – the '254' didn't stand for its engine size, but 250cc four-cylinder. This is the MkII version, which made its debut in 1979.

l. **1960s BMW R69S,** 594cc, overhead-valve horizontally-opposed twin, 4-speed foot-change gearbox, shaft final drive, traditional BMW black finish with white pinstriping.
£6,000+ *PC*

This particular machine was constructed from new components during 1996–98 in Germany. Its specification includes Denfeld dual seat, US-version handlebars and a 24 litre Hoske tank. It has virtually zero mileage.

r. **1980 BMW R65,** 649cc, overhead-valve flat-twin, 82 x 61.5mm bore and stroke, 5-speed gearbox, ATF brake callipers, Bing CV carburettors.
£1,650–2,000 *PS*

The ultra-short-stroke 650 R65 supplanted the old R60/7 during 1978. The R65 could reach 105mph and won many friends with its good combination of light weight and reliability in service. There was also a very similar R45 model, but with a single disc front brake.

l. **1939 Brough-Superior SS80,** 990cc.
£5,700–6,500 *BKS*

One of the stalwarts of the Brough range throughout the 1930s, the side-valve SS80 adopted the Matchless V-twin engine in 1935. It utilised this powerplant until production ceased in 1939, when the company turned to precision engineering work for the war effort. This example is not entirely original.

*r.***1929 BSA S29,** 493cc, overhead-valve twin-port single, concours condition.
£3,750–4,250 *VER*

The first BSA single was built in 1910 and founded a tradition of solid, reliable transport that was to last for over 60 years.

l. **1930 BSA Sloper,** 499cc, twin-port single, 3-speed hand-change gearbox.
£3,000–3,250 *PM*

A classic in its day, the famous Sloper model was equally suitable for solo or sidecar use.

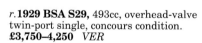

l. **1935 BSA W35 Blue Star,** 499cc,
overhead-valve twin-port single,
85 x 88mm bore and stroke.
£3,500–4,000 *BKS*

*The Blue Star was typical of BSA's
single-cylinder models built during
the mid-1930s with its vertical
cylinder and twin-port head.
Production ran from 1932 until the
end of 1935, when it was replaced
by the Empire Star models.*

r. **1948 BSA B33,** 499cc, overhead-
valve single, 4-speed gearbox, rigid
frame, telescopic front forks,
pillion pad, fully restored.
£2,200–2,400 *AT*

*The B33 and its smaller 348cc
B31 brother were very much the
workhorse models of BSA's post-
war B-Series range of singles.*

l. **1951 BSA B34,** 499cc.
£4,000–4,500 *BLM*

*The first post-war Gold Star was the
B32 ES of 1949, and by 1951 it had
been joined by the larger engined
version. Plunger rear suspension was
standard. The Gold Star soon built
an enviable reputation as not only
a sports roadster, but also a racer,
scrambler and trials mount.*

r. **1952 BSA M21,** 591cc, sidevalve
single-cylinder engine, telescopic forks,
plunger rear suspension.
£1,600–1,800 *BKS*

*By increasing the stroke of the existing
496cc M20 from 94 to 112mm and
retaining the bore of 82mm, BSA were
able to offer a 591cc Model 21 with
ample amounts of engine torque for the
dedicated sidecar enthusiast. The M21
ran from 1946 until 1963, thanks
mainly to its continued use by bodies
such as the RAC and AA.*

l. **1952 BSA ZB32,** 348cc, overhead-valve
single, fully restored.
£4,000–4,500 *PC*

*Much of the Gold Star legend stems from the
type's dominance of the Isle of Man Clubman's
race series during the 1950s. In 1952, the
model was still designated ZB, and this was
the final year of it having a plunger frame.
New for this year was a Bert Hopwood engine
design incorporating a separate rocker box and
modified cylinder head and barrel.*

l. **1952 BSA C10L,** 249cc, sidevalve single-cylinder engine, 63 x 80mm bore and stroke, restored.
£750–950 *BLM*

This machine has cycle parts very similar to the Bantam two-stroke.

r. **1953 BSA D1 Bantam,** 123cc, plunger rear suspension, original, completely rebuilt.
£625–675 *PS*

Developed from the German DKW RT125, the famous Bantam was one of BSA's most popular models.

l. **1953 BSA A7,** 497cc, overhead-valve pre-unit twin, plunger frame.
£1,300–1,500 *PC*

The A7 and Star Twin were revised in line with the larger A10 for 1951, many components being shared. The engine capacity was changed to 497cc, and a plunger frame was offered as an option (standard on the Star Twin).

r. **1956 BSA DB32 Gold Star Clubman,** 348cc, overhead valves, RRT2 gearbox, 190mm front brake, alloy rims, Amal GP carburettor.
£6,000–7,000 *BLM*

The DB32 replaced the CB32 Gold Star for the 1955 model year. It benefited from racing experience in the Isle of Man.

l. **1956 BSA DB34 Gold Star,** 499cc, later chrome Lucas headlamp, no rev-counter, otherwise largely stock, touring trim.
£5,000–5,500 *CStC*

Besides the well-known and highly prized Clubman's models, the Gold Star roadster was also offered in touring trim with conventional handlebars.

BSA Unit Twins

January 1962 was only a few days old when the BSA factory announced its new unit twins to the world's motorcycling press. The newcomers were considerably lighter than the old pre-unit A7/10 series, which they replaced.

The new machines had engine sizes of 499cc (74 x 65.5mm) for the A50 and 654cc (75 x 74mm) for the A65. In other respects, the two models were largely identical, each having a compression ratio of 7.5:1, four-speed gearboxes and full-width brakes. Power outputs of 28.5bhp (A50) and 38bhp (A65) were obtained in a relatively low state of engine tune. Soon more sporting versions appeared, including the Lightning, Spitfire and Thunderbolt. Besides widespread use as motive power for many sidecar racers, the BSA unit twin helped Mike Hailwood achieve a notable victory in the 1965 Silverstone Production race ahead of the entire Triumph works team.

r. **1959 BSA A10 Super Rocket,** 646cc, 70 x 84mm bore and stroke. **£2,800–3,200** *BKS*

First seen in late 1957, the Super Rocket replaced the Road Rocket. Both models were sporting versions of the A10 Golden Flash tourer with a higher state of engine tune.

l. **1960 BSA C15,** 247cc, overhead valves, 67 x 70mm bore and stroke, unit construction, 4-speed gearbox, full-width brake hubs. **£900–1,200** *MAY*

The C15 was launched in September 1958 and became the basis for an entire unit-construction range of single-cylinder machines.

r. **1960 BSA A10 Super Rocket,** 646cc, overhead-valve, pre-unit twin, non-standard pillion grab rail, older restoration, very good condition. **£2,400–2,650** *CotC*

For the 1960 model year, the A-Series pre-unit twins saw a change of clutch design to one using only four springs adjusted by self-locking nuts.

l. **1964 BSA C15,** 247cc. **£800–900** *PS*

This was the last year that points were located in a separate housing at the rear of the cylinder on C-Series singles. Earlier in 1962, BSA had introduced a number of changes on the C15, including a higher-compression piston, a new horn, improved ignition and a 60 watt alternator.

l. **1968 BSA B25 Starfire,** 247cc, overhead valve unit single, twin-leading-shoe front brake.
£600–800 *MAY*

Based on the earlier C25 Barracuda model, the B25 Starfire made its debut for the 1968 model year. Effectively, it was a replacement for the longer-running C15.

r. **1969 BSA Victor Special BV44 VS,** 441cc, overhead-valve unit single, 79 x 90mm bore and stroke, original.
£1,200–1,400 *PC*

Based on an earlier B44 VE (Victor Enduro), this was the new model for the 1969 season, with coil ignition 8in front brake and full lighting equipment.

l. **1971 BSA B25 SS Gold Star,** 247cc.
£1,200–1,500 *BKS*

BSA-Triumph's range for 1971 included five BSA singles, all with the new oil-bearing frame and conical-hub brakes. The two 250s continued to use the B25 engine, virtually unchanged, while the larger B50 models were a full 500cc. In both capacities, there was an SS – Street Scrambler – which featured an 8in front brake and high-level exhaust. The famous Gold Star name was revived for the duo. Despite good performance and excellent handling, the newcomers were swamped by the financial problems that soon overtook BSA-Triumph. The 250s disappeared in August 1971, and the 500s the following year.

r. **1932 Calthorpe Ivory Minor,** 247cc, 2-stroke engine, Villiers top end and crankshaft.
£2,500–3,000 *PC*

This marque appeared before WWI, and by the end of the 1920s was best known for the Ivory models.

l. **1961 Cotton Continental,** 249cc, 50 x 63.5mm bore and stroke, Villiers S33/3 carburettor, 15bhp at 5,500rpm, 4-speed gearbox, completely original condition.
£1,500–2,000 *COEC*

Gloucester-based Cotton entered the 1960s with a range of five models: three for the road and two for competition. All used Villiers two-stroke engines. The Continental twin was new for 1961; production ceased in 1963.

l. **1950 Douglas 90 Plus,**
348cc, overhead-valve flat-twin.
£4,250–4,750 *VER*

The 90 Plus was the sports model in the Douglas catalogue. Examples were raced successfully in the annual Clubman's TT in the Isle of Man during the early 1950s. Today, the Plus 90 is the most collectable, and thus valuable, of all Douglas post-war motorcycles.

r. **1957 Douglas Dragonfly,** 348cc.
£2,000–2,500 *MAY*

This was the last of the famous line of Douglas flat-twins – to many, the British BMW. Unfortunately for Douglas, the Dragonfly was not a sales success, being seen as neither a tourer nor a sports model, and production ceased at the end of 1957.

1960 Ducati 175 Sport, 174cc, single cylinder with bevel-driven single overhead camshaft, original specification including twin Silentium silencers and jelly-mould tank, factory options of alloy rims and Veglia tachometer, concours condition.
£3,500+ *PC*

l. **1975 (built 1974) Ducati 350 Desmo,**
340cc, double-sided drum front brake, Marzocchi forks.
£3,200–3,600 *IVC*

The first of the wide-case singles made their debut in 1968. By 1969, there were three versions: MkIII, Scrambler (SCR) and Desmo. This is the final version of the Desmo series.

1977 Ducati Darmah SD, 864cc, Desmo 90° V-twin, original specification including Campagnolo wheels, seamed Lafranconi silencers, stainless steel mudguards, hydraulic steering damper, ND clocks and instrumentation, fully restored to concours condition.
£2,900+ *PC*

1980 Ducati 500SL Pantah, 498.89cc, overhead-camshaft, Desmo V-twin, 74 x 58mm bore and stroke.
£2,200–2,400 *IVC*

1982 Ducati 500SL Pantah, Desmo 90° V-twin, 2-into-1 exhaust, concours condition.
£2,500+ *IMO*
The paintwork on this Pantah is based on the Mike Hailwood Replica 900.

r. **1979 Ducati 350 GTV,** 349cc, chain-driven overhead camshafts, parallel twin cylinders, 5-speed gearbox, electric start, standard specification, completely restored.
£1,600–1,800 *DUC*

Based on the Sport Desmo parallel twin, the GTV employed conventional valve springs and debuted at the 1977 Milan show. It was offered in both 350 and 500 versions.

1985 Ducati 650SL Pantah Special,
649.56cc, Desmo 90° V-twin,
82 x 61.5mm bore and stroke, GPM body
kit including tank, seat, fairing and front
mudguard, Biturbo rear shock absorbers,
concours condition.
£3,000+ *PC*

r. **1959 Gilera Sport,**
172cc, original specification
including alloy rims and
Silentium silencer.
£950–1,100 *PS*

c1930 FN Twin Port, 500cc, overhead single,
girder forks, rigid frame, concours condition.
£5,000+ *PC*

*FN, based at Herstal near Lüttich, made
motorcycles from 1903. The first model had
a single-cylinder, four-stroke, 250cc engine
mounted in a reinforced cycle frame. From
the 1930s, FN built a range of sturdy single-
cylinder models for the Belgian army and
civilian use.*

l. **1931 Harley-Davidson Model V,**
1206cc, concours condition.
£12,650–14,000 *BKS*

r. **1964 Honda CB92,** 124cc, overhead-camshaft twin, 44 x 41mm bore and stroke, 15bhp at 10,500rpm, 18in wheels, leading-link forks, swinging-arm rear suspension.
£3,000–3,500 *VJMC*

The CB92 and its C92 touring brother arrived in 1959. They introduced a level of sophistication unmatched at the time by any machine of similar capacity made in Europe.

l. **1971 Honda CB750,** 736.5cc, single-overhead-camshaft across-the-frame 4, 61 x 63mm bore and stroke.
£3,250–3,750 *BKS*

Honda did not rest on their laurels following the introduction of the CB750 in 1969 – 1970 saw a revised model K0, which featured an amended throttle control, followed by the K1 in 1971. The latter benefited from further mechanical revisions, notably to the lubrication system, and cosmetic revisions to the petrol tank, side panels and seat.

r. **1977 Kawasaki KH250 B2,** 249.5cc, 45 x 52.3mm bore and stroke, 32bhp at 8,000rpm, 5-speed gearbox.
£700–800 *BKS*

The first of Kawasaki's 250 triples, the S1, appeared in 1971; the last, the KH250 B5, in 1980. The biggest change was from a drum to disc front brake.

l. **1981 Laverda Jota,** 981cc, double-overhead-camshaft triple, non-standard Stuck fairing.
£2,000–2,200 *BKS*

Developed from the 3CL for production racing, the Jota was the fastest machine available at the time of release. Fitted with a free-flow exhaust system, revised cams and minus its airbox, the Jota was the Mr Hyde to the 3CL's Dr Jekyl. To many it epitomised the concept of the superbike. Exceptionally fast and noisy, it required a strong hand if it was to give its best but, ridden as intended, it could leave any other machine then produced in its wake.

l. **1951 Matchless G80,** 497cc, overhead-valve pre-unit single, 82.5 x 93mm bore and stroke. **£2,000–2,500** *BLM*

Matchless and AJS were among the first manufacturers to introduce swinging-arm frames on their production roadsters. In their case, the year was 1949.

r. **1955 Matchless G9,** 498cc, overhead-valve twin. **£3,000–3,500** *BKS*

AMC announced its twin-cylinder models – the AJS model 20 and the Matchless G9 – in late 1948. Both featured a third, central, main bearing between the two crank throws.

l. **1955 Matchless G3LS,** 348cc, overhead valves, single cylinder, front-mounted magneto, restored. **£1,700–1,900** *PC*

Changes for 1955 included brake hubs, headlamp shell, Amal Monobloc carburettor and auto-advance. The famous 'jampot' rear shocks were also modified, together with the front forks.

r. **1958 Matchless G9,** 498cc, overhead valves, twin cylinders, completely restored. **£2,600–3,000** *AT*

The 1958 G9 twin still had the lovely megaphone silencers, but had had its 'jampot' rear shocks replaced by conventional units. For that year, the pilot lights on each side of the headlamp were dropped. There were also an alloy chaincase and modified rear units giving a lower ride height.

r. **c1955 Moto Guzzi Milano/Taranto,** 498.4cc, overhead-valve single.
£10,000–12,000 *AtMC*

This machine was specially built for Italian long-distance events, with alloy rims, SS Dell'Orto racing carburettor, larger tank, etc. The speedo drive was from the front wheel, while the tacho drive was from the timing cover.

l. **1972 Moto Guzzi Nuovo Falcone,** 498.4cc, overhead-valve unit-construction single, 12 volt electrics, electric starter, full-width drum brakes.
£1,800–2,000 *NLM*

This ex-police machine is fitted with a civilian dual seat and chromed double-barrel silencer.

r. **1981 Moto Guzzi V50 II,** 490cc, overhead-valve 90° V-twin, 5-speed gearbox, shaft final drive.
£1,000–1,400 *IVC*

The De Tomaso-funded V35 and V50 middleweight V-twins made their debut at the Cologne show in Germany in September 1976. This machine has an SP-type fairing from a V655P model.

l. **1975 Moto Morini 3½ Sport,** 344cc, 72° V-twin with Heron heads.
£2,400–2,800 *IVC*

The first Morini V-twin was the 3½ Turismo, which made its public debut at the Milan show in November 1971, entering production the following year.

1974 MV Agusta 750S, 743cc, 65bhp, clip-ons, rear-sets, 4 megaphone silencers, twin-loop cradle frame, shaft final drive.
£16,250–18,000 *BKS*

This machine is from the second series with twin disc front brakes and is equipped with the optional full factory fairing.

*r.***1972 MV Agusta 350B Elettronica,** 349cc, overhead-valve twin, electronic ignition.
£2,600–3,000 *BKS*

l. **1937 New Imperial Model 46,** 346cc, overhead-valve single with inclined cylinder, 70 x 90mm bore and stroke, unit construction, high-level exhaust, pillion pad, girder forks.
£3,800–4,000 *VER*

r. **1972 MV Agusta 750S,** 743cc, double-overhead-camshaft across-the-frame 4 cylinder engine, 5-speed gearbox, shaft final drive.
£13,250–15,000 *BKS*

The 750S made its debut at the Milan show in November 1969, but didn't enter production until 1971. This 1972 machine is of the first series, which sported wire wheels and drum brakes.

l. **1914 New Imperial Light Tourist,** 293cc, sidevalve JAP engine.
£5,000–5,250 *VER*

New Imperial was founded in 1892 and, as such, was one of the real pioneers of the British motorcycle industry. From 1900 it was run by Norman Downs.

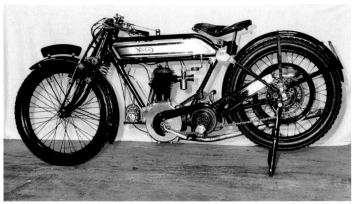

l. **1922 Norton Model 16H,** 490cc, sidevalve single with adjustable tappets, chain final drive.
£6,750–7,250 *BKS*

The late, great motorcycle enthusiast and special builder, Bert Fruin, restored this Model 16H many years ago, and it won a Banbury Run concours while still in his hands. The 16H first appeared in 1921, and the number arose from a frame change, the initial 'H' being for Home. There was also the Model 17C (Colonial).

r. **1925 Norton Model 18,** 490cc, overhead-single.
£9,250–10,000 *BKS*

The Norton factory was always willing to be at the forefront of racing, featuring a TT model from its early production days. It was 'Pa' Norton who pushed the engine format to an overhead-valve design, and in 1922 the first new model was introduced to the public at the Earl's Court show, called the Model 18. By 1925, the Model 18 had thoroughly established itself as a competition model, Alec Bennett winning the Senior TT of 1924.

l. **1936 Norton Model 30 International,** 490cc, overhead-camshaft single, 79 x 100mm bore and stroke, Manx-type fuel tank.
£5,200–5,800 *BKS*

By 1931, Norton engines were so developed that they won virtually every Senior and Junior TT race for almost a decade, thus promoting the sporting singles which by 1936 had become known as International models. The name was derived from Norton's entry in the ISDT in 1933.

r. **1949 Norton ES2,** 490cc, overhead-valve single.
£2,500–3,200 *PM*

Post-war, the ES2 single entered production in 1947 with plunger rear suspension, as on the overhead-camshaft models. The engine was modified for 1948 with a new timing case, direct-action tappets and a one-piece rocker box.

r. **c1959 Norton Dominator 99,** 597cc, overhead-valve twin, wideline chassis, concours condition.
£4,500–5,000 *AtMC*

Making its debut in 1956, the 99 soon built up a strong following thanks to its outstanding combination of roadholding, braking and performance. It was superseded in 1962 by the famous 650 series, which offered even higher performance.

l. **1955 Norton Model 19S,** 597cc, overhead-valve single, 82 x 113mm bore and stroke.
£2,400–2,700 *AT*

The 19S was introduced in 1954 and ran through to 1958. Although it used Roadholder forks and swinging-arm rear suspension, it did not employ the duplex Featherbed chassis. It was intended as a more modern replacement for the sidevalve Big 4.

1970 Norton Commando Fastback, 745cc, overhead-valve twin.
£2,800–3,200 *PC*

All models of Commando were given a disc front brake from mid-1972, but this is an earlier model with Inter modifications, plus alloy wheel rims.

1975 Norton Commando Interstate MkIII, 829cc, overhead-valve twin with American Prestolite electric start, left-hand gear change, concours condition.
£4,000–4,500 *BKS*

The final version, the 850 Commando Electric Start, came in 1975 with Manx silver colour scheme.

1975 Norton 850 Commando, 829cc, overhead-valve twin, US export model with small tank, high handlebars.
£2,500–2,750 *BKS*

The US model of the 850 electric-start model had Prestolite electric start and left-hand gear change.

1963 Panther Model 120, 645cc, overhead-valve twin-port single, excellent condition.
£3,000–3,500 *BKS*

Although used as a solo, Panther's Model 120 is more famous as a sidecar machine.

EXCELSIOR (*British 1886–1964*)

1929 Excelsior, 147cc, Villiers single-cylinder
2-stroke, hand-change gearbox.
£1,300–1,500 *PM*

*Excelsior dates from 1874 in its original guise,
when it manufactured penny-farthing cycles; it
became involved with motorcycles in 1896. From
the turn of the century, Excelsior (not to be
confused with the American manufacturer of the
same name) appeared in track races, later running
at Brooklands and in the Isle of Man TT. But it
was not until 1929 that the company gained its
first TT victory, in the lightweight (250cc) event.
The production models of the late 1920s were
normally equipped with Villiers or JAP engines,
the latter usually overhead-valve four-strokes.*

1954 Excelsior F4 Consort, 99cc.
£800–900 *BKS*

*Besides their Talisman twin-engined series,
Excelsior's 1950s production centred on small
commuter models with Villiers engines. In April
1953, the range was joined by the F4 Consort,
an ultra-lightweight motorcycle fitted with a
99cc Villiers 4F engine and two-speed gearbox.*

Don't Forget!
*If in doubt please refer to the 'How to Use'
section at the beginning of this book.*

 **Miller's
Motorcycle Milestones**

Excelsior Manxman (*British 1935*)
Value £4,500–8,500
In the history of motorcycling, four companies
have carried the Excelsior logo on their fuel
tanks. One was Éxcelsior Fahrradwerke of
Brandenburg, Germany, which manufactured
motorcycles from 1901 until the outbreak of
WWII. Another was the little-known Excelsior
company based in Munich, while much larger
was the Excelsior Manufacturing and Supply
Corp of Chicago, USA. Last, but certainly not
least, was the British Excelsior Motor Company
of Birmingham.

The British marque, which belonged to the
Walker family (no relation to the editor!), began
manufacturing motorcycles in 1896. At first,
they employed bought-in engines from the likes
of Minerva, de Dion-Bouton and MMC. These
were fitted into Excelsior-made frames. Soon,
the Excelsior name began appearing in the
race results.

After WWI, Excelsior went from strength to
strength, its output ranging from humble 98cc
commuter two-strokes to 998cc JAP-powered
V-twin machines. The company's greatest

racing success was its victory in the 1933
Lightweight (250cc) Isle of Man TT, with the
248cc Ike Hatch-designed 'Mechanical Marvel'.

But without doubt, Excelsior's most famous
model was the Manxman, which was built in
both sports and racing versions. The first of
these, in 246 and 349cc engine sizes, arrived
in 1935. Both shared a common stroke and
were of straightforward, but substantial,
design, with a single overhead camshaft
driven by a shaft and bevel gears on the offside.
The valve gear was fully enclosed, and the
bevel cover was embossed with the 'Three
Legs of Man' insignia. The mag-dyno was
positioned at the rear of the cylinder, where
it was driven by a train of gears. These also
operated the two gear-type oil pumps and a
Smiths rev-counter. Lubrication was of the
dry-sump variety.

The Manxman range was extended to include
a larger 496cc version for 1936.

After WWII, Excelsior mainly produced two-
strokes, either with Villiers engines or its own
243 and 328cc twin-cylinder units. Production
ceased in 1964.

1961 Excelsior Consort C12, 98cc, Villiers 6F
2-stroke engine, 2-speed foot-change gearbox,
completely restored, original metallic blue
paintwork, excellent condition throughout.
£600–800 *BTS*

1962 Excelsior Talisman ETT8, 243cc.
£1,800–2,000 *BTS*

*The same basic machine, with a 328cc engine,
was offered in 1961 as the ETT9.*

FAIRY (*British 1901–23*)

1923 Fairy Lady's Model, 169cc, single-cylinder Hobart 2-stroke engine, direct belt-drive transmission, restored.
£1,100–1,400 *BKS*

Fairy offered machines that were similar to those of the McKenzie company, and were almost certainly manufactured by the same firm, Hobart of Coventry. In existence from 1901 to 1923, the latter was a major supplier of components – including frames and engines – to the motorcycle industry, and built complete machines of its own.

FB MONDIAL (*Italian 1948–79*)

1952 FB Mondial TV175, 174cc, overhead camshaft, single cylinder, matching frame and engine numbers.
£1,700–1,900 *PS*

This model was based loosely on the company's 125cc, world championship-winning, double-overhead-camshaft unit.

r. **1955 FB Mondial Constellation 200,** 198cc, overhead valves, single cylinder, 62 x 66mm bore and stroke.
£1,800+ *PC*

The Constellation was an uprated version of the 200cc, overhead-valve Turismo model. Its specification included a forward-operating kickstarter on the offside, telescopic front forks, swinging-arm rear suspension, aluminium wheel rims, conical brake hubs (made by Mondial themselves), Silentium cigar-shaped silencer, touring handlebars and a dual seat.

FRANCIS-BARNETT (*British 1919–64*)

This well-known marque – best remembered for its lightweight commuter motorcycles and an inter-war frame constructed from lengths of straight tube bolted together – originated in 1920 when Gordon Francis and Arthur Barnett built their first machine. Following the end of WWII, 'Fanny B', as the marque was often called, returned to the market in 1946 with two models, an autocycle and a lightweight motorcycle.

In 1947, the company became part of the AMC (Associated Motorcycles) group, but it was some time before this had any great effect. The first AMC-powered Francis-Barnett arrived in 1957, in the shape of the 249cc Cruiser 80. Although its engine had an ultra-smooth appearance, this was only skin deep. It was the work of an Italian designer, who accepted the brief – and fee – then quickly departed for home before his handiwork had been developed or tested!

Unfortunately for AMC and, of course, Francis-Barnett's luckless management, the engine proved poor in both operation and reliability. However, AMC not only continued with this unit, but also introduced smaller versions in 171 and 199cc capacities. Eventually, though, common sense prevailed and the company returned to Villiers power, at least for twins and competition mounts.

In 1962, Francis-Barnett production was moved to the Greet factory, which was occupied by James, also part of the AMC group. Thus, the two marques – once great rivals – were built side by side and, inevitably, grew closer as each day passed.

Also in 1962 the 89 Cruiser Twin was introduced, which marked a return to the use of a Villiers engine. This was the 249cc, 2T twin-cylinder unit with four-speed gearbox.

From a 1964 high of nine models, by the beginning of 1966, the range had dropped to six. By then, the firm's days were numbered due to the troubles of the parent group, and in October 1966 production ceased. It was a sad day for many motorcyclists who regarded the marque with a fondness virtually unequalled in the world of small-capacity British two-strokes.

l. **1940 Francis-Barnett K39 Cruiser,** 249cc, single-cylinder Villiers 2-stroke.
£1,500–1,700 *PS*

The Cruiser began life in 1933 as the model 32. It was a popular and unusual machine with a unique type of frame construction. This incorporated an I-section forging that formed the head lug and downtube. From the lug, two channel-section members ran back under the tank to the rear wheel. These and the other sections of the frame were braced by additional struts. In addition, a large proportion of the frame was enclosed.

1954 Francis-Barnett Kestrel 66, 122cc Villiers 13D engine, 50 x 62mm bore and stroke, 3-speed gearbox.
£400–500 *BKS*

1955 Francis-Barnett Falcon 70, 197cc Villiers 8E engine, 59 x 72mm bore and stroke, 3-speed gearbox.
£500–550 *PS*

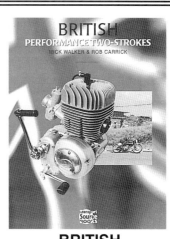

1955 Francis-Barnett Cruiser 75,
224cc Villiers 1H engine.
£650–700 *PS*

1955 Francis-Barnett Falcon 74, 197cc,
Villiers 8E 2-stroke engine, 3-speed gearbox,
fully restored, excellent condition.
£900–1,000 *BTS*

l. **1957 Francis-Barnett Falcon 74,** 197cc,
Villiers 8E engine, 3- or 4-speed gearbox.
£350–400 *PS*

GILERA (*Italian 1909–*)

1956 Gilera Nettuno, 247cc.
£2,600–3,000 *BKS*

Gilera first sprang to prominence in the late 1930s, when their supercharged four-cylinder racers trounced BMW in Grands Prix and snatched the world speed record from the German marque. Throughout the early 1950s, the racers continued to grab the headlines, taking five manufacturer's titles and six individual championships in the hands of riders such as Duke, Liberati and Masetti. The best known and most successful large-capacity Gilera roadster of the period was the 500cc Saturno. Less familiar outside Italy was its baby brother, the Nettuno (Neptune), a 247cc, overhead-valve, four-stroke single. Like its larger contemporary, the Nettuno employed the horizontally-sprung, friction-damped, swinging-arm rear suspension first seen on the pre-war blown four.

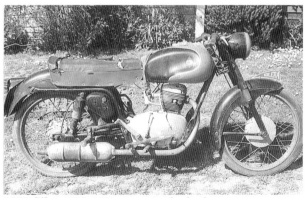

1957 Gilera 150, 152cc, non-standard exhaust,
requires restoration.
£300–400 *MAY*

Miller's
Motorcycle Milestones

Gilera 499cc Saturno (*Italian 1946*)
Value £4,000–6,000
Gilera is one of the truly great names of Italian motorcycling. Born on 21 December 1887, Giuseppe Gilera built his first motorcycle – a 317cc single – in 1909. But with the outbreak of war in 1914, Gilera's efforts were transferred to the production of pedal cycles for the Italian military.

After the end of WWI, there was a massive demand for motorcycles in Italy, but it was not until 1920 that Gilera was able to capitalize on this – after moving out of Milan to a much larger factory at Arcore, a few kilometres outside the urban sprawl of the city, and not far from Monza park, where the famous race circuit would soon be built.

Before long, a series of single-cylinder four-stroke machines appeared, including the Turismo (1920–24), Sport (1923–28), Gran Sport (1929–31), L-SS (1931–36) and *Sei Giorni* – Six Days – (1931–34). The last came about through the marque's success in the International Six Days Trial (ISDT).

Then came the VT series, with pushrod-operated valves and class-leading performance. These were built during 1935–41 and, in truth, were the forerunners of the Saturno, Gilera's most famous production motorcycle.

The Saturno was created in 1939 by Ing. Giuseppe Salmaggi, from an original 1933 design by Mario Mellone. The prototype won the last Targa Florio – a classic road race in Sicily – just prior to Italy's entry into WWII in June 1940.

After the war, the Saturno was put into production in 1946. Its 498.76cc (84 x 90mm) single-cylinder engine sported an alloy cylinder head and pushrod-operated valves. The design was of semi-unit construction with a four-speed gearbox and multi-plate clutch.

Like its British counterpart, the BSA Gold Star, the Saturno was developed over a number of years, and also saw service as a racer, trials bike and motocrosser.

The original model sported girder forks and Gilera's own rear suspension, embodying a swinging fork and horizontal compression springs. In 1950, the Saturno Sport appeared with oil-damped telescopic front forks, while in 1952 the series received a brand-new frame with swinging-arm rear suspension controlled by twin shock absorbers.

The Saturno was very successful in every field it entered. In all, 6,450 examples were built (including 170 racers) before production finally came to an end in 1959.

1958 Gilera Sport, 172cc, overhead-valve unit-construction engine, original, including rare alloy silencer.
£1,000–1,150 *RIM*

1959 Gilera B300, 304cc, pushrod-operated parallel valves, unit construction, 4-speed gearbox.
£1,300–1,500 *NLM*
This model had an unusual spark plug location at the rear of the cylinder head.

1959 Gilera B300 Extra, 304cc.
£900–1,000 *PS*
This particular machine has a fully enclosed chain.

1961 Gilera Sport, 172cc.
£1,000–1,400 *BLM*

r. **1963 Gilera Jubilee,** 98cc, overhead-valve single, unit construction, original except for seat.
£400–500 *MAY*

HARLEY-DAVIDSON (*American 1903–*)

l. **1917 Harley-Davidson Model F,** 989cc, inlet-over-exhaust V-twin, unrestored, paintwork heavily crazed, little nickel plating remaining, lining and tank badges still present, but badly faded.
£11,500–13,000 *BKS*

1950 Harley-Davidson FL, 1207cc, overhead-valve V-twin, 4-speed foot-change gearbox, fully restored.
£10,500–12,000 *PC*

1974 Harley-Davidson Super-Glide, 1200cc, modified with drag-style exhaust pipes, front brakes improved with 4-piston calipers, Japanese front fork assembly, very good condition.
£5,500–6,500 *CotC*

1978 Harley-Davidson Electra-Glide, 1340cc, overhead-valve V-twin.
£5,000–6,000 *PC*

This particular machine has been customised using Harley-Davidson and other parts and accessories.

l. **1979 Harley-Davidson SXT125,** 124cc, single-cylinder 2-stroke engine, oil-pump lubrication, 5-speed gearbox.
£300–350 *PC*

This particular model was built as an HD Cagiva in the first year of Cagiva's operation, but using parts that dated back to Harley-Davidson's ownership of the Varese factory.

HONDA (*Japanese 1946–*)

Founded in 1948 by Sochira Honda in Hamamatsu, the Honda Motor Co has become the world's largest manufacturer of powered two-wheelers. The company has production facilities around the globe, including factories in Europe and the United States, home of the Gold Wing.

Although two-strokes have featured in the company's inventory, Honda is best known as a producer of four-strokes. Notable among the firm's products is the C model 'Cub', with over 20 million examples having been made to date. The Honda 750-4 was responsible for establishing the Superbike class and proving that a four-cylinder engine was viable and practical for road use, while the mighty CBX1000-6 was a demonstration of the company's unsurpassed engineering skill.

Throughout Honda's history, competition has played an important part in developing the firm's products. During the 1960s, multis ridden by Mike Hailwood and Jim Redman proved extremely competitive and paved the way for sophisticated road-going models later in the decade.

Today, there is increasing affection for Japanese motorcycles from the period 1960–80. This has led to a growth in demand for Benlys, Street Scramblers, Monkey Bikes and early-model fours.

1964 Honda CB92, 124cc, overhead-camshaft twin, 44 x 41mm bore and stroke, 15bhp at 10,500rpm, leading-link forks, full-width hubs, 2LS front brake.
£2,500–3,000 *MAY*

In 1959, Honda introduced the C95 touring twin and its sporting brother, the CB92. They continued an angular styling first seen on the 247cc C70 model two years before in 1957. Their specification and equipment, together with an excellent finish, put European machines of similar engine size to shame. Only the handling and roadholding were open to criticism. Today, the CB92 is considered one of the true classics of the early Japanese motorcycle industry.

1964 Honda CB92, 124cc, suitable for parts only.
£250–300 *MAY*

Don't Forget!

If in doubt please refer to the 'How to Use' section at the beginning of this book.

1964 Honda CB160, 161cc, chain-driven single overhead camshaft, 50 x 41mm bore and stroke, twin cylinders with 360° crankshaft, electric starter, fully restored.
£1,600–1,700 *VJMC*

1964 Honda CB77, 305cc, barn-stored 1974–96, meticulously restored to factory specification using genuine Honda parts, engine rebuilt by P. D. Engineering.
£2,500–3,000 *BKS*

Honda's twin-cylinder CB77 was in production from 1963 to 1967, being fitted with the 305cc overhead-camshaft engine. With a compression ratio of 9.5:1, this engine developed 28.5bhp at 9,000rpm, giving the machine a top speed of 95mph. The CB77 retained many of the mechanical and design features of the Hawk 250.

1965 Honda C77, 305cc, 60 x 54mm bore and stroke.
£1,200–1,500 *BKS*

Introduced in 1963, the C77 replaced the C76 touring twin, with which it shared the slightly angular styling that was synonymous with Honda machines of the period, utilising pressed-steel frames and fittings. The major difference between the new model and its predecessor was that it had a wet-sump engine lubrication system. The C77 was equipped with an electric starter, indicators, a dual seat and full mudguards as standard.

1966 Honda CB72, 247cc, 54 x 54mm bore and stroke, concours condition.
£2,500–3,200 *BKS*

Introduced in 1960, the CB72 featured a twin-cylinder, 180°, overhead-camshaft engine that produced 24bhp at 9,000rpm, endowing the well equipped model with a top speed of 90mph. Although more expensive than many of its quarter-litre rivals, when compared with machines of similar performance, its price was very reasonable, leading to healthy sales.

l. **1966 Honda CB450,** 444.9cc, double overhead camshafts, torsion-bar valve springs, 4-speed gearbox in unit with engine, completely restored.
£1,700–2,000 *S*

The infamous 'Black Bomber' was Honda's much-feared, mid-1960s entry into the larger-capacity class. In the event, the British twins of the day held their ground, possibly inducing the company into an earlier launch – barely two years later – of the sensational 'K' model four. Today, these high-specification, mid-range CB450 twins are well regarded by British enthusiasts.

1969 Honda CB90Z, 89.5cc, overhead camshaft, single horizontal cylinder, 50 x 45.6mm bore and stroke.
£520–550 *BKS*

1970 Honda CB250, 249.3cc, 5-speed gearbox, original, unrestored.
£230–300 *BKS*

First offered in 1968, the CB250 replaced the CB72. It featured a new 249.3cc (56 x 50.6mm) overhead-camshaft engine.

1971 Honda CB500/4, 498.5cc, single-overhead-camshaft four, 56 x 50.6mm bore and stroke, 50bhp at 9,000rpm, 5-speed gearbox, single 260mm front disc, 180mm drum rear brake.
£2,800–3,000 *VJMC*

1974 Honda CB400F, 408.6cc, single overhead camshaft, 4 cylinders, 51 x 50mm bore and stroke, non-standard seat, fairing and silencer, non-original black paintwork.
£750–950 *MAY*

The Japanese home-market version of this model had a smaller 398.8cc engine.

l. **1974 Honda CB750K2,** dry-sump lubrication with separate oil tank, pillion footrests between the silencers, non-original exhaust.
£2,500–3,000 *PM*

l. **1977 Honda CB750F2,** 738cc, single overhead camshaft, 4 cylinders, Comstar wheels, disc brakes front and rear, 2-into-1 exhausts on each side, original condition.
£1,600–1,800 *SKC*

The CB750F2 was the final model with the single-overhead-camshaft engine imported into the UK.

1978 Honda CBX Super Sport, 1047cc, double overhead camshafts, 6 cylinders, 64.5 x 53.4mm bore and stroke, twin-shock rear suspension.
£2,500–5,000 *CBX*

Featuring four valves per cylinder, the CBX six also had no less than seven main bearings. With a compression ratio of 9.3:1, it produced 105bhp at 9,000rpm. Motor Cycle Weekly achieved 139.2mph in a road test shortly after the CBX was launched in Japan during 1977. In all, 24,000 CBX Super Sports were built.

1978 Honda CB400F2, 408.6cc.
£920–1,000 *BKS*

Although given an amended title, the CB400/4 F2 differed in only minor detail from the previous F model, which in no way detracted from the machine's performance and fine handling. Now regarded as a classic, the smallest of the CB fours to be imported into the UK was responsible for laying to rest a number of myths. It is widely regarded as being the first Japanese multi to 'handle', and is endowed with a great deal of character.

1979 Honda CBXL125S, 124cc, overhead-camshaft single, 56.5 x 49.5mm bore and stroke, 5-speed gearbox, high-level exhaust, concours condition.
£700–900 *VJMC*

1982 Honda CBX1000C Pro-Link, 1047cc, 98bhp, Pro-link (monoshock) rear suspension, original and unrestored.
£2,000–4,000 *CBX*

This was the later touring version of the CBX, which was produced during 1981–82. Equipped with a fairing and matching luggage, it did not have the power of the original Super Sport model. In all, 6,000 were produced, but only 289 were sold in the UK, most of the remainder going to the USA and Canada. Although rarer than the early CBX model, it does not command such a high price.

1980 Honda CBX, 1047cc, 6 cylinders, double overhead camshafts, 24 valves, 6 carburettors, 64.5 x 53.4mm bore and stroke, 105bhp, fitted with crashbars, period carrier and 6-into-1 exhaust, otherwise original.
£3,200–3,500 *BKS*

The late 1970s witnessed an extraordinary horsepower battle between the four Japanese manufacturers, each attempting to outdo their rivals with increasingly sophisticated machinery. Honda fielded the mighty double-overhead-camshaft, six-cylinder, 105bhp CBX in 1978 as their range leader. This new model utilised the powerplant as a stressed member, and was equipped with twin disc brakes at the front to retard the 545lb machine.

HUMBER (*British 1900–30*)

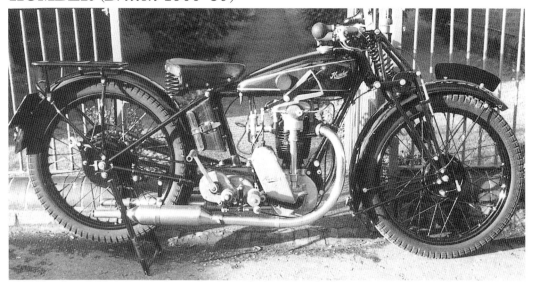

1928 Humber OCS, 349cc, single overhead camshaft, single cylinder, 75 x 79mm bore and stroke.
£6,500–7,000 *VER*

The Humber company had its origins in the cycle industry and was involved with two-, three- and four-wheel powered vehicles from the earliest days. Humber won the 1911 Junior (350cc) TT and also achieved some success at Brooklands in pre-WWI days, but was not a major marque during the 1920s. Then, in 1928, they introduced a neat 349cc overhead-camshaft engine, which remained in production until 1930. Now extremely rare, the machine never sold in large numbers. Subsequently, Humber decided to concentrate on the four-wheel sector.

INDIAN (*American 1901–53*)

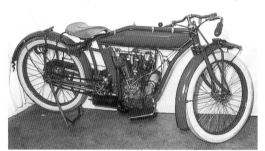

1913 Indian Twin 7hp, 1000cc,
inlet-over-exhaust V-twin.
£9,500–10,500 *IMC*

1915 Indian 5hp, 750cc, inlet-over-exhaust V-twin,
3-speed hand-change gearbox, multi-plate clutch,
gear-driven magneto, automatic engine oiling.
£8,500–9,000 *BKS*

In the years preceding WWI, American companies made an impact upon the British motorcycling public, helped largely by Indian V-twins taking the first three places in the Senior TT. Thoroughly beaten, the British manufacturers were shaken to the core by the success of these advanced and powerful machines. As a result, Indian motorcycles sold steadily in Britain until the outbreak of war in 1914.

1952 Indian Brave, 248cc, sidevalve single,
rigid frame, telescopic forks, concours condition.
£1,300–1,500 *IMC*

This particular machine was made by Brockhouse Engineering, of Southport, Lancashire, for export to the USA. In 1954, a swinging-arm-frame model was introduced. Production ceased in 1955.

r. **1953 Indian Chief,** 80cu in.
£14,000–16,000 *IMC*

JAMES (British 1902–64)

1953 James Captain J8, 197cc,
completely original, fully restored.
£700–800 *BTS*

*In later years, James became part of the AMC group,
which brought them ever closer to their old rivals,
Francis-Barnett. This led to badge-engineering in the
mid-1950s, but in the early post-war years, the Greet,
Birmingham factory followed its own path. It had
done so since its first motorcycle had appeared in
1902. Early models often had four-stroke engines,
some with V-configuration. However, from the mid-
1930s, the firm concentrated on the commuter market
and continued to do so thereafter. Like Francis-
Barnett, James were dragged down by the collapse
of AMC during the mid-1960s.*

JAWA (Czechoslovakian 1929–)

1934 Jawa, 350cc, overhead-valve
single-cylinder engine.
£2,700–3,000 *JCZ*

*Jawa was formed in 1929 by Ing. Frantisek Janecek,
the name being a contraction of Janecek and Wanderer.
The latter was a German manufacturer of considerable
repute during the vintage and veteran era. As for
Janecek, he had been an engineer for many years, and
during WWI had worked in arms production. To make
a speedy entry into motorcycle manufacturing, Janecek
built Wanderers under licence. Then, in 1932, Jawa
added a model with a British-designed two-stroke
Villiers engine. The British rider/designer George
Patchett joined Jawa in 1931 and went on to create
a range of in-house sidevalve, overhead-valve and
overhead-camshaft four-strokes. He also rode Jawas
in the Isle of Man TT during the 1930s.*

r. **1963 Jawa Californian,** 246cc, twin-port single-
cylinder 2-stroke, rare early American export model.
£1,200–1,500 *JCZ*

1955 James Colonel K12, 225cc, Villiers IH
single-cylinder 2-stroke engine.
£700–900 *BTS*

1960 James Commodore L25,
249cc, AMC engine.
£500–550 *PM*

KAWASAKI (*Japanese 1962–*)

1976 Kawasaki KH500 A8, 499cc, 3-cylinder piston-port 2-stroke, 60 x 58.8mm bore and stroke, 5-speed gearbox.
£900–1,000 *BKS*

Originally introduced in September 1968, the Kawasaki 500 triple shocked the motorcycling establishment. Capable of nearly 125mph and near 12 second standing quarters, the Mach III set new levels of performance for a road bike. By the time the final KH500 was introduced in 1976, Kawasaki had been forced to subdue their unruly offspring. The newcomer produced less power and was equipped with a disc front brake, resulting in a more civilised machine, but fortunately it still retained some of the character of the original model.

1982 Kawasaki Z1300 A4, 1286cc, double overhead camshafts, water-cooled, 6 cylinders, original.
£2,300–2,500 *PC*

For 1982, the Z1300 A4 featured transistorized ignition with electronic advance for the first time. The Z1300 was a massive machine. It had a dry weight of 653lb, and in its day only exceeded by that of the Honda Gold Wing and Harley-Davidson Electra-Glide.

1983 Kawasaki Z1000R, 1015cc, double-overhead-camshaft across-the-frame four, 70 x 66mm bore and stroke, 5-speed gearbox, imported to UK from USA.
£1,150–1,350 *BKS*

The Z1000R was produced in response to Eddie Lawson's success in the American Superbike series. This required machines to maintain the outward appearance of the road-going variants from which they were derived, but allowed a great deal of freedom in tuning the machine. The Z1000R had the outward appearance of Lawson's Z1000 race bike, but was not so highly tuned. The result was one of the most handsome motorcycles of the period. Resplendent in its lime green team colours with a cut-down seat, bikini fairing and matt black exhaust system, the new model represented the end of a decade of development for the air-cooled 'Zed'.

1979 Kawasaki KH250 B4, 249.5cc, original, unrestored.
£500–750 *MAY*

This model was discontinued in 1980.

1983 Kawasaki GPz1100, 1089cc, double overhead camshafts, air-cooled, 4 cylinders, 72.5 x 66mm bore and stroke.
£1,800–2,000 *PC*

The 1983 GPz1100, with digital fuel injection (DFI), achieved a top speed of 150mph in an American magazine road test. At that time, it was the fastest production roadster ever tested.

KERRY (*British 1902–early 1960s*)

l. **1904 Kerry 3½hp,** inlet-over-exhaust single-cylinder engine.
£4,000–4,500 *BKS*

Manufactured by the Belgian company of Saroloa, who were among the first producers of complete motorcycles and manufacturers of proprietary single-cylinder and V-twin engines, the Kerry was probably one of the first examples of badge-engineering within the motorcycle trade. Mr Kerry, the managing director of the East London Rubber Co, entered into an agreement with Sarolea whereby they put his name on the crankcase and tank of their 3½hp motorcycle, enabling him to import the machines between 1904 and 1906 and sell them as Kerry motorcycles. Only seven Kerrys are known to survive.

LAVERDA (*Italian 1949–*)

1978 Laverda 3CL, 981cc, double-overhead-camshaft 3 cylinder engine, 75 x 74mm bore and stroke.
£1,800–2,000 *BKS*

1981 Laverda Mirage TS, 1115cc, double overhead camshafts, 3 cylinders, 80 x 74mm bore and stroke, completely original, excellent condition.
£3,000+ *PC*

The Mirage was announced in 1978, being basically a 1200T with some Jota tuning goodies. Then, in 1980, it was replaced by the Mirage TS. This machine featured a standard 1200-series engine with Jota head and downpipes. To reduce primary-drive noise, a couple of springs connected the rear two clutch friction plates, of which there were eight instead of seven. The Mirage TS had an all-silver finish.

l. **1981 Laverda Formula Mirage,** 1115cc, original, fully restored, Astrolit wheels, hydraulic clutch, specially tuned engine.
£8,000+ *PC*

This bike was one of only 17 made.

Miller's Motorcycle Milestones

Laverda 744cc SFC (*Italian 1975*)
Value £6,000–9,000
Laverda's first motorcycles were humble 75cc push-rod singles, which debuted at the end of the 1940s.

Success in the Italian long-distance road races of the 1950s helped establish the marque's sporting credentials. But it was really the appearance of a prototype 654cc (75 x 74mm) parallel twin that really set the ball rolling on an international scale. This had a four-bearing, 180° crankshaft, a duplex-chain-driven single overhead camshaft, triplex chain for the primary drive, a multi-plate clutch and a five-speed gearbox.

By the Milan show at the end of 1967, it was clear that the production Laverda big twin would be a 750. This was achieved by increasing the bore size to give 743.9cc.

Just as they had done years earlier with their tiny singles, Laverda decided to enter the racing arena to publicise their new twin. At first, this was done unofficially, but by 1970 Laverda had won the first 500km race for production motorcycles at Monza.

Then came a purpose-built machine, the 750SFC. This was launched in 1971 as an endurance racing version of Laverda's SF series,

the 'C' standing for 'Competizione'. The SFC duly won its first event, the gruelling Barcelona 24 hours at Montjuich Park.

Although derived from the touring SF model, the SFC displayed a number of important differences. Its engine was not only more highly tuned, but also more robust, having larger bearings and a higher-capacity oil pump. Its chassis incorporated a revised frame as well as the racing-style half fairing, seat unit and controls.

However, these features did not deter enthusiastic road riders from using a large number of SFCs on the street. Initially equipped with Laverda's own drum front brake, the SFC was one of the fastest machines on the road in the early 1970s. Although expensive, there were always more potential buyers than the 100 or so built in the first three years of production.

In 1974, the SFC was updated with triple disc brakes, thicker forks and tubes, and other more minor changes. Later SFCs came with electronic ignition, and some even had cast alloy wheels. The final batch were the quickest, having a special camshaft that delivered 135mph.

During its six-year production life, only 549 examples were built, helping to make the 750SFC particularly valuable today.

LEVIS (British 1911–39)

1922 Levis Popular, 211cc.
£2,000–2,200 *BKS*

One of the pioneers of the two-stroke motorcycle, Levis began manufacture of their 211cc, single-gear lightweight in 1911. Dubbed the 'Popular', it became a huge success for the Birmingham marque, remaining in production until 1926.

1930 Levis Model A2, 346cc, twin-port overhead-valve single, gas lamp, high-level exhaust pipe.
£2,600–3,000 *BLM*

Levis also made an A1 model, which had a single exhaust port.

MATCHLESS (British 1901–69, revived 1987)

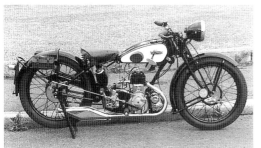

1930 Matchless R/4, 249cc, sidevalve single-cylinder engine, hand-change gearbox, 62.5 x 80mm bore and stroke.
£1,800–2,000 *PM*

> **Miller's is a price GUIDE not a price LIST**

1921 Matchless H2, 998cc, inlet-over-exhaust V-twin engine.
£5,200–5,500 *BKS*

The Collier brothers' Matchless H2 featured an inlet-over-exhaust MAG engine displacing 1000cc and driving through a three-speed gearbox. It had a fully-sprung frame featuring girder front forks and a pivoted-fork rear end controlled by leaf springs. Aimed at the discerning rider seeking a powerful combination, the model was normally supplied with a sidecar, also of Matchless manufacture.

1931 Matchless Silver Hawk, 593cc.
£8,750–9,000 *BKS*

First seen at the 1931 Olympia show, the Silver Hawk was an attempt by Matchless to provide a refined motorcycle with performance, a quality lacking in their previous luxury model, the Silver Arrow V-twin. The new machine featured an overhead-camshaft, 26° V4 engine with fully enclosed valve gear driven by a vertical shaft on the right of the engine, flanked on each side by the exhaust pipes. The mag-dyno drive was taken from the base of the valve drive shaft. The unit sat above the four-speed gearbox on the right of the machine, while the carburettor was centrally located on the left. The frame incorporated a triangulated rear end with twin springs and friction dampers, which combined with the front girder forks to produce a comfortable ride. Unfortunately, Ariel unveiled their Square Four at the same time, and this offered similar performance and refinement for £5 less. As a result, it dominated the limited luxury market at the expense of the Matchless.

1951 Matchless G9 Spring Twin, 498cc, overhead-valve vertical twin, 66 x 72.8mm bore and stroke, correct short megaphone silencers, half-width brake hubs, jampot rear units, silver anodised wheel rims.
£2,000–2,400 *BLM*

1955 Matchless G80, 497cc, overhead-valve single-cylinder engine.
£2,250–2,500 *AT*

A pilot light on each side of the headlamp arrived for the 1954 season. For 1955, the G80 (along with most other Matchless and AJS models) received an Amal Monobloc carburettor, together with another full-width front hub, the pins of which had a barrel profile. There was a full-width rear hub to match, and a deeper headlamp shell to accommodate the speedometer.

1957 Matchless G9, 498cc, overhead-valve twin-cylinder engine.
£2,000–2,200 *BKS*

Introduced in 1949, the G9 and its AJS counterpart, the Model 20, were unusual in having a third, central bearing for the crankshaft, and in being available only in pivoted-fork form. The model formed the basis for a range of machines that would grow to 750cc in later years. While gaining horsepower, the machine lost some of the initial smoothness and flexibility.

1958 Matchless G80CS, 497cc, overhead valves, single cylinder, 86 x 85.5mm bore and stroke, 4-speed foot-change gearbox.
£3,500–3,700 *BKS*

Although clearly derived from the heavyweight road-going singles, the CS of 1958 had become a specialised competition machine. It had a short-stroke, all-alloy engine with a larger carburettor, higher compression ratio and hotter camshafts. The cycle parts reflected their intended role, with a smaller petrol tank, alloy mudguards, tucked-in exhaust system, and smaller headlamp (when fitted). The model met with considerable success in scrambles in the UK, and proved popular in American desert races.

r. **1964 Matchless G12,** 646cc, overhead valves, twin cylinders, 3 bearing crank, largely original.
£2,300–2,500 *PC*

The Matchless (and AJS) twin's style for 1964 included Norton brake hubs and Roadholder forks.

1959 Matchless G9, 498cc.
£1,850–2,250 *AT*

The first year in which Burgess-type silencers were fitted instead of megaphones was 1959.

MILLER-BALSAMO (*Italian 1921–59*)

l. **1932 Miller-Balsamo Record Breaker,** 174cc, overhead-camshaft single-cylinder engine, external flywheel, blade forks, rigid frame, comprehensive aluminium streamlined bodywork.
£3,000+ *PC*

This machine broke no less than nine world speed records in the 175cc category in 1932.

MINERVA (*Belgian 1895–1909*)

1903 Minerva, 211cc, Pioneer Certificate, unused for several years, requires full mechanical and safety checks.
£3,500–3,700 *BKS*

Although a latecomer to bicycle manufacture, the Belgian Minerva concern was among the first to offer viable engines for motorcycles. Nominally of 1hp, the 211cc unit was designed for attachment ahead of the cycle's front downtube and was of advanced configuration, employing a mechanically-operated inlet valve instead of the automatic type favoured by rival manufacturers. As well as building complete machines, the company supplied engines to many Continental and British manufacturers. Larger-capacity engines, including V-twins, were developed, but the inevitable increase in bulk meant that these had to be mounted conventionally within the frame. Despite commercial and competition successes on two wheels, Minerva's plans lay elsewhere, and the company abandoned motorcycle production after 1909 to concentrate on cars.

MOTO GUZZI (*Italian 1921–*)

r. **c1929 Moto Guzzi Tipo Sport 14,** 498.4cc, inlet-over-exhaust horizontal-single-cylinder engine, 88 x 82mm bore and stroke, fully restored.
£8,500–9,000 *AtMC*

1954 Moto Guzzi Falcone Turismo, 498.4cc, overhead valves, horizontal single cylinder, 88 x 82mm bore and stroke, external flywheel, alloy rims, pillion pad, inverted control levers, sports handlebars.
£3,000–3,400 *IVC*

1980 Moto Guzzi Le Mans MkII, 844cc, overhead-valve V-twin, 83 x 78mm bore and stroke, shaft final drive, original except for mirror and fork gaiters.
£1,400–1,600 *BLM*

This particular example has been ridden rather than polished, hence the price.

1981 Moto Guzzi Imola V35, 346cc.
£1,400–1,800 *PC*

r. **1983 Moto Guzzi California MkII,** 948.8cc, missing screen and panniers, seat recovered in non-original all-black scheme (instead of white and black).
£2,000–2,250 *PC*

The California II went on sale in early 1982, after making its debut at the Milan show in November 1981.

1983 Moto Guzzi Imola MkII V35, 346cc, overhead-valve 90° V-twin, 16in diam wheels.
£1,000–1,400 *BLM*

The V35 Imola was built between 1979 and 1983, and its swoopy lines were shared with the V50 Monza II, the V65 Lario and the Le Mans 1000.

MOTO MORINI (*Italian 1937–*)

1975 Moto Morini 3½ Strada, 344cc, 72° V-twin, 68 x 57mm bore and stroke, square-slide VHB Dell'Orto carburettors, drum brakes.
£1,400–1,800 *IVC*

1978 Moto Morini 500, 478.6cc, 72° V-twin engine, 69 x 64mm bore and stroke.
£1,800–2,100 *BLM*

This larger version of the Morini V-twin debuted in 1977 and was marketed in the UK as the Maestro. From 1982, a revised model with six-speed gearbox was offered.

1977 Moto Morini 3½ Sport MkII, 344cc, cast alloy wheels, new seat, black headlamp shell.
£2,400–2,600 *IVC*

MOTOSACOCHE
(*Swiss 1899–1957*)

1910 Motosacoche, 211cc.
£3,500–4,000 *VER*

Motosacoche was formed in 1899 when brothers Henri and Armand Dufaux opened a bicycle factory in Geneva, using the trade name MAG. Early Motosacoche motorcycles often had pedal cycle frames. Later, the company produced engines up to 1200cc in size. MAG engines were fitted by a number of motorcycle manufacturers, including Ariel, Matchless and even Brough-Superior. The company entered a number of speed events, and one of its first successes came through the Clément marque, which won the 1913 French GP with a MAG engine.

MV AGUSTA (*Italian 1945–78*)

1952 MV Agusta Lungo, 123cc, single-cylinder
2-stroke, 53 x 56mm bore and stroke, blade forks,
swinging-arm rear suspension, completely restored.
£1,250–1,500 *BKS*

*Although best known for their racing and road-going
four-cylinder four-strokes, MV Agusta also built
lightweights, and in the early days listed small two-
strokes and even a scooter. Indeed, one of the marque's
earliest Grand Prix results – fifth place in the 1950
Dutch 125 round – was achieved by a two-stroke.
Much better engineered than any British contemporary,
the 125 MV was powered by a neat, unit-construction,
single-cylinder engine which, somewhat unusually for
a post-war design, featured detachable transfer ports.
The twin-downtube, swinging-arm frame was fitted
with blade-type girder forks.*

1958 MV Agusta 175CSS,
172.4cc, original, unrestored.
£12,000–16,000 *PC*

*Built in very small numbers from 1955 to 1958,
the 175CSS was sold in road trim, but its main
purpose was as a clubman's type racing mount.
There was even a special off-road version, coded
SDMX (Six Day Moto Cross), which was a cross
between an enduro bike and a motocrosser.*

l. **1958 MV Agusta Turismo Rapido Lusso,**
123.5cc, overhead-valves, single cylinder, 54 x 54mm
bore and stroke, unit-construction, 4-speed gearbox,
original legshields, requires restoration.
£400–450 *MAY*

1967 MV Agusta SC6, 591.8cc, double overhead camshafts, 4 cylinders, shaft final drive, fully-enclosed
rear shock absorbers, small lockable metal panniers, single silencer for each pair of exhaust pipes,
mechanically-operated Campagnolo dual front disc brakes.
£12,000–16,000 *PC*

*Compared to the prototype, which debuted at the Milan show in December 1965, the production 600 Four
(coded SC6) displayed a number of changes. These included a revised exhaust system, a stepped seat, a
finned rear-drive bevel box, 24mm UBF Dell'Orto carburettors, a larger battery carrier and generally
smoother lines.*

Miller's
Motorcycle Milestones

MV Agusta 743cc 750S (*Italian 1971*)
Value £10,000–16,000
While its machines were ridden to unparalleled success on the race circuits of the world, MV (Meccanica Verghera) never achieved the same success with its standard production models. As far back as 1950, the company had displayed a road-going version of its illustrious GP double-overhead-camshaft four at the Milan show. However, although the public was treated to occasional tantalising glimpses of this sole prototype over the following years, customers were only able to buy much less exciting lightweight singles and twins.

Then, 15 years later, at the 1965 Milan show, Count Domenico Agusta surprised show goers by displaying a 591.8cc (58 x 56mm) four. Enthusiasts craved a road-going version of the 500GP model, but the newcomer was very much a touring mount, while the engine size was obviously intended to thwart any attempt to create a replica of the factory racer.

Count Agusta had also succeeded in creating what was probably the ugliest motorcycle of the post-war era. It was finished in a sombre black, rather than the racer's Italian red, and was a combination of strange humps and angles with garish chrome, as seen on Japanese commuter bikes of the period. In all, only 135 examples were built between 1967 and 1972.

But MV made amends when, at the 1969 Milan show, it launched the new 750S. This silenced critics who had labelled the 600 staid and dull. By contrast, the S (Sport) was stylish and exciting, displaying all the glamour and colour its forebear lacked.

Entering production in 1971, the 743cc (65 x 56mm) double-overhead-camshaft four was a true dream machine, a Ferrari on two wheels. And just like its four-wheel compatriot, it was very expensive to produce, hence its sky-high price, which was over four times the cost of a Honda CB750.

Like the 600, the 750's engine made use of 1950s GP technology. This meant a mass of expensive gears, bearings and shims, all of which consumed valuable time on the assembly line. Like the racer, the four-cylinder MV roadster became a means of generating publicity and glamour. And although the 750 might have appeared totally divorced from the 600, it owed many of its technical features – including shaft drive – to the earlier machine.

Other versions followed, including the America and Monza, before production ceased in late 1977. In over 10 years, fewer than 2,000 MV fours were sold – compared to over 61,000 CB750s during the first three years in the USA alone!

1972 MV Agusta 350B Elettronica, 349cc, overhead valves, parallel twin cylinders, unit construction.
£2,000–2,300 *IVC*

Considered by many to be the best MV twin of all, the 350B sports model made its debut, along with the 350GT tourer, at the close of the 1960s. In October 1972, both gained 12 volt electrics and electronic ignition, hence the Elettronica name.

1977 MV Agusta Type 216 350 Sport, 349cc, overhead valves, parallel twin cylinders, unit construction, 63 x 56mm bore and stroke, 34bhp at 8,500rpm, 5-speed gearbox, twin carburettors, gear primary drive.
£1,150–1,350 *BKS*

r. **1977 MV Agusta 750S America,** 789cc, double-overhead-camshaft four, 67 x 56mm bore and stroke, partially dismantled, supplied with detached parts including fairing, panels, gearbox cover and complete Magni exhaust system.
£10,500–11,500 *BKS*

The 789cc 750S America project was the work of New York-based Chris Garville and Jim Cotherman.

1974 MV Agusta 750, 743cc, double-overhead-camshaft four, 65 x 56mm bore and stroke, 69bhp at 8,500rpm, shaft final drive, second-series machine fitted with AP-Lockheed front disc brakes in place of original Scarab set-up.
£13,500–14,500 *BKS*

Developed from MV Agusta's long line of successful multi-cylinder racers, the first road-going four – a twin-carburettor, 600cc tourer – appeared in 1965. But the public demanded something more exciting, and the Gallarate marque duly obliged in 1969, upping capacity to 743cc and boosting maximum power to 69bhp by fitting a quartet of Dell'Orto carburettors to the revised 750GT. Also in the line-up was the more sporting 750S, which continued in production after the GT's demise in 1973. It bowed out in 1975 to make way for the 750S America, rated by Bike *magazine as 'one of the most dramatic-looking bikes made' and 'the real stuff of legend'.*

NEW HUDSON (*British 1909–57*)

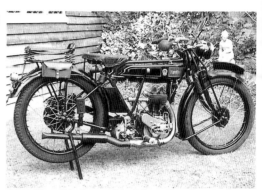

1923 New Hudson, 211cc, single-cylinder 2-stroke, belt final drive, restored to concours condition.
£2,000–3,000 *PVE*

1927 New Hudson 350, 2¾hp, sidevalve single-cylinder engine, acetylene lighting set, leather tool boxes, period accessories.
£2,250–2,500 *BKS*

NEW IMPERIAL (*British 1910–39*)

Prior to WWII, New Imperial was a well-known name in British motorcycling circles, for both road-going production machines and competition bikes. The company's origins can be traced back to 1892, but things really began when Norman Downs took over in 1900. In those early days, New Imperial fitted proprietary engines – usually of JAP or Precision manufacture – into frames of their own design.

Like many companies, New Imperial had to weather the storm at the end of the 1920s and early 1930s caused by the Depression. But they responded in the best possible way, by thinking ahead. This led to the announcement, in August 1931, of their unit-construction models, which were remarkably modern in specification.

In addition to having the engine and gearbox in a common crankcase, the new machines also featured wet-sump lubrication, the oil being carried in a housing at the front of the crankcase. And it wasn't just the engine assembly that showed great forethought, for not only was there rear suspension, but also a form of monoshock.

The first two unit models to arrive had twin-port heads, inclined cylinders and fully enclosed valve gear. More unit-construction models soon followed.

One of the most famous of all New Imperial models was the Grand Prix, its name having been chosen to reflect the marque's racing triumphs. For example, New Imperial won six TT races, all in the 250cc class, except in 1924, when they did the double and took honours in the 350cc (Junior) event as well. Their final TT victory came in 1936 – the same year that the works team finished a magnificent 1–2 in the Ulster GP, which saw a side-by-side dash to the chequered flag.

However, following the death of Norman Downs, the company ran into financial trouble and was sold to Jack Sangster (of Ariel and Triumph fame). Then the war intervened, and Sangster's plan to move New Imperial to the Triumph works in Coventry came to nothing. The result was that only four models (all of unit construction) survived into 1940, but then simply faded away. Like many other marques, New Imperial was not revived after the war.

l. **1914 New Imperial Light Tourist,** 293cc, sidevalve vertical-single-cylinder, JAP engine, right-hand gearchange, belt final drive, acetylene headlamp, bulb horn, leather tool pannier.
£5,000–5,500 *BKS*

r. **1930 New Imperial Model 2,** 344cc, sidevalve single-cylinder engine, 74 x 80mm bore and stroke.
£750–850 *PS*

The Model 2 was one of two 350 sidevalves in the 1930 New Imperial catalogue. It had a single-loop frame, and it qualified for the lower tax rate thanks to its light weight.

NORMAN (*British 1937–61*)

1961 Norman B4 Sports, 249cc, piston-port twin-cylinder 2-stroke Villiers 2T engine, completely restored.
£1,500–1,800 *AT*

Norman was based in Ashford, Kent, where they made bicycles, but they entered the motorcycle field with two models for 1939. Post-war, they built machines for both themselves and Rudge, and by 1960 no less than nine Norman motorcycles and mopeds were listed. The top models were a pair of twins powered by the 249cc, Villiers 2T engine, the B3 Roadster and B3 Sports. For 1961, these were superseded by the definitive B4 series. Norman's last year of production was 1962.

1962 Norman B4, 249cc, twin-cylinder 2-stroke Villiers 2T engine, leading-link front forks, swinging-arm frame, restored over 5 years, concours condition.
£1,600+ *PC*

This bike is one of only three 1962 Norman twins known to exist in the UK.

NORTON (*British 1902–*)

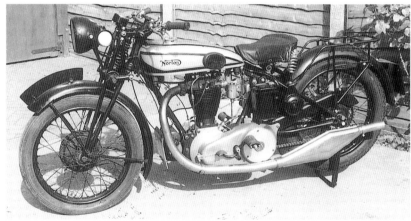

l. **1930 Norton Model 18,** 490cc, overhead-valve single.
£3,000–3,300 *AtMC*

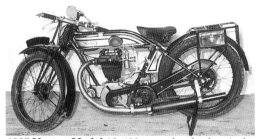

1925 Norton Model 18, 490cc, overhead-valve single.
£11,000–12,000 *BKS*

Norton relied on the sidevalve engine until the 1920s, when their well-tried 490cc unit was used as the basis for their first overhead-valve design. Penned by James Lansdowne Norton himself, and first seen in prototype form in 1922, the overhead-valve Norton made little impact in that year's Senior TT, but at Brooklands D. R. O'Donovan raised the world 500cc kilometre record to over 89mph using the new motor. A road version, the Model 18, was listed for 1923 and quickly established a reputation for speed and reliability when a standard engine was used to set a host of records. Racing continued to improve the breed, the Model 18 gaining Webb forks and better brakes for 1925 – when Alec Bennett won the Senior TT for Norton – as a direct result of the works team's experiences. The Model 18 retained its essentially vintage characteristics until 1931, when the range was redesigned.

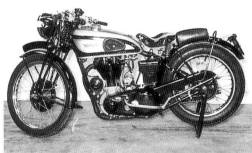

1936 Norton Model 30 International, 490cc, single overhead camshaft, fitted with optional conical hubs.
£6,000–7,000 *BKS*

In 1927, Norton produced their first overhead-camshaft engine, which led to a long association with sporting and racing camshaft singles that lasted into the 1960s. As the engines were developed during this period, they ensured that the company remained world leaders in their field and that the 'Unapproachable Norton' was the greatest road-racing and sporting motorcycle ever produced. In 1933, camshaft Nortons were entered in the ISDT, and a very successful period followed, the machines dominating sporting events at home and abroad. Thus was born the name 'International', which stayed with the sporting single until its demise in 1958.

l. **1936 Norton ES2,**
490cc, overhead-
valve single,
79 x 100mm bore
and stroke, girder
forks, rigid frame,
concours condition.
£4,500–5,000 *BKS*

1936 Norton Model 40 International, 348cc,
single overhead camshaft, 71 x 88mm bore and
stroke, recently restored, excellent condition.
£5,000–5,500 *CotC*

1937 Norton Model 50, 350cc, overhead-
valve single, 71 x 88mm bore and stroke,
very good condition.
£2,200–2,500 *CotC*

The Model 50 was introduced in 1933.

1942 Norton 16H, 490cc, sidevalve single,
79 x 100mm bore and stroke.
£1,400–1,500 *OxM*

*This particular machine is an ex-WD model
converted for civilian use.*

r. **1946 Norton Model 18,** 490cc, overhead-
valve single.
£3,500–3,750 *VER*

*The 1946 Model 18 was very similar to that year's
ES2, but it had a rigid frame instead of the latter's
plunger type. They shared the same telescopic forks
and revised gearbox end cover.*

1949 Norton ES2, 490cc, overhead-valve single, telescopic forks, plunger frame.
£2,500–3,200 *AT*

1954 Norton Big 4, 634cc, sidevalve single, 82 x 120mm bore and stroke, original, excellent condition.
£2,000–2,350 *CotC*

The Big 4 and the 16H of 1954 were the last of Norton's sidevalve line, and they could trace their ancestry back to the first belt-driven Norton single. The Big 4's real strength was as a sidecar tug.

1956 Norton Model 19S, 597cc, overhead-valve single, 82 x 113mm bore and stroke.
£2,300–2,500 *BKS*

1947 Norton Model 30 International, 490cc, over-head-camshaft single, telescopic forks, plunger frame.
£7,000–8,000 *VER*

Make the most of Miller's

Condition is absolutely vital when assessing the value of a Classic Motorcycle. Top class bikes on the whole appreciate much more than less perfect examples. However a rare, desirable machine may command a high price even when in need of restoration.

Miller's
Motorcycle Milestones

Norton Model 99 597cc (*British 1956*)
Value £2,500–5,000
Designed by Herbert 'Bert' Hopwood, the
original 497cc (66 x 72.6mm) Dominator 7
arrived in 1948, with Roadholder forks and a
plunger frame. The early models had a single
downtube, and it was not until November 1951
that the news filtered out of a Dominator with a
road-going version of the famous Featherbed
swinging-arm frame.

When it arrived in time for the 1952 season, the
Model 88 not only employed a Featherbed frame,
but also shortened forks, deeply valanced
mudguards and pear-shaped silencers. It was
intended for export only at first, and was an
immediate success with buyers abroad, quickly
establishing the reputation of the Featherbed's
legendary roadholding. By 1953, the machine
had been given more sporting lines, but it was
still listed as an export model only.

In 1954, the Model 88 became available on the
home market at last. It had gained a more

effective 8in front brake, but still retained a
bolted-up frame and iron head.

For 1955, the Featherbed twin was fitted with a
light alloy head, together with the new Amal
Monobloc carburettor. At last, the frame was not
only made from heavier-gauge tubing, but also the
complete sub-frame was welded to the main loops,
instead of being bolted-up. Other improvements
included full-width alloy hubs, a new dual seat
and polished fork sliders. The Model 88 became
known as the 88 De Luxe late in 1955 and was
joined by a big brother – the 99 – powered by an
enlarged version of the twin-cylinder engine with
dimensions of 68 x 82mm, which gave 597cc.

A *Motor Cycling* test of the 99, early in 1957,
found that the larger model was like the 500, but
with extra performance and better acceleration –
and no additional vibration. Later, the engine
was enlarged still further: first to 646cc in 1961,
then 745cc in 1963. However, although faster,
these later machines were never quite as smooth
or long lasting in use.

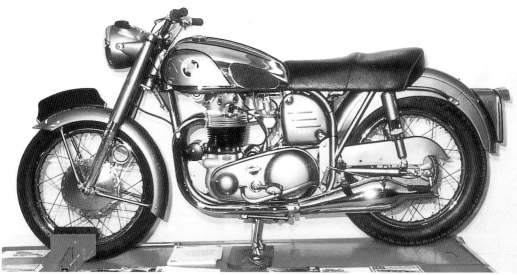

1956 Norton Dominator 99, 597cc,
overhead-valve parallel twin, restored
to concours condition.
£5,000+ *PC*

1960 Norton Dominator 99, 597cc, overhead-
valve twin, non-standard alloy wheel rims.
£5,200–5,500 *BKS*

*Norton's 500 twin appeared in the racing singles'
Featherbed frame in November 1951. Initially for
export only, the Dominator Model 88 was the first
production Norton to feature the lightweight, race-
proven chassis. Introduced for 1956, the 596cc 99 was
outwardly identical to its smaller brother. Although
endowed with greater power and higher gearing,
which enabled it to top the magic 'ton', the 99 retained
the excellent ride and handling associated with the
Featherbed chassis. The model remained essentially
unchanged – apart from gaining alternator/coil-
ignition electrics for 1958 – until dropped in 1962.*

1958 Norton Dominator 88,
497cc, overhead-valve twin.
£2,200–2,500 *PM*

*The famous Featherbed frame with heavily-braced
headstock and welded-on sub-frame was adopted
for the Dominator twin in 1955, replacing the
earlier Featherbed design. In late 1959, the model
received the slimline version of the frame.*

1970 Norton Commando Fastback, 745cc, overhead-valve twin, 73 x 89mm bore and stroke, Isolastic rubber engine mountings, drum brakes.
£4,400–4,700 *BLM*

Voted Machine of the Year in 1968 by Motorcycle News *– following its launch in late 1967 – the Commando went on to win this award five years in a row, a record achievement unmatched before or since. The Commando design was begun in January 1967 under the guidance of Dr Stefan Bauer, who had been appointed by Dennis Poore of Manganese Bronze Group, which had taken over Norton following AMC's collapse in the previous year.*

l. **1973 Norton Commando Roadster,**
745cc, overhead-valve twin.
£3,600–3,800 *BLM*

In 1972, the 750 Roadster received new crankcases, a roller-bearing main, a non-timed breather and an external oil filter. Mid-season, the model was given the Combat engine and a disc front brake. This 1973 model is equipped with all of those improvements.

1975 Norton Commando Interstate MkIII,
829cc, left-hand gear-change, American Prestolite electric starter.
£3,250–3,550 *BKS*

Initially marketed in 750 form with the Combat engine, the Interstate was designed to appeal to those who wished to ride long distances at high speed. As such, it was equipped with a 5 gallon petrol tank to create, in effect, what would be called a sports-tourer today. By 1975, when this particular example was produced, the highly-strung Combat engine had been replaced by the less-stressed, but equally powerful, 829cc engine.

1988 Norton Rotary Classic, 588cc, twin-rotor air-cooled rotary engine.
£5,500–6,500 *PC*

Only 101 examples of this model were produced. Of all the Dr Felix Wankel-inspired rotary engines employed for motorcycle use, the Norton was the best looking and probably most successful. It was also fitted into a touring model using Yamaha-sourced components, the F1 sports bike, the works racing motorcycles and even drone target planes for military use.

l. **1976 Norton 850 Commando Interstate,**
829cc, left-hand gear-change, American Prestolite electric starter.
£5,900–6,200 *BKS*

One of the very last Commandos to be built, this particular 850 Interstate MkIII has never been registered and has only recorded 1½ miles.

NSU (German 1901–67)

Miller's Motorcycle Milestones

NSU Max 247cc (German 1952)
Value £2,000–3,000

Among the real pioneers of the motorcycle, NSU (Neckarsulmer Strickwaren Union), built their first machine in 1901; five years later, they introduced their first car. The first NSU motorcycle employed a single-cylinder Swiss Zedal engine, but later the company produced machines with their own engines, including a line of V-twins from 496 to 996cc.

In 1929, the leading British designer Walter Moore joined NSU from Norton. During the 1930s, he was responsible for a series of rapid single-cylinder models, before returning home just prior to the outbreak of war in 1939.

During the war years, NSU built thousands of motorcycles and pedal cycles, also the *Kettenrad*. This was a small, tracked personnel carrier with motorcycle front forks and a 1478cc Opel car engine.

Albert Roder became chief designer in 1947. Under his leadership, NSU enjoyed unparalleled success during the next decade. The two most important – and successful – models were the Max motorcycle and the Quickly moped. An amazing 1.1 million of the latter were sold between 1953 and 1965.

September 1952 had seen the debut of the very unorthodox 247cc (69 x 66mm) Max. It utilised the pressed-steel chassis and leading-link front forks of the Fox and Lux models, but the overhead-camshaft engine was completely new

and featured a type of valve gear unique among motorcycle engines. Known as the *Ultramax* system, the drive to the overhead valve gear was by long connecting rods housed in a tunnel cast integrally on the nearside of the cylinder. Eyes at the ends of the rods encircled counterbalanced eccentric discs, which were connected to the half-time pinion and the overhead camshaft. As the engine revolved, the eccentrics imparted a reciprocating motion, which was transferred to the valve gear. Hairpin valve springs were used, and the entire mechanism was enclosed. Production of the new Max hit its stride in 1953 when 24,403 units were built.

In 1955, a racing version of the Max, the Sportmax, was sold to customers, while Hermann Peter Müller took the 250cc world road racing title on a semi-works version. That year, the Special Max also went on sale. Then, in 1956, the definitive model, the Supermax, hit the streets.

The last Supermax rolled off the production lines in 1963. In just over a decade, many thousands of Max-based models had been sold. It is also acknowledged as being one of the very best-quality motorcycles to have ever reached series production.

The last NSU two-wheelers were built in 1965. In early 1969, NSU merged with the Volkswagen Group, making it Germany's largest automobile manufacturer.

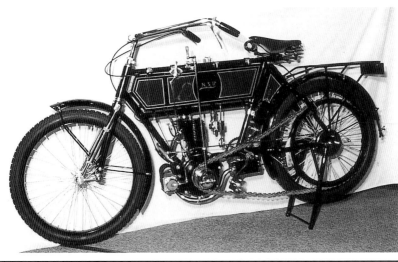

l. **1907 NSU,** 398cc, completely restored to original condition.
£7,500–8,000 *GB*

After using Swiss Zedal engines for their first motorcycles, NSU switched to engines of their own design, including the 398cc single in this particular machine.

OK SUPREME (British 1899–1939)

l. **1925 OK Sports,** 2¾hp, overhead valves, single cylinder.
£4,400–4,600 *BKS*

The OK company was formed in 1899, and its early machines were fitted with various engines, including the De Dion and Minerva. Later, they adopted Blackburne and Bradshaw units, one of the latter being used in this particular machine. In 1926, after the partners split, one of the founders, Ernie Humphries, took control of the company and added 'Supreme' to the title. In the 1930s, motorcycle production expanded considerably, models such as the Silver Cloud and Flying Cloud being listed. OK Supreme built some machines with engines of their own design, notably 246 and 346cc overhead-camshaft units. However, most OK models sported bought-in power units, but by then from JAP and Matchless. Production ceased in 1940 and did not resume after WWII.

PANTHER (*British 1900–66*)

1912 Panther P & M, 499cc, inlet-over-exhaust single, requires restoration.
£3,700–4,000 *BKS*

Like many early pioneers, Jonah Phelon's initial attempt at motorcycle production, in his West Riding engineering works, consisted of little more than replacing the front downtube of a standard pedal cycle with a De Dion Bouton engine. By 1906, he had formed a partnership with Richard Moore, and their machine featured a two-speed gearbox with selective clutch, which was also used by nearby rival Alfred Angus Scott.

1936 Panther Model 30 Red Panther, 348cc, overhead-valve single, 71 x 88mm bore and stroke, wet-sump lubrication, original, unrestored.
£1,200–1,400 *PAN*

1937 Panther Model 20 Red Panther, 249cc, overhead-valve single, 60 x 88mm bore and stroke.
£1,000–1,250 *PM*

This machine displays Panther's traditional inclined cylinder layout.

1963 Panther Model 120, 645cc, overhead-valve single.
£2,750–3,000 *BLM*

r. **1962 Panther Model 120,** 645cc, overhead-valve single, inclined cylinder, twin exhaust ports, 88 x 106mm bore and stroke, original, unrestored, paintwork and some chromework need attention.
£1,300–1,500 *PS*

Introduced in 1958, the Model 120 shared its cycle parts with the 594cc Model 100. It was a big, heavy machine that was ideal for sidecar duty.

PARILLA (*Italian 1946–67*)

c1953 Parilla 175 Turismo, 174cc, high overhead
camshaft, valves operated by short pushrods, unit
construction, 4-speed gearbox, gear primary drive.
£1,900–2,100 *PC*

1955 Parilla 175, 175cc, high overhead camshaft,
single cylinder, 59.8 x 62mm bore and stroke,
unit construction, requires restoration.
£500–600 *PC*

 **Miller's
Motorcycle Milestones**

Parilla 174cc Fox (*Italian 1952*)
Value £1,600–2,500.
Giovanni Parrilla was the son of Spanish
parents who emigrated to southern Italy in
the 1920s. During WWII, he found himself a
new home in the north, in that industrial
heartland, Milan, where he opened a small
business specialising in the repair of
agricultural diesel pumps and injectors. At the
end of the war, much of the northern part of
Italy, including Milan, was left in a shattered
state, and Parrilla took an early decision to
transfer his attention to motorcycles. Bearing in
mind his humble background, the growth of
Parilla (the second 'r' having been deleted) was
quite sensational, particularly given its creator's
lack of financial backing.
  Parilla's first design was a single-overhead-
camshaft, 247cc model, which made its debut as
a racer in October 1946. It was quickly
developed into the company's first production
roadster, which created much favourable
comment in the Italian press when launched the
following year – here was a proper motorcycle,
when rivals were mainly building hoards of
cheap and cheerful, two-stroke commuter
motorcycles and scooters.
  In 1948 came the Biaberro (twin-camshaft)
racer. Power output from the 66 x 72mm engine
(dimensions shared with its roadster brother)

was a healthy 18.5bhp, giving a maximum speed
of almost 100mph.
  More Parillas followed, both four- and two-
strokes. But the model that was to have the
most effect on the company's future appeared at
the end of 1952, in the shape of the unorthodox
175 Fox, with its high-camshaft engine. The
valves were controlled by short, splayed
pushrods operated by a single chain-driven cam,
mounted at the top of the timing case and kept
in adjustment by a Weller-type tensioner. The
engine's capacity was 174cc (59.8 x 62mm).
  The 'high-cam' concept was seen by Giovanni
Parrilla as the way to go for both his street
bikes and racers. The design was the work
of two men, Giuseppe Salmaggi and Alfredo
Bianchi, both famous for several other
notable designs.
  During the mid- to late 1950s, the 175 high-
cam appeared in a wide range of models,
including the GS (Gran Sport). By 1960, there
was also an MSDS. Built to conform with Italian
Formula 3 racing regulations with an open
exhaust, this could achieve 100mph.
  The following year, 1961, Parilla upped the
motor to 199cc (64 x 62mm), then 246.95cc
(68 x 68mm). The latter was mainly aimed at
the American market, in touring and GS forms.
  Parilla quit bikes during 1967 to concentrate
on the manufacture of kart engines.

PREMIER
(*Czechoslovakian 1913–33*)

1913 Premier 3-speed, 3½hp, sidevalve single,
twin exhaust, 3-speed hub, belt drive, restored,
concours winner.
£6,000–7,000 *SUN*

PUCH (*Austrian 1903–*)

1965 Puch SVS, 174cc, 2-stroke split single,
4-speed gearbox, US export model.
£600–800 *BKS*

*In the years preceding WWII, the Austrian
manufacturer Puch developed the concept of the
split single, continuing production after the war.
The engine featured two cylinders and pistons that
shared a common combustion chamber, which was
thought to aid the efficiency of the motor.*

RALEIGH (British 1899–1930s)

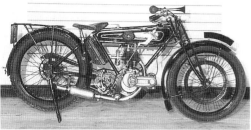

1926 Raleigh 5S.
£2,500–2,750 *HCH*

Famous for their pedal cycles, Raleigh Industries of Nottingham also built motorcycles from 1899 to 1906, then again from 1919 until the early 1930s.

1926 Raleigh Model 16, 350cc, 2¾hp, acetylene headlamp, bulb horn.
£3,500–3,750 *RSS*

The Model 16 was a typical Raleigh inlet-over-exhaust single of the period. The company also owned the well-known Sturmey-Archer concern, which supplied many British and foreign manufacturers with gearboxes and engines. This particular machine is fitted with a 'cocking a snook' mascot, which were very popular with motorcyclists in the 1920s and 1930s.

l. **1928 Raleigh 21,** 549cc, twin-port overhead-valve single, forward-mounted magneto, single carburettor, hand-change gearbox, girder forks.
£4,000–5,000 *RSS*

ROYAL ENFIELD (British 1901–70)

1925 Royal Enfield Lightweight Sports,
348cc, sidevalve single.
£2,000–2,200 *BKS*

In 1924, Royal Enfield introduced two new JAP-engined 350s: the sidevalve Model 350 and overhead-valve Model 351. Also that year, Stan Greening, of JAP's experimental department, appeared at Brooklands with a Royal Enfield fitted with a racing JAP engine. This was the first of many successful entries in sporting events with these machines.

1932 Royal Enfield Cycar Model Z1, 148cc, single-cylinder 2-stroke, 50 x 56mm bore and stroke, original, unrestored.
£1,500–1,850 *AT*

This is a very rare 2-stroke machine, with engine enclosure.

1926 Royal Enfield 8hp, 976cc, inlet-over-exhaust V-twin.
£4,750–5,000 *BKS*

Intended primarily as a sidecar tug, the 8hp model came equipped with footboards and chain final drive incorporating Enfield's cush-drive system. By 1926, it had the option of electric lighting.

1933 Royal Enfield Sport Bullet, 248cc, overhead-valve single, inclined cylinder, 64 x 77mm bore and stroke, original.
£1,400–1,700 *AT*

Bullet 250 production commenced in 1933.

1934 Royal Enfield Model K, 976cc, sidevalve V-twin, 85.5 x 85mm bore and stroke, good condition.
£2,500–3,000 *AT*

After initially being built for export only, the Model K was given a capacity increase to 1140cc (85.5 x 99.25mm).

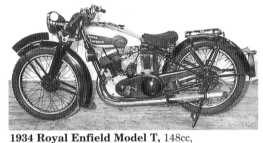

1934 Royal Enfield Model T, 148cc, 56 x 60mm bore and stroke.
£1,300–1,500 *BKS*

Introduced for the 1934 season, the 148cc overhead-valve model had been created specifically for the new 15s (75p) tax bracket for machines under 150cc. It was one of the very few four-strokes in a class dominated by two-strokes.

1939 Royal Enfield RE125, 126cc, 2-stroke, 54 x 55mm bore and stroke.
£2,600–2,800 *BKS*

Manufactured by Royal Enfield in great numbers, the RE125 was offered to the military as well as civilian use. In fact, it had been designed originally for export, but found immediate favour with the Airborne Division of the British Army, who decided that it could easily be dropped by parachute for active service with the Red Berets, who affectionately christened it the 'Flying Flea'. This particular machine is a civilian version, which was despatched from the factory in 1939, but to 1940 specification. As, by that time, the majority of production had been allocated to military projects, this machine is comparatively rare.

1946 Royal Enfield Model G, 346cc, overhead-valve single, 70 x 90mm bore and stroke, separate gearbox, rigid frame.
£1,500–1,700 *BKS*

Following the end of WWII, Royal Enfield introduced the 350 Model G and 500 Model J, which had telescopic forks from the outset. The machines were virtually identical except for their engine capacities.

r. **1957 Royal Enfield Ensign MkII,** 148cc, 2-stroke single, 56 x 60mm bore and stroke, good condition.
£550–600 *PS*

1957 Royal Enfield Bullet, 499cc, overhead-valve single, 84 x 90mm bore and stroke, double-sided drum front brake.
£2,800–3,200 *BLM*

1959 Royal Enfield Bullet, 499cc, overhead-valve single, 84 x 90mm bore and stroke.
£3,000–3,500 *BLM*

Examples of 500 big-head Bullets are difficult to find and are priced accordingly.

1962 Royal Enfield Constellation, 692cc, overhead-valve pre-unit twin, excellent condition, fully restored.
£3,000–3,500 *CotC*

The Constellation was the performance model in Enfield's 1962 range. Besides a hotter engine, it sported a siamesed exhaust system and chromed mudguards.

1964 Royal Enfield Crusader Sports, 248cc, overhead-valve single, 70 x 64.5mm bore and stroke, unit construction, 4-speed gearbox, good condition.
£700–1,000 *BLM*

The Crusader Sports was as quick as many heavyweight 350s.

1966 Royal Enfield Continental GT, 248cc, overhead-valve single, 70 x 64.5mm bore and stroke, 5-speed gearbox.
£1,500–2,300 *BLM*

Created in response to the café racer cult sweeping Britain at the time, the Continental GT demonstrated that Royal Enfield was more in tune with customers' needs than many of the larger factories.

1965 Royal Enfield Turbo Roadster, 249cc, Villiers 4T 2-stroke twin-cylinder engine, restored.
£1,800–2,000 *BTS*

l. **1970 Royal Enfield Interceptor Series II,** 736cc, overhead-valve twin, 71 x 93mm bore and stroke.
£3,000–3,300 *BKS*

Until the launch of the Norton Atlas, the Interceptor – developed from the company's Constellation model – had been the largest-capacity vertical twin produced in Great Britain. Endowed with vast amounts of torque, the model was redesigned in 1968, adopting wet-sump lubrication, a Norton front end and a pair of Amal Concentric MkI carburettors.

RUDGE (British 1910–40)

1913 Rudge Multi, 499cc.
£5,300–5,500 *S*
This particular Rudge Multi was entered by John Rennison in the 10th Pioneer Run in April 1939, after having been found on a scrapheap in the previous year.

1924 Rudge Multi, 499cc.
£3,500–4,000 *CotC*

1937 Rudge Special, 499cc, overhead-valve twin-port single, girder forks, rigid frame, black and gold finish.
£2,750–3,250 *AT*

SCOTT (British 1909–69)

1912 Scott Twin, 486cc, water-cooled 2-stroke engine, unused for several years, requires recommissioning.
£7,700–8,000 *BKS*

Bradford-born Alfred Scott's experiments with 2-stroke motorcycle engines began in the closing years of the 19th century. The first Scott motorcycle followed in 1908, its twin-cylinder engine, two-speed foot-change gearbox and all-chain drive making it an exceptionally advanced design for its day. Light weight, ample power and sure-footed handling were Scott virtues from the outset. Not surprisingly, the machine soon made a name for itself in trials events, often with its inventor aboard; in 1909, the marque made its first appearance in the Isle of Man TT. Revisions to the design saw a water-cooled, rather than air-cooled, cylinder head and barrel. Chain-driven rotary valves were used by the works racers in 1911, but without success, leading to a switch to gears for 1912. This would prove a breakthrough year for Scott, as works rider Frank Appleby won the Senior TT, having led from the start. It was the first time such a feat had been achieved, and the first Senior victory for a two-stroke.

1919 Scott Standard, 532cc, water-cooled
2-stroke twin, inclined cylinders, 2-speed
gearbox, deeply valanced mudguards, footboards,
'pull-back' handlebars, vintage-type fuel canister,
original condition.
£5,000+ *SUN*

1925 Scott Super Squirrel, 498cc, water-cooled
2-stroke twin, 3-speed gearbox.
£2,400–2,600 *BKS*

*Although recognisably derived from Alfred Scott's
earliest designs, the Scott motorcycle of the 1920s
gained steadily in complexity and weight.
A three-speed countershaft gearbox had been
introduced for 1923, and as a result of the racing
programme, there was a new duplex fame and
bigger brakes for 1927. For the traditionalists,
the old-style two-speed model soldiered on into
the 1930s.*

l. **1928 Scott Flying Squirrel Sports,** 499cc,
water-cooled 2-stroke twin, 68.25 x 68.25mm bore
and stroke, siamesed exhaust, concours condition.
£5,000–5,500 *VER*

r. **1930 Scott Flying
Squirrel,** 499cc,
68.25 x 68.25mm
bore and stroke.
£3,700–4,000 *BKS*

1950 Scott Flying Squirrel, 598cc, water-cooled 2-stroke twin, 73 x 71.4mm bore and stroke,
Dowty forks, rigid frame.
£2,800–3,200 *BKS*

*During the spring of 1950, Scott Motors (Saltaire) Ltd went into voluntary liquidation, but in December it was
announced that manufacture of the 1951 range would take place in Birmingham, following acquisition of the
rights by Matt Holder of the Aerco Jig & Tool Co. This particular machine was despatched from the Shipley
works on 23 March 1950, making it one of the very last of 600 machines built post-war by Scott Motors.*

SERTUM (*Italian 1922–51*)

1950 Sertum 250, 249cc, sidevalve engine, unit construction, 4-speed gearbox, blade-type girder forks, pillion pad.
£4,000–5,000 *IVC*

This once famous Milan factory originally made precision instruments, but in 1922 its owner, Fausto Alberti, decided to enter the two-wheel market. The company's first design was a 174cc sidevalve model. Thereafter, throughout the 1920s and 1930s, Sertum grew to considerable size, thanks to the excellence of its dependable singles and twins – in sidevalve, overhead-valve and even overhead-camshaft form. Sertum were also actively involved in motorcycle sport, notably the ISDT and long-distance road races such as the famous Milano-Taranto epic. But after a promising post-war start, things went rapidly downhill, to the point in 1951 where the company was forced to close.

SUNBEAM (*British 1912–57*)

1913 Sunbeam 2¾hp, 347cc, sidevalve single-cylinder engine.
£7,000–7,500 *BKS*

Already established as manufacturers of high-quality bicycles, Sunbeam entered the world of powered two-wheelers in 1912 with an advanced design having a two-speed gearbox and all-chain drive. At 347cc, the machine was regarded as a lightweight, but its exceptional finish and quality placed it firmly in the premium sector of the market, contemporary advertising describing it as the 'Gentleman's Motorcycle'.

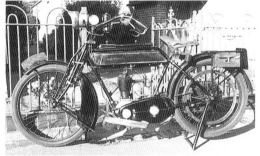

1913 Sunbeam 2¾hp, 347cc, sidevalve single, vertical cylinder, footboards, tyre pump on top frame rail, original, unrestored condition.
£7,000+ *VER*

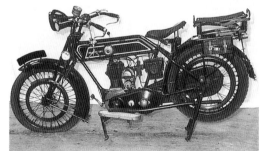

1923 Sunbeam 3½hp Longstroke Model, substantially original, unused for some time, requires recommissioning.
£3,500–4,000 *BKS*

After the launch of their first motorcycle in 1912, Sunbeam quickly established a reputation for sporting prowess, achieving second place in the 1914 Isle of Man Senior TT, and winning the 1920 race. Overhead-valve engines were introduced in the mid-1920s, but early successes were achieved with sidevalve machines, most notably the 492cc 'longstroke', which secured a debut win at the 1921 French Grand Prix. In road-going form, this engine remained in production until WWII.

1925 Sunbeam Sports, 499cc sidevalve single, hand-change gearbox, all-chain drive, kickstart, small drum brakes.
£3,200–3,500 *BKS*

The 1925 'longstroke' sports was sometimes known as the 'Speedman's Machine'.

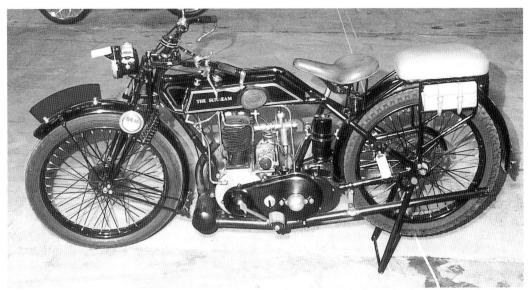

1925 Sunbeam Model 6, 499cc, sidevalve single, original racing camshaft, engine bottom end rebuilt.
£4,500–5,000 *BKS*

John Marston was born in 1836 at Ludlow, Shropshire. After serving an apprenticeship in the tinplate business, he began making bicycles in 1888, registering the trademark 'Sunbeam'. His machines soon gained a reputation for quality, and his motorcycles followed suit, being renowned for their deep, lustrous black finish. Marston died in 1918, and his company became a part of Nobel Industries, but production of high-quality motorcycles continued.

1926 Sunbeam Model 7 4½hp, 600cc, sidevalve engine, 4-speed gearbox, interchangeable wheels, used regularly since full restoration 27 years ago.
£4,500–5,000 *SUN*

1927 Sunbeam 6 Longstroke, 492cc, sidevalve engine, 77 x 105.5mm bore and stroke, 3-speed gearbox, Amac carburettor, Lucas mag-dyno lighting set, fitted with optional steering damper and beaded-edge rims and tyres rather than wired-on tyres, restored 1977, used regularly since.
£3,700–4,000 *SUN*

1928 Sunbeam Model 8, 346cc, overhead-valve single, 70 x 90mm bore and stroke, girder forks, rigid frame.
£2,500–2,800 *BKS*

1935 Sunbeam Model 16, 248cc, overhead-valve single-port high-camshaft engine, 64 x 70mm bore and stroke, original exhaust and silencer.
£1,500–2,000 *AT*

The Model 16 was made only in 1935.

l. **1936 Sunbeam Model 9,** 493cc, overhead-valve single-port engine, fully enclosed final-drive chain.
£3,700–4,000 *BKS*

For the 1936 season, the touring Model 9 reverted to a single-port head. It gained a new cradle frame and, with many others in the Sunbeam range, adopted a Burman gearbox. This moved the final drive to the nearside of the machine.

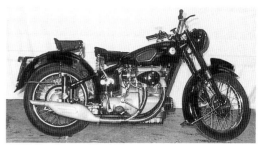

1939 Sunbeam Model B25, 497cc, overhead-valve
single-port high-camshaft single, 82.5 x 93mm bore
and stroke.
£2,000–2,500 *OxM*

This model was first produced in 1939.

1952 Sunbeam S8, 489cc.
£2,400–2,600 *BKS*

*The S8 Sunbeam was introduced in March 1949
as a more sporting version of the Erling Poppe-
designed S7.*

1949 Sunbeam S7, 489cc, overhead-camshaft all-alloy in-line vertical twin, 70 x 63.5mm bore and stroke,
unit construction, shaft drive, plunger rear suspension, 16in balloon tyres, restored to concours condition.
£3,800–4,000 *VER*

*After being sold to AMC in 1937, Sunbeam passed to the BSA group in 1943. In early 1946, the company
released details of one of the few really new post-war British motorcycles, the S7.*

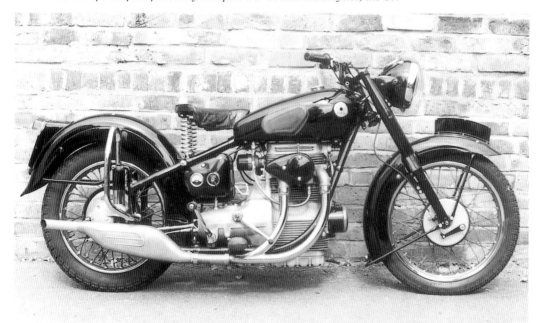

1958 Sunbeam S8, 489cc, overhead-valve in-line twin, cast alloy silencer, restored, excellent condition.
£2,300–2,500 *CotC*

This particular example was one of the last S8s to be built, with production ceasing in 1958.

SUZUKI (*Japanese 1952–*)

1965 Suzuki M15 Sportsman, 50cc, single-cylinder piston-port, 2-stroke, 41 x 38mm bore and stroke.
£750–1,000 *BKS*

The M15 Sportsman was built from 1963 to 1967.

1976 Suzuki GT550A, 544cc, 3 cylinder 2-stroke, 61 x 62mm bore and stroke, 50bhp at 6,500rpm, original, unrestored.
£1,300–1,500 *SKC*

Although similar in appearance to the GT380, the GT550 was considerably faster. It also had a five-speed gearbox instead of the former's six-speed unit. One drawback of this model is that the chrome cylinders cannot be rebored. Good examples are hard to find, but some parts – such as indicators, mudguards and wheels – are interchangeable with other models.

1972 Suzuki GT 750J, 739cc, 3 cylinder water-cooled 2-stroke, piston-port induction, 70 x 64mm bore and stroke, completely restored.
£3,300–3,600 *SOC*

The GT 750J was the first of Suzuki's water-cooled triples to be put on to the market (in 1972), and was the company's answer to Honda's CB750 four. It had a four-leading-shoe front brake, which later was changed to twin discs. A true Grand Tourer, it was not only fast and comfortable, but also proved long-lived.

1974 Suzuki RE5M, 497cc, Wankel rotary engine, 6-speed gearbox, unrestored, superb condition.
£3,500–3,800 *SOC*

Prices for this model start at £800 for tatty examples. The later version (RE5A) was produced with GS750-type clocks instead of the cylindrical canister seen on this early model.

 # Miller's Motorcycle Milestones

Suzuki T500 492cc (*Japanese 1967*)
Value £1,200–1,900
The T500 was Suzuki's first large-capacity motorcycle, and the initial batch of machines reached Britain in late 1967, although the model had gone on sale in the USA earlier that year. The Stateside name, Titan, was not used in Britain because a leading motorcycle dealer of the era, Read Titan of Leytonstone, had already registered the name. Thus, the Titan became the Cobra in the UK.

When the 250cc T20 model was launched in 1965, few observers could have foreseen that two years later, Suzuki would introduce another, similar machine, but with double the capacity. Like the T20, the newcomer employed a piston-port, twin-cylinder 2-stroke engine, but the larger 70 x 64mm bore and stroke dimension gave a displacement of 492cc. With a 6.6:1 compression ratio, the engine developed a maximum power output of 46bhp at 7,000rpm. The overall appearance of the larger engine was clearly based on the T20, but it differed from the smaller unit in many details.

The bottom end of the 500 was almost a carbon copy of the 250, with needle bearings for both the big- and small-ends, three main bearings and four crankshaft seals; the alternator was on the nearside, and the helical-

gear primary drive on the offside. Unlike the smaller engine, the 500 employed five instead of six gears.

Both the cylinder and heads were of aluminium, the former with replaceable cast iron liners. Early engines featured 34mm carburettors, but from 1969 these were replaced by 32mm instruments.

In standard road-going form, the T500 could top 110mph, but later specially-prepared racing versions showed that its real potential was far greater.

Like most Suzukis of the period, lubrication was provided by a pump and separate oil tank. This did much to gain the 2-stroke new friends and buyers, who might otherwise have been put off by having to mix their own oil and petrol to a specific ratio.

Robust and simple to work on, the 500 Suzuki twin proved ultra reliable in service. Another star feature was its economy, which for a large-capacity 2-stroke was amazing: 50mpg was easily obtainable with the minimum of oil consumption.

The final version, the GT500A, was introduced in 1976, gaining a disc front brake, electronic ignition and a steering damper. The model was deleted from Suzuki's range at the end of 1977, after a decade of continual development.

1976 Suzuki GT550, 544cc, air-cooled 3 cylinder 2-stroke, 5-speed gearbox, completely restored.
£2,500+ *SOC*

1977 Suzuki GT380B, 371cc, 54 x 54mm bore and stroke, 38bhp at 7,500rpm.
£800–1,300 *BKS*

The GT380 entered production in 1972. It featured a six-speed gearbox and had a frame clearly based upon the 750 triple. It was a true 100mph machine, which was marketed as the Sebring in the USA. The final year of production was 1979.

1977 Suzuki GT380B, 371cc, 3 cylinder 2-stroke, completely original.
£800–1,300 *SKC*

r. **1977 Suzuki GT750B,** 739cc, 3 cylinder 2-stroke, 70bhp at 6,500rpm, original, concours condition.
£2,800–3,000 *SKC*

Unlike many machines, the GT750 improved in later years, both in specification and performance.

l. **1977 Suzuki RV125,** 123cc, 2-stroke single, 56 x 50mm bore and stroke, 10bhp at 6,000rpm, 5-speed gearbox, 14in front and 12in rear tyre, original.
£1,000–1,200 *SKC*

The all-terrain RV125 was equally at home on road, mud, sand, dirt or snow – a two-wheeled 'Land Rover' in fact. It was built from 1973 to 1977. Suzuki also produced 50, 75 and 90cc versions, but these had four-speed gearboxes. This particular model is now very rare.

1978 Suzuki GS550E, 549cc, double-overhead-camshaft air-cooled 4-stroke, 56 x 55.8mm bore and stroke, 6-speed gearbox, imported to UK from Italy.
£650–700 *MAY*

r. **1984 Suzuki Katana 1000SZ,** 998cc, double-overhead-camshaft air-cooled four, restored, modified with 36mm Mikuni carburettors (from 29mm), RF600 front end, GSX600F rear wheel and hand-made swinging arm, concours condition.
£4,000+ *SOC*

TERROT (*French 1901–early 1960s*)

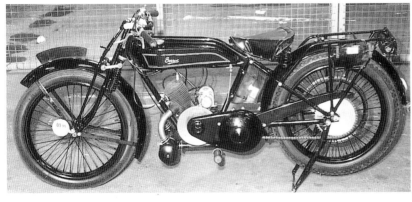

l. **1920s Terrot Tourist,** 175cc, twin-port 2-stroke single, chain final drive, rigid frame, flat tank.
£1,300–1,500 *PS*

r. **1927 Terrot Model HSS,** 349cc, overhead-valve single-port engine, hand gear-change, restored.
£2,500–2,800 *AT*

TRIUMPH (TWN) (German 1903–57)

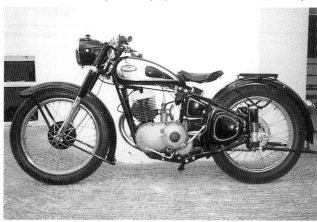

l. **1953 Triumph BDG 250H,** 246cc, split-single 2-stroke, 11bhp at 3,800rpm, original, 101 miles from new, very good condition, very rare.
£1,650–1,850 *CotC*

Although known as TWN in Germany's export markets to avoid confusion with the British Triumph marque, in many ways the German company had as much claim to the name as its British counterpart. Not only did the Germans Siegfried Bettman and Mauritz Schulte found the British company in Coventry in 1897, but they also opened a factory at Nuremberg in 1903. It was this plant that went on to build the German Triumphs. The factory was absorbed into the massive Grundig electrical combine in 1958, after which no more motorcycles were built.

TRIUMPH (British 1902–)
The Early Days

Most enthusiasts probably consider Triumph to be the most British of British motorcycles, but in truth the marque originated mainly through the efforts of a young German, Siegfried Bettman, who had moved to England in 1884. In 1887, he was joined by another young German, Mauritz Schulte. With Bettman handling the business side and Schulte the engineering, they put their early efforts into the manufacture of pedal cycles, the pair setting up a small factory in Coventry during 1888.

But Bettman had bigger ideas, while Schulte had become interested in the developing motor industry. Thus, in 1902, Triumph built their first motorcycle. This combined a Belgian-made 2¼hp Minerva engine with a Triumph bicycle frame.

By 1905, they had designed and built their own 3hp, single-cylinder, sidevalve engine, which spawned a range of models. Thanks to sound design and good quality, these soon built a reputation for reliability that was second to none. This was followed by competition success in the TT of 1908.

During WWI, the term 'Trusty Triumph' was coined, the company being major suppliers of motorcycles to the British and Allied armed forces. Following the end of the conflict, Triumph continued to offer a wide range of machines for the burgeoning civilian market, although they were not particularly innovative, mainly being based on pre-war designs. One model that stood out from this crowd of largely uninteresting machines was the four-overhead-valve Model R (Ricardo). However, although its advanced engine caused a stir, its running gear let it down, being standard sidevalve tackle.

The Depression, which had begun with the Wall Street Crash of October 1929, caused Triumph severe financial problems during the early 1930s. And even though the noted designer Val Page joined Triumph from Ariel in 1932, the company did not stave off the financial crisis. This was only overcome when John Young Sangster (known as Mr Jack or JYS) bought Triumph and appointed Edward Turner as chief designer and managing director. Turner's legendary Speed Twin, which appeared in 1937, set a standard that the rest of the industry could only admire, then copy. With the Turner-created Tiger singles, the Speed Twin gave Triumph a strong product range that made the company profitable once more.

1921 Triumph Model H, 550cc, sidevalve single-cylinder engine.
£2,650–2,850 *BKS*

The Model H was developed for military use during WWI and was a popular bike with despatch riders, earning the marque the accolade of 'Trusty Triumph'. It remained in production from 1915 until 1927, alongside a range of similar 500 and 550cc machines and, of course, the 225cc Junior model.

1924 Triumph Model 3-46, 346cc, sidevalve single.
£3,000–3,500 *BKS*

The 3-46 was essentially a larger version of Triumph's innovative, unit-construction, three-speed, 250cc LS model. Like its smaller brother, it was one of the first machines in the Triumph range to feature drum brakes.

1935 Triumph 5/3, 549cc, sidevalve single, good condition, suitable for solo or sidecar use.
£1,500–1,750 *CotC*

r. **1939 Triumph T100,** 498.76cc, overhead-valve twin, 63 x 80mm bore and stroke, 4-speed foot-change gearbox.
£6,000–6,750 *VER*

Edward Turner followed his success with the Tiger singles of 1936 by designing the Speed Twin, which debuted in 1937. Initially known as the Model T, it soon became the Speed Twin or 5T. The more sporting T100 followed in 1939. This particular machine was one of the very first T100s built.

1938 Triumph Tiger 80, 349cc, overhead-valve single, 70 x 89mm bore and stroke.
£5,000–6,000 *BKS*

Suffering from financial difficulties, Triumph was taken over by Ariel's boss, Jack Sangster, in early 1936. One of his first moves was to instruct Edward Turner (designer of the Ariel Square Four) to create a new breed of Triumph single. The result was the 249cc Tiger 70, 349cc Tiger 80 and 493cc Tiger 90, all of which debuted that same year. Turner's changes were simple, but very effective. He had given the existing models a more sporting specification and new names, adding additional sparkle with extra chrome and eye-catching colours.

1946 Triumph 3T, 349cc, overhead-valve pre-unit twin, 55 x 73.4mm bore and stroke, telescopic forks, rigid frame.
£2,900–3,200 *VER*

The 3T was the smallest of the immediate post-war twins, being introduced in 1946. It was similar in appearance to the 500cc twin, but had significant changes to the design of its engine.

Miller's
Motorcycle Milestones

Triumph 149cc T15 Terrier (*British 1953*)
Value £600–1,400
It was in November 1952 that Triumph announced a brand-new single, just in time to be launched at the annual Earls Court show. The machine represented a new approach by the company, signalling a return to the commuter market. Ultimately, it spawned not only the famous Tiger Cub, but also a whole family of BSA unit singles, starting with the C15 in 1958 and ending with the Victor 500 in 1971.

Designer Edward Turner (famous for the Ariel Square Four and Triumph Speed Twin) decided that the Terrier could get away with a capacity of 149cc (57 x 58.5mm) while providing adequate performance. It would also need to look like the larger Triumphs – to encourage owners to move on to the larger twin-cylinder models.

Turner chose a four-stroke engine when virtually every other British manufacturer of mainstream lightweights used two-strokes. He reasoned that although it would be more expensive to buy, it could provide more rider features – many copied from the twins – and a much lower fuel consumption. He also chose an overhead-valve design rather than an overhead-camshaft arrangement.

The engine construction was unusual, for the crankcase was not split on the vertical centre-line, but to the left of the crankshaft. Once the latter was installed, a 'door', carrying the drive-side main bearing, was fitted to complete its support. This extended to the rear to form the inner primary chaincase, reducing the number of castings and providing a rigid assembly.

A 1953 advertisement for the model read, 'A Real Triumph – in miniature! The Triumph Terrier 150cc ohv, unit construction engine/gearbox, 4-speed, foot operated gearbox, telescopic forks and spring frame.'

Although the Terrier was taken out of production in 1956, its successor, the 199cc T20 Tiger Cub (which had followed in late 1953), had a much longer life. It was 15 years old when production ceased in 1968.

But it was the Terrier that had started it all and, therefore, deserves a special place in British motorcycling folklore.

1949 Triumph TR5 Trophy, 498.76cc, overhead-valve pre-unit twin.
£4,000–4,500 *BKS*

Introduced in 1949 and drawing on the company's experience in the ISDT, the Trophy had an engine based on the Speed Twin, but fitted with the alloy head and block from the Grand Prix racing model. A special frame with a short wheelbase and good ground clearance was utilised, while the remainder of the components reflected the model's intended off-road purpose.

1954 Triumph Tiger 110, 649cc, overhead-valve twin, 42bhp, original, partly restored.
£3,500–4,000 *PC*

In October 1953, a sports version of the Thunderbird was shown at the Paris show and featured many changes. Among these were high-compression pistons, a higher-lift camshaft and a larger carburettor. The model was named the Tiger 110 and was the first Triumph to be offered with swinging-arm rear suspension.

1951 Triumph T100, sprung hub.
£2,800–3,200 *AT*

A race kit was available for the T100, allowing the owner to compete in Clubman's racing. Bernard Hargreaves won the 1952 Senior Clubman's TT on just such a machine, averaging 82.45mph for the four-lap, 151 mile race.

1954 Triumph T100, 498.76cc, overhead-valve parallel twin, Isle of Man racing history, restored, concours condition.
£5,000–6,000 *CotC*

At the end of 1953, the Tiger 100 gained a swinging-arm frame and an 8in front brake as standard.

One of the few changes for the 1957 Triumph range was the adoption of the now famous checkerboard tank badge and chrome strip. These made a useful colour break when a two-tone finish was applied. Other more important, but less obvious, refinements included the replacement of the single-sided front brake and hub with a full-width component on the Speed Twin and 650cc models.

1958 Triumph 3TA Twenty-One, 349cc, overhead-valve unit construction twin, 58.25 x 65.5mm bore and stroke, restored to original specification, including two-tone seat. **£1,750–2,000** *CotC*

The name 'Twenty-One' was chosen to celebrate Triumph's 21st birthday, and also because in the USA, a 350cc engine falls into the 21cu in class.

1957 Triumph 6T Thunderbird, 649cc, original except for aftermarket carrier. **£2,700–3,000** *PC*

1959 Triumph TR6 Trophy, 649cc, overhead-valve pre-unit twin, all-alloy engine, single carburettor, siamesed high-level exhaust, not completely original. **£4,400–4,600** *BLM*

1960 Triumph T20 Cub, 199.5cc, overhead-valve unit-construction single, 63 x 64mm bore and stroke, original except Zenith carburettor replaced by superior Amal Monobloc. **£800–1,100** *MAY*

1960 Triumph T100A, 490cc.
£2,500–3,000 *S*

The first year of production for the T100A was 1960. Basically, it was a 5TA with special cams, a higher compression ratio of 9:1, an energy-transfer ignition system, a five-plate clutch and a different silencer. It was finished in black except for the lower section of the fuel tank, which was painted ivory.

1961 Triumph T120R Bonneville, 649cc, overhead-valve pre-unit twin, restored, original except for Amal Mk1 Concentric carburettors instead of Monoblocs.
£5,500–6,000 *PA*

The 1960–61 T120R Bonneville is one of the most sought after of all Triumph motorcycles. Arguably, it is the most desirable of all Bonnevilles, with its famous powder blue and silver finish.

1961 Triumph TR6 Trophy, 649cc, overhead-valve pre-unit twin.
£3,500–4,000 *BLM*

The Trophy reappeared in early 1961, but it was far removed from the earlier TR5. In fact, it was really a single-carburettor version of the T120R Bonneville.

1961 Triumph Tiger 110, 649cc, overhead-valve pre-unit twin.
£3,000–3,300 *BLM*

Fastest of all the Triumph 'bathtub' models, the Tiger 110 was built from September 1959 to the end of 1962. It shared its styling with the 6T Thunderbird (and the 3TA, 5TA and T100A unit models) of the same era.

Triumph – Staying in front

Triumph remain the leading manufacturers of motorcycles in the UK, continuing a trend that began in the 1930s with Edward Turner's ground-breaking 500cc Speed Twin. That machine established a blueprint for twins which became central to the British industry for the following four decades, and it provided the basis for all models turned out during Triumph's halcyon days, with the exception of their lightweight Cub/Terrier series. Machines such as the Tiger 100 and 110, Thunderbird, Daytona, Bonneville and Trident owe their ancestry to this one model. Equally, the Triumph twin proved one of the most successful and versatile competition engines, scoring victories in every field of motorcycle sport.

The more recent intervention and capital investment of Midlands businessman John Bloor have provided a new range of machines that are modern in all respects. They have been enthusiastically received by the trade, by the press and by riders, ensuring the marque's continued presence in the motorcycle market for the next century.

l. **1962 Triumph T100SS,** 490cc, overhead-valve pre-unit twin, semi-'bathtub' rear enclosure, siamesed exhaust as standard. **£1,750–2,000** *PM*

The 7in front drum brake of the T100SS was not powerful enough to cope with the machine's performance.

1963 Triumph Tiger 90, 349cc, overhead valves, unit construction. **£2,000–2,200** *BKS*

Launched in October 1962, the Tiger 90 featured a tuned engine equipped with a siamesed exhaust and a revised ignition system. The latter employed points instead of the previous distributor.

1965 Triumph Tiger Cub, 199.5cc, overhead-valve unit single. **£600–800** *VER*

From 1963, all Cub models had contact points in the timing cover, a clutch cable access hole in the cover, and finned rocker box inspection covers.

1966 Triumph T120 Bonneville, 649cc, overhead-valve unit twin, later twin-leading-shoe front brake. **£3,000–3,500** *BLM*

From the 1963 model year, all Triumph 650s switched to a unit-construction layout with a new nine-bolt cylinder head. The tank badges were also restyled that year.

1967 Triumph T100T Daytona, 490cc, overhead-valve unit twin, 8in front brake. **£2,750–3,250** *BLM*

The Daytona was first produced in 1967, with the big Bonneville front brake.

1967 Triumph Tiger 90, 349cc, overhead-valve unit twin, unrestored.
£1,500–1,800 *MAY*

1968 Triumph Daytona T100T, 490cc, overhead-valve unit twin.
£2,500–2,700 *BLM*

New Daytona features for 1968 were a twin-leading-shoe front brake, twin carburettors, a modified frame and separate points.

1969 Triumph Trophy TR25W, 249cc, overhead-valve single, 67 x 70mm bore and stroke, 24bhp at 8,000rpm.
£600–800 *BLM*

Launched in 1968, the TR25W was based on the 250cc BSA. Built in trail form, it had an upswept exhaust tucked close to the frame on the offside. The twin-leading-shoe front brake was new for 1969, while the exhaust ran outside, rather than inside, the frame tube.

l. **1969 Triumph Trophy TR6,** 649cc, overhead-valve pre-unit twin, restored, excellent condition.
£4,000+ *CotC*

For 1969, the 650cc Triumph gained exposed rear springs and an exhaust balance pipe. This particular bike is a British model with twin silencers.

> **Don't Forget!**
> *If in doubt please refer to the 'How to Use' section at the beginning of this book.*

l. **1969 Triumph TR6 Trophy,** 649cc, overhead valve unit twin, export version with high-level exhaust.
£2,000–2,300 *PS*

l. **1924 Raleigh,** 350cc, 2¾hp, inlet-over-exhaust single, calliper brakes, inverted control levers.
£3,000–3,500 *RSS*

Famous for its pedal cycles, the Nottingham-based Raleigh concern was once equally well known for its motorcycles. It also built Sturmey Archer gearboxes, which were sold to rival manufacturers throughout Europe.

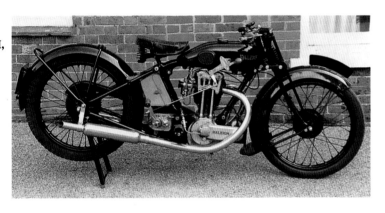

r. **1928 Raleigh Model MH,** overhead-valve twin-port single, forward-mounted magneto.
£4,250–4,650 *VER*

The MH model continued until the end of 1933, when the company switched to building three-wheeler cars and vans, which it had begun in 1930. In 1935, the three-wheelers also ceased and the firm returned to bicycles production.

l. **1934 Royal Enfield Model K,** 976cc, sidevalve V-twin, 85.5 x 85mm bore and stroke.
£2,500–3,000 *HCH*

During the early 1930s, the Royal Enfield range was headed by the K-Series V-twin. Basically an old design, it was largely intended for sidecar use. Later, a larger 1140cc (85.5 x 99.25mm) engine was introduced, which ran up to 1939.

Enfield India

During 1956, Royal Enfield set up a subsidiary in Madras, India, to manufacture the famous Bullet single-cylinder model in its 350cc form under licence. The Indian plant did nothing more than faithfully reproduce the original – keeping largely to the 1955 British specification. This was very much in the same tradition as another factory, which produced the Indian-built Morris Oxford car.

When the British Royal Enfield factory eventually closed its doors at the beginning of the 1970s, after a move to Bradford-on-Avon, Wiltshire, the Enfield India enterprise simply kept on going. By this time, a 175cc Crusader model, powered by an Indian-built Villiers two-stroke engine, had joined the range.

Later came a 499cc version of the Bullet – again very much a replica of the original British model. From the late 1970s, these machines have been imported into Britain, first by Slater Bros (the then Laverda importers) and later by an Indian living in southern Britain.

Since the 1956 licence agreement, Enfield India has produced hundreds of thousands of motorcycles, and continues to do so as we approach the 21st century. Certainly quantities produced of both the four-stroke and two-stroke models have long since overtaken the original British production figures.

Another twist to the Enfield India saga came in 1986, when it was announced that the company would also produce the German Zündapp K80 commuter model under yet another licencing agreement.

l. **1960 Royal Enfield Constellation,** 692cc, overhead-valve twin, 70 x 90mm bore and stroke, leading-axle fork, double-sided front drum brake.
£3,300–3,600 *PS*

Nicknamed the 'Connie', the Constellation arrived in April 1958. The engine was based on the Super Meteor unit fitted with 8.5:1 pistons, magneto ignition, Amal TT carburettor and siamesed exhaust system. This pushed the power up to 51bhp at 6,250rpm. Motor Cycling took one to Belgium and timed it at 115mph.

r. **1965 Royal Enfield Turbo Sports,** 249cc, Villiers 4T engine, restored.
£2,000+ *BTS*

The Turbo twin was essentially a set of Crusader cycle parts propelled by a Villiers 4T engine. The silencers and carburettor were also sourced from Villiers. The sports version had a special finish, including extra chrome plate on items such as the tank and mudguards.

l. **1923 Rudge Multi,** 499cc.
£4,500–5,000 *VER*

The British company Rudge Whitworth manufactured motorcycles from 1911 until 1940. The Multi model earned its name from its gearbox, which offered no less than 20 gear stages. Production continued until 1923.

r. **1937 Rudge Sports Special,** 499cc, overhead-valve twin-port single, 85 x 88mm bore and stroke, high-level exhaust, concours condition.
£3,500–4,000 *PM*

First offered in 1937, the Sport Special featured a pent-roof, four-valve cylinder head with enclosed valve gear. Production ceased in 1940.

r. **1930 Scott Flying Squirrel,** 499cc, water-cooled twin with inclined cylinders, leather tool carrier.
£3,250–3,750 *VER*

Founded by Alfred Angas Scott, this famous company was based in Shipley, West Yorkshire. Much later, in 1950, it moved to Birmingham. The 1930 range offered two engine sizes – 499cc and 597cc. Known as 'Short Stroke' units, these were still very much based on the original Scott technology of some two decades earlier.

l. **1936 Scott Flying Squirrel,** 497cc, water-cooled 2-stroke twin, 66.6 x 71.4mm bore and stroke.
£4,800–5,200 *BKS*

This machine is to virtually standard specification. It was totally restored between 1990 and 1992 by the specialist, J. W. Tennant-Eyles.

r. **1926 Sunbeam Model 7,** 600cc, oil bath chaincase, valanced mudguards, alloy footboards, traditional Sunbeam black and gold finish.
£5,000–5,500 *BC*

Sunbeam was famous for quality and finish, achieved by doing much work 'in-house'. They bought in basic casting, and the usual proprietary components, such as carburettor and magneto, but otherwise it was all their own work. Machining, plating and painting were all done on the premises to the very high standards set by the founder, John Marston. In 1928, Sunbeam became part of the giant ICI organisation, which ultimately was to have an effect on quality – for the worse.

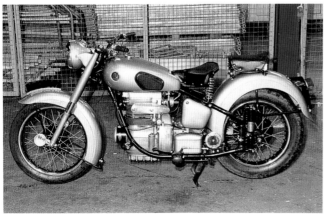

l. **c1950 Sunbeam S8,** 489cc.
£2,000–2,300 *PS*

Never as popular as the original S7 model, the S8 was nonetheless blessed with the majority of features that made the former such an interesting machine, including a short-stroke overhead-camshaft engine and gearbox in unit, wet-sump lubrication and car-type clutch. This example is finished in the alternative silver paint scheme.

r. **1975 Suzuki GT750M**, 739cc, original specification with correct metallic silver/grey livery, excellent condition.
£2,000–2,300 *BKS*

First offered in 1972 (although shown in 1971), the liquid-cooled GT750 featured a double drum brake on the J model, and twin discs for the K and L models. Later, the L model received a gear indicator and CV carburettors. Finally, the M model arrived with more power and no fork gaiters.

l. **1976 Suzuki GT550A**, 544cc.
£2,500+ *VJMC*

The GT550A featured ram-air, five speeds, electric start, a rev-counter (crankshaft driven from M model), chrome cylinder bores, a double drum brake for the J model, and a disc for K and later versions, including the final A series. This example of the last-but-one 550 has been painstakingly restored to original condition.

1974 Suzuki GT750K, 739cc, totally restored, concours condition.
£4,500–5,000 *SKC*

Rarest of all Suzuki's GT750 models, the K was only built for eight months.

1983 Suzuki TS185ER, 184cc, single-cylinder piston-port 2-stroke engine.
£425–475 *PS*

The ER series of trail bikes was built in 100, 125, 185 and 250 sizes and proved popular in the early 1980s.

1977 Suzuki GT185B, 184.8cc, 2-stroke twin, 49 x 49mm bore and stroke, 5-speed gearbox, totally restored, concours condition.
£800–1,200 *SKC*

Built from 1973 until 1979, this model had kick and electric start, and a disc front brake.

1983 Suzuki Katana 1100, 1100cc, double overhead camshafts, 4 cylinders, non-standard Lazer 4-into-1 exhaust, anti-dive forks.
£2,200–2,500 *PC*

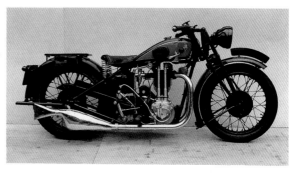

r. **1930 Triumph CTT,** 498cc, overhead-valve twin-port single, 80 x 99mm bore and stroke, hand gear-change.
£4,250–4,850 *VER*

First sold in the late 1920s, the CTT was one of the more sporting Triumphs of its era, but due to the effects of the Depression was only offered until 1931 – a great shame, as it was a machine of considerable character.

l. **1954 Triumph Speed Twin,** 498.76cc, overhead-valve parallel twin, restored, very good condition.
£2,300–2,500 *CotC*

This model was the last of the sprung-hub Speed Twins. For 1954 only, it was fitted with an 8in front brake.

r. **1954 Triumph Tiger 110,** 649cc, overhead-valve twin, 71 x 82mm bore and stroke.
£3,200–3,500 *BKS*

The Tiger 110 ran from 1953 through to 1961. It made its debut at the Paris show in October 1953 and was the first Triumph model to be offered with swinging-arm rear suspension.

l. **1959 Triumph 5TA Speed Twin,** 490cc, overhead-valve unit twin, 69 x 65.5mm bore and stroke.
£2,000–2,200 *BKS*

Launched in September 1958, the 5TA was basically a larger displacement version of the 3TA Twenty-One. Most machines were sold with the famous Speed Twin Amaranth Red paint scheme.

1959 Triumph T120 Bonneville, 649cc, overhead-valve pre-unit twin.
£5,000–5,500 *PM*

The Bonneville was launched in September 1958. This is one of the first, with headlamp nacelle, valanced mudguards, old-style dual seat and pearl grey / tangerine paint finish.

1961 Triumph 3TA Twenty-One, 349cc.
£1,400–1,600 *MAY*

Launched in 1957, the Twenty-One earned its name in celebration of Triumph Engineering's 21st birthday.

l. **1962 Triumph Bonneville T120R,** 649cc.
£6,000–7,000 *BLM*

Production of what is generally seen as the ultimate expression of Edward Turner's vertical twin, the pre-unit Bonneville, ceased in 1962.

r. **1962 Triumph T20 Tiger Cub,** 199.5cc, overhead-valve unit single, totally restored to showroom condition. **£1,400–1,600** *AT*

For many years after its launch, at the end of 1953, the Tiger Cub followed the Terrier's crankcase design. Then, for 1960, the crankcase split line was moved to the conventional position in line with the centre of the cylinder.

l. **1963 Triumph Tiger 90,** 349cc, overhead-valve unit twin. **£1,800–2,100** *MAY*

In October 1962, the 3TA was joined by a sports version called the Tiger 90. It made its public debut at the Paris show and followed the general lines of the Tiger 100SS in its styling with separate headlamp and partial rear enclosure. The only year of semi-bathtub and white finish was 1963.

r. **1967 Triumph Tiger 90,** 349cc, overhead-valve unit twin, restored. **£1,800–2,200** *MAY*

For 1966, the T90 gained 12 volt electrics, followed in 1967 by a new frame from the T100T model. These changes were also shared by the T100SS. The T90's partial rear enclosure had been deleted from the 1964 season onwards.

l. **1968 Triumph T120R Bonneville,** 649cc, overhead-valve unit twin, concours condition. **£4,250–4,850** *VER*

For 1968, the Bonneville gained a twin-leading-shoe front brake. This is an export model with high bars and side reflectors.

l. **1970 Triumph Bonneville,** 649cc, overhead-valve parallel twin, unit construction, 4-speed gearbox.
£4,000+   *PC*

This is the final model in export guise – prior to the new oil-in-frame version designed at Umberslade Hall, which appeared the following year.

r. **1971 Triumph T150 Trident,** 740cc, overhead-valve across-the-frame 3 cylinder engine, unit construction, 4-speed gearbox, US export model with side reflectors.
£4,000+   *PC*

A total of 27,544 of all Trident versions were built.

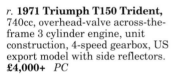

l. **1973 Triumph T150V Trident,** 740cc, pushrod across-the-frame 3 cylinder engine, original condition.
£4,000–5,000   *PC*

This model has a 5-speed gearbox (right-hand side) and a single disc front brake.

r. **1977 Triumph Silver Jubilee Bonneville,** 740cc, overhead-valve unit twin.
£2,800+   *PC*

This example is a US export version of the Silver Jubilee Bonneville. In all, 1,000 examples were built for the Stateside market.

l. **1982 Triumph Bonneville 750 Limited Edition,** 744cc, overhead-valve unit twin, 76 x 82mm bore and stroke.
£2,500–3,000   *BLM*

The Bonneville 750 Limited Edition was also known as the Executive Electro. It came fully equipped for touring with a cockpit fairing, panniers and top box. Only a small number were produced from 1981 to 1983.

l. **1936 Velocette KSS MkII,**
348cc, overhead-camshaft single,
alloy head, one-piece cam box, 4-speed
foot-operated gear-change.
£4,500–4,800   *VER*

*Like Norton's International, the Velocette
KSS overhead-camshaft single was
many riders' dream machine during
the 1930s. Certainly both were premier
sporting models, which drew heavily
on their respective marque's successes
in Grand Prix and TT racing events.*

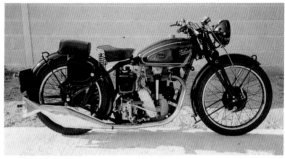

r. **1947 Velocette KSS MkII,**
348cc, overhead-camshaft single.
£4,750–5,000   *BLM*

*Post-war, the KSS continued until
1948, with little changed from the
1930s. It was axed on cost grounds,
the engine needing the same level of
skill to build as the KTT racing model.*

l. **1949 Velocette LE MkI,**
149cc, concours condition.
£800–1,000   *LEV*

*Introduced for the 1949 model year,
the LE departed completely from the
usual Velocette design concepts.
It was a small-capacity, sidevalve,
horizontally-opposed, twin with water-
cooling. It also sported shaft final drive,
hand-lever starting, a monocoque frame
and comprehensive weather protection.
Finally, it was just about the quietest
motorcycle ever built.*

r. **1956 Velocette Viper,** 349cc,
overhead-valve single, 72 x 86mm
bore and stroke, telescopic forks,
swinging-arm frame, single-level dual
seat, V-belt-driven dynamo, chrome
mudguards, excellent condition.
£3,000–3,500   *AT*

*In 1956, Velocette introduced the Viper
(350) and Venom (500) sports models.
These high-performance machines
featured a 7½in front brake, full-width
hubs and a deep headlamp shell, which
carried the instruments in its top section.
The Viper engine differed from the
touring MAC unit by having a shorter
stroke. It was more akin to the 500 MSS
unit on which the Venom was based.*

1956 Velocette Venom, 499cc, clip-ons, rear-
sets, swept-back pipe, Thruxton-type seat,
matching speedometer and tacho, fork gaiters,
chrome headlamp, restored in Clubman's trim.
£4,250–4,750   *AT*

1956 Velocette Venom, 499cc, overhead-valve single,
86 x 86mm bore and stroke, touring trim, excellent
condition throughout.
£3,000–3,250   *CotC*

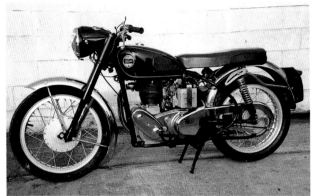

l. **1960 Velocette Venom,** 499cc, overhead-valve single, original specification, except for primary and final drive covers being chrome-plated alloy wheel rims..
£3,000–3,400 *AT*

The Venom, and its smaller-engined brother, the Viper, appeared in 1956. They were high-performance sports models with 7½in front brakes, full-width brake hubs and deep headlamp shell which carried the instruments in their top surfaces.

r. **1960 Velocette Viper,** 349cc, overhead-valve single, rebuilt using some non-Velocette components, excellent condition.
£2,500–3,000 *VER*

The Viper used the same running gear as the Venom, but had a smaller-capacity 349cc engine with long-stroke 72 x 86mm bore and stroke dimension. The Venom's were square at 86 x 86mm.

l. **1967 Velocette Venom Clubman's,** 499cc, overhead-valve single, all-alloy engine, 4-speed gearbox.
£3,700–4,200 *BKS*

This example has been completely rebuilt using a number of Thruxton components. It features a twin-leading-shoe front brake, alloy rims with stainless steel spokes, clip-ons, humped seat, swept-back exhaust, rear-sets, matching tacho and speedo, and the Thruxton oil tank incorporating a heat shield.

r. **1949 Vincent-HRD Black Shadow,** 998cc, overhead-valve V-twin.
£13,000–15,000 *BKS*

This particular example is a converted Rapide B with C-Series Girdraulic forks, but it retains features of the B-Series, such as the HRD badging. The 15mph advantage that the Black Shadow enjoyed over the Rapide was the result of several tuning measures, including an increase in carburettor bore size to 1⅛in (from 1¹⁄₁₆in) and a rise in compression ratio to 7.3:1. These improvements, allied to careful final assembly, resulted in an additional 10bhp.

l **1927 Zenith 680,** 677cc, sidevalve V-twin JAP engine, 70 x 88mm bore and stroke.
£4,000–4,500 *BKS*

In many ways a rival to the Brough Superior, the Zenith used similar JAP (James Arthur Prestwich) V-twin engines for its motive power.

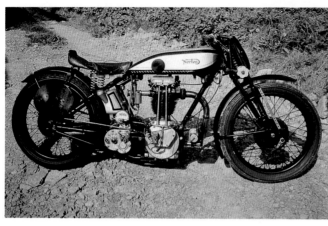

l. **1929 Norton Model 18,** 490cc, overhead-valve single.
£7,500–8,500 *BKS*

The Model 18 made its debut at the Olympia show at the end of 1922 and was to run right through until as late as 1954, albeit with changes along the way. During this time, it slotted in between the cheaper, slower sidevalves and more expensive, faster overhead models.

r. **1935 Excelsior Manxman,** 349cc, 4 valves, bronze alloy cylinder head, Amal carburettor, BTH magneto, Albion gearbox, forced lubrication with dry-sump crankcase.
£9,500–11,000 *BKS*

Tyrell Smith, Syd Gleave and 'Ginger' Wood, among others, put the Excelsior name firmly on the racing map during the 1930s, riding the Manxman to many victories, notably in the Isle of Man. It was Gleave who rode the 250cc, four-valve, Ike Hatch-designed 'Mechanical Marvel' to victory in the 1933 Lightweight TT, probably inspiring the company to produce the Manxman.

l. **1956 CZ Works Prototype,** 125cc, double-overhead-camshaft single, wet sump lubrication, magneto ignition, Dell'Orto carburettor, unit construction, 5-speed gearbox.
£11,500–13,000 *RIM*

This works prototype double-overhead-camshaft 125 CZ made its debut at the Austrian Grand Prix in May 1956. It was a development of similar machines first seen in 1955.

r. **1956 MV Agusta 175 CSS,** 172.4cc, overhead-camshaft single, 59.5 x 62mm bore and stroke.
£4,200–4,600 *IVC*

Also known as the Disco Volate (Flying Saucer), the CSS could be used for either fast road or clubman's type racing events. There was also an off-road version for use in long-distance trials events, such as the ISDT.

l. **c1958 NSU Max Racer,** 247cc, overhead-camshaft single, converted Max Roadster, conical front brake, Sportmax replica tank and seat, Krober electronic rev-counter.
£1,300–1,500 *BKS*

This machine, as with many others, is a Max roadster made to look like the pure-bred Sportmax racer. The latter was not only good enough to dominate everything except the world championships during the late 1950s, but was also outright 250cc World Champion in the hands of H. P. 'Happy' Müller in 1955.

1962 Royal Enfield Crusader Sports Racer, 248cc, overhead-valve unit single, race-kitted roadster, special crankshaft, piston, valves, camshaft and carburettor, 5-speed gearbox.
£675–750 *PS*

1964 Cotton Telstar, 247cc, Villiers Starmaster engine, 68 x 68mm bore and stroke, 4-speed gearbox.
£2,000–3,000 *COEC*

Production ceased in 1967, with 66 examples built.

r. **1963 Honda CR93,** 124.8cc, double overhead-camshafts, 43 x 43mm bore and stroke, 360° crankshaft, unit construction, 5-speed gearbox.
£22,000–25,000 *AtMC*

The CR93 was produced in two forms, the first offered for sale in Japan during May 1962. In road trim (complete with lights, silencers and even a rear view mirror!), the machine could reach 84mph, whereas the racing version produced 20bhp and exceeded 100mph. This is an early example with the double-sided, single-leading-shoe front brake. From 1964, this was replaced by a single-sided, twin-leading-shoe component.

l. **1968 Linto Racer,** 496.6cc, overhead-valve horizontal twin, 72 x 61mm bore and stroke, 360° crankshaft, 6-speed gearbox, totally original.
£25,000+ *PC*

This machine is one of only 15 made. Designed by Ing Lino Toni, the Linto engine was essentially a pair of 250 Aermacchi top ends mounted on a special crankcase assembly. Although promising much, its racing life was cut short by a combination of teething problems and the arrival, in 1969, of the TR2 Yamaha twins.

l. **1968 Yamaha YAS1 Racer,** 124cc.
£1,200–1,400 *BKS*

Introduced on to the British market in 1968, the YAS1 featured an air-cooled twin-cylinder engine and 5-speed gearbox. Realising the machine's potential on the race circuit, Yamaha also marketed an official race kit. Many examples were raced during the late 1960s and early 1970s with considerable success, even winning national championships with riders such as Steve Machin, Austin Hockley and Clive Horton.

r. **1974 Yamaha TZ250,** 247.3cc, water-cooled 2-stroke twin, restored to original condition.
£5,500–6,000 *GB*

During the early 1970s, the TZ250 and 350 were virtually unbeatable – even by much larger machines. This was due to their ability to provide an overall package of handling, braking and performance, whereas other machines had a weakness in at least one of those areas.

l. **1976 Yamaha TZ750,** 748cc, 4 cylinder water-cooled 2-stroke, 66 x 54mm bore and stroke, 140bhp at 10,700rpm, 6-speed gearbox, excellent condition.
£9,000–10,000 *GB*

This bike has never been raced.

r. **1978 Yamaha Maxton TZ250,** 247.3cc, TZ250 engine in Maxton chassis.
£2,600–3,000 *VJMC*

Built by Ron Williams of Maxton Engineering to special order, this machine is similar to one ridden to victory by Charlie Williams (no relation) in the Isle of Man TT.

l. **1986 Yamaha FZ750,** 748cc, 4 cylinders, 20 valve double-overhead-camshaft engine.
£3,000–3,500 *IVC*

The FZ750 and the Suzuki GSR750 were the foremost street bikes in their capacity class, and were extremely successful in both sports machine and endurance racing. This ex-Team Loctite bike was ridden by Keith Heuwen in the 1986 British Championship series.

r. 1992 BSA Rocket 3 Replica,
overhead valves, 3 cylinders, 850cc
conversion kit, Rob North-type
chassis, AP Lockheed triple disc
brakes, race-ready condition.
£8,000+ *GB*

l. 1993 Norton Replica 30M Manx, 499cc.
£15,000–17,000 *BKS*

This pristine example of the 500cc variant was built by Bernie Allen during 1993. The machine conforms to the 1961 specification in most respects and, at the time of manufacture, cost £24,000. Fittings include Akront alloy rims laced to conical hubs and fitted with Dunlop racing tyres, a KR73 rear and KR76 front. The Summerfield-based engine breathes via an Amal GP carburettor, with ignition being provided by a BTH magneto. It is housed in a frame constructed from Reynolds 531 tubing. The machine is unused and has been stored in ideal conditions.

r. 1994 Cotton Telstar Replica, 247cc.
£3,500–4,000 *COEC*

Constructed by the Fluff Brown AJS Motorcycles company, this Telstar Replica has a double-sided Italian Grimeca front brake, MP forks and Avon-type fairing. It has a standard 4-speed gearbox and an FB Villiers Starmaker engine.

l. 1997 Benelli 350 Four Replica,
double overhead camshafts, air-cooled,
4 cylinders, as-new condition.
£85,000+ *GB*

Constructed in 1997, this is a faithful replica of Benelli's 1969-type 350 Four, as raced by Renzo Pasolini; it was built by George Beale Racing.

r. 1997 Matchless G50 Replica,
496cc, as-new condition.
£22,000+ *GB*

This is a specially-built lightweight G50 Replica with Ceriani forks, four-leading-shoe front brake, belt primary drive and modern carburettor. It was built by George Beale Racing.

1962 Lambretta Li 150 Series 2, 149cc.
£1,200–1,400 *MAY*

A total of 162,040 Li 150 Series 2 machines were built between October 1959 and November 1961. A major difference between it and the Series 1 model was that the headlamp was moved from the apron to the handlebars. This not only gave improved styling, but also meant that the lamp turned with the handlebars.

1962 Lambretta Li 150 Series 2, 149cc.
£1,200–1,500 *MAY*

Together with the Series 1, the Series 2 Li 150 was one of the most popular scooters of its era.

1967 Lambretta SX 200, 198cc, restored.
£2,000–2,200 *MAY*

1971 Triumph Squire TR6 with Sidecar, 649cc, overhead-valve unit twin.
£2,400–2,700 *PC*

r. **1925 FN M50,** 748cc, 4 cylinder inlet-over-exhaust engine, calliper brakes on both wheels.
£10,250–12,000 *BKS*

At the end of 1924, FN's new chain-driven machine, designated the M50, featured an inlet-over-exhaust, four cylinder engine with a bore and stroke of 52 x 88mm, resulting in a displacement of 748cc. The gearbox was attached to the rear of the crankcase in automotive fashion, presenting an imposing sight. This machine was discovered a number of years ago in four boxes and was painstakingly restored. Among the collection of parts was a Mills Fulford chassis, for which an unrestored body was sourced at an autojumble, enabling the restoration to be completed.

l. **1928 Indian Big Chief with Princess Sidecar,** 1200cc, sidevalve V-twin, 3-speed hand gear-change, electric lighting.
£9,000–10,000 *BKS*

Indian announced the 'World's Most Complete Cycle Line' for 1928, and included the sidevalve 1200cc V-twin Indian Big Chief, a smooth and powerful machine particularly well suited for sidecar work. With that in mind. Indian placed the kickstarter on the left. This machine was shipped to Finland in 1928 and is said to have been used to run alcohol during Prohibition. From 1948 to 1969, it stayed with the owner of a wood mill, who rode it into the ground. It was restored in 1969, ridden regularly and eventually was put on museum display in Finland in 1984.

l. **1995 LMC Replica Veteran Motorcycle,** 499cc. **£2,300–2,600**   *BKS*

This machine represents the ingenuity of a Cornishman who decided to make his own motorcycle with whatever parts he could find. His model was a BAT, made in Penge from 1902 to 1906. He took measurements from an enlarged photograph, made a jig and built the frame as accurately as he could. He adopted Saxon front forks, a brake drum from an Escort car, and a hand brake from an American ACE. The basis of the engine is a VB Ariel; the piston is from a Montego, while the barrel is standard Ariel. The cylinder head is his own design. The transmission pulley is grafted to a cleverly disguised Honda 175 clutch, attached to the Ariel crank.

r. **c1954 Norton Special,** 490cc. **£2,200–2,500**   *PS*

This Norton single-cylinder special has been built in road-racing style, using both genuine and aftermarket components. It features alloy tanks, clip-ons, rear-sets, a racing seat and fly screen.

l. **c1960s Triton Special,** 649cc, pre-unit Triumph T110 engine to Bonneville specification, slimline Norton frame, special petrol and oil tanks, flat handlebars, swept-back pipes and Gold Star-type silencers. **£2,800–3,000**   *PC*

This bike is typical of many home-built machines of the era, and a surprising number have survived as testament to their original builders.

r. **c1967 Triumph Vendetta Special,** 490cc. **£1,500–1,700**   *PS*

Vendetta was a small Welsh company that sprang to prominence during the late 1960s and early 1970s with frame kits for several British engines. This is a 490cc Triumph Daytona unit engine in a Vendetta-made frame to café racer specification.

l. **1971 Norton Commando Café Racer,** 745cc. **£2,300–2,600**   *CStC*

This café racer was based on an early 750 Commando, with racing tank, seat, front mudguard, clip-ons and rear-set foot controls. The London-based Gus Kuhn dealership offered a wide range of accessories for Commandos during the early 1970s.

A brochure for the Velo Solex
motorised bicycle, 1952.
£6–8 *DM*

A brochure for Francis-Barnett motorcycles, 1939,
8 x 10½in (20.5 x 26.5cm).
£25–30 *DM*

A brochure for the Triumph Automatic
T10 scooter, 1965, 8 x 9½in (20.5 x 24cm).
£3–5 *DM*

A set of 4 Manx Telecom phonecards, depicting
1988 Isle of Man TT racers.
£180–200 *JCa*

A poster advertising Norton motorcycles, 1959,
19 x 28in (48.5 x 71cm).
£150–200 *LE*

Tommy Robb, *From TT to Tokyo*,
1974, 9 x 6in (23 x 15cm).
£12–15 *DM*

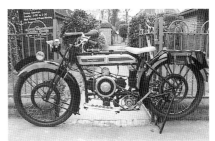

1970 Triumph Daytona T100T, 490cc,
twin carburettors, US export model.
£2,200–2,700 *PC*

1971 Triumph TR6R Tiger 650,
649cc, single carburettor.
£1,750–2,000 *PC*

*For 1971, the 650cc range comprised three models:
the T120R, TR6C and TR6R (or Tiger 650). The
main change that year was to the frame, which was
designed to contain the engine oil. There were also
new forks, hubs and many detail changes.*

1971 Triumph Bonneville T120, 649cc,
overhead-valve unit twin, US export model,
fitted with non-standard silencers.
£2,300–2,600 *HIST*

r. **1972 Triumph T120R Bonneville,** 649cc,
overhead-valve unit twin, US specification, largely
original, non-standard Route 66 'roll' below headlamp.
£2,500–2,800 *S*

l. **1975 Triumph T160
Trident,** 740cc, overhead-
valve 3 cylinder engine,
67 x 70mm bore and
stroke, unit construction,
5-speed gearbox.
£2,800–3,200 *BKS*

*The NVT (Norton Villiers
Triumph) revised Trident,
the T160, featured an electric
starter, front and rear disc
brakes and a new teardrop-
style fuel tank. Its engine
layout resembled that of
the BSA Rocket 3, with
sloping cylinders, a left-hand
gear-change and a 4-into-2
exhaust system.*

1976 Triumph Bonneville T140V, 744cc, overhead-valve unit twin, 5-speed gearbox, front and rear disc brakes, left-hand gear-change, US export model.
£2,400+ *HIST*

1978 Triumph T140 Bonneville, 744cc, original, unrestored, fair condition.
£2,000–2,250 *BLM*

1977 Triumph Silver Jubilee Bonneville, 740cc, overhead-valve parallel twin, 67 x 70mm bore and stroke.
£2,800+ *PC*

In 1977, to mark the 25th year of Queen Elizabeth's reign, Triumph built the Silver Jubilee Bonneville. The machine was based on the standard T140V with a silver finish highlighted in red, white and blue. The primary chain case and timing cover were chrome plated. Each machine had a white panel on each side cover, bearing a Union Jack, and the legends 'Silver Jubilee 1977' and 'Limited Edition'. A thousand of these machines were built for sale in the UK, each with a certificate of authentication. A similar quantity went to the USA, and a further 400 to other markets around the world.

1982 Triumph Thunderbird, 649cc, overhead-valve unit twin, 76 x 71.5mm bore and stroke.
£2,200–2,800 *PC*

In April 1981, Triumph revived the Thunderbird name for a reduced-cost 650. This was achieved by shortening the stroke to 71.5mm, which required a new crankshaft and shorter block. Also to cut costs, a drum rear brake and points ignition were fitted.

l. **1982 Triumph TSX,** 744cc, overhead-valve unit twin, concours condition.
£3,000+ *PC*

One of the final Meriden Co-operative models was the custom version of the Bonneville, the TSX. This had Morris cast alloy wheels, a 16in rear tyre, high bars and megaphone silencers. Today, it is a very rare machine.

VELOCETTE (*British 1904–68*)

1934 Velocette KTS MkI, 348cc, overhead-camshaft single, 74 x 81mm bore and stroke, chain final drive, rigid frame.
£2,600–2,800 *BKS*

A motorcycling dynasty was behind the Velocette name, and this was reflected in the quality of the design and manufacture of these unique machines. The family were the Goodmans, and three generations were to guide the company over the years. The first Velocettes were two-strokes, but by the dawn of the 1930s, the marque had established its name in racing circles with a trio of victories in the Junior (350cc) TT in 1926, 1928 and 1929, using an overhead-camshaft single. This resulted in the KTS, s sports roadster version of the TT replica KTT model. There was also a KSS variant, known as the Supersport.

1934 Velocette MAC, 349cc, overhead-valve single, 68 x 96mm bore and stroke.
£2,700–3,000 *VER*

Introduced in 1934, the MAC came about by extending the stroke of the 250 MOV to 96mm, copying the dimensions of an experimental long-stroke KTT. In other respects, it was a replica of the smaller model and went on to enjoy an even longer production life. The cut-away engine shows the various working components of the pushrod MAC unit.

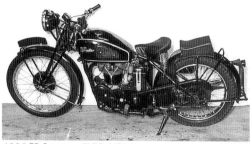

1936 Velocette KSS MkII,
348cc, overhead-camshaft single.
£3,000–3,500 *BKS*

The 1936 model year saw the introduction of considerably revised versions of the KTT racer and KSS Supersport. Both featured a one-piece alloy cylinder head and camshaft box, which enclosed the valve gear. This was equipped with coil springs and eccentric rocker spindles.

1937 Velocette KSS MkII, 348cc, overhead-camshaft single, original, 839 miles since new, unrestored.
£4,500–5,000 *BKS*

1951 Velocette MAC, 349cc, overhead-valve single, requires restoration.
£1,500–1,650 *AT*

For 1951, the pushrod MAC single gained telescopic forks and an alloy top half for the engine.

1953 Velocette MAC, 349cc, non-standard exhaust minus original fishtail silencer, requires restoration.
£1,500–1,800 *AT*

The swinging-arm MAC was the first produced in 1953.

1954 Velocette MSS, 499cc, overhead-valve single, iron head and barrel, 86 x 86mm bore and stroke, telescopic forks, swinging-arm frame.
£2,300–2,500 *BKS*

Introduced in 1935, the MSS in its original 495cc (81 x 96mm) form was taken out of production in 1948. It made a return in 1954 with a new 499cc engine and updated cycle parts. The latter allowed adjustment of the rear suspension setting by moving the shock absorber top mounts through an arc.

l. **1956 Velocette Venom Clubman's,** 499cc, completely restored, Amal Concentric carburettor, clip-ons, rear-sets, alloy rims, fork gaiters, swept-back exhaust, rev-counter, twin-leading-shoe front brake, black and gold finish, concours condition.
£3,500–4,000 *PC*

r. **1956 Velocette MSS,** 499cc.
£1,800–2,000 *BKS*

Eugene Goodman designed the first of the 'M' series – the 250 MOV – in 1933. It was followed in 1935 by the 350 MAC and the 495cc MSS, which originally had been conceived as a sidecar tug.

1957 Velocette Valiant, 192cc, overhead-valve flat-twin, shaft final drive.
£400–600 *BRIT*

The Valiant was first produced in 1957. This popular lightweight had an overhead-valve air-cooled engine based on the water-cooled sidevalve unit used in the LE model.

1958 Velocette MAC, 349cc, overhead-valve single, original except for tank finished in earlier style, unrestored.
£1,800–2,000 *PS*

l. **1959 Velocette Viper,** 349cc, overhead-valve single, fitted with later Veeline fuel tank and aftermarket rear carrier.
£2,200–2,500 *CotC*

r. **1959 Velocette Venom,** 499cc, touring trim, alloy wheel rims, unrestored.
£2,000–2,200 *BKS*

1960 Velocette Viper, 349cc, restored to original specification, concours condition.
£4,000+ *PC*

1960 Velocette Venom Clubman's Café Racer, 499cc, overhead-valve single, alloy barrel and head, Thruxton exhaust, close-ratio gearbox, clip-ons, rear-sets, rev-counter, twin-leading-shoe front brake, alloy wheel rims.
£2,800–3,300 *BLM*

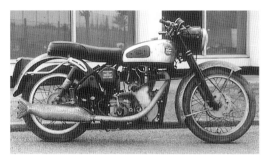

1960 Velocette Venom, 499cc, overhead-valve single, Thruxton exhaust, rear-sets, 8,000rpm rev-counter, alloy wheel rims, original, requires restoration.
£2,200–2,400 *S*

1962 Velocette LE MkIII, 192cc.
£550–650 *PM*

By 1962, the LE model had reached MkIII form, having been updated with a foot-change, four-speed gearbox and a conventional kickstarter.

1967 Velocette Thruxton, 499cc, overhead-valve single, fitted with Mitchenhall (Avon) fairing.
£8,000–9,000 *BKS*

Derived from the Venom, the Thruxton arrived for 1965. It featured a revised cylinder head with a 2in diameter inlet valve, an Amal GP carburettor, close-ratio gearbox, alloy wheel rims, a twin-leading-shoe front brake, rear-sets and clip-ons. Tested by The Motor Cycle at 114mph, it also recorded numerous production race victories, including a class win in the 1967 Isle of Man TT for sports machines.

VINCENT-HRD (*British 1928–56*)

1947 Vincent-HRD Rapide, 998cc, fully restored, concours condition.
£15,000+ *GODE*

1948 Vincent-HRD Rapide, 998cc, overhead-valve V-twin, 45bhp at 5,300rpm, original, good condition.
£9,500–10,250 *AT*

1950 Vincent Comet Special, 499cc, overhead-valve single, Norton wideline dual seat, British Hub Co front brake, Norton Dominator rear hub, Lucas chrome headlamp, alloy wheel rims, standard Vincent frame and suspension, older restoration, very good condition.
£3,250–3,500 *CotC*

Miller's Motorcycle Milestones

Vincent-HRD Series C Grey Flash 499cc
(*British 1949*)
Value £7,000–10,000
The Series C Grey Flash is famous for being the first racing motorcycle to bring to the public's attention that great two- and four-wheel world champion, John Surtees.

The Grey Flash was based on the Comet, a 499cc (84 x 90mm) single, which in turn was half a Vincent V-twin. It was launched for the 1949 season and was actually built in three guises: as a pukka racer, as a sports roadster with full lighting equipment and silencer, and as a roadster supplied with racing equipment for easy conversion into racing trim.

The Grey Flash was tuned to Black Lighting specification and, to live up to its name, the tank and frame components were painted in grey-green to distinguish it from the standard Comet roadster. Weighing 330lb and costing £230 excluding purchase tax, the Grey Flash produced 35bhp at 6,200rpm. In the 1952 TT, Ken Bills rode one to 12th place in the Senior race, averaging 83.79mph. Moreover, George

Brown and the young John Surtees put up some impressive performances on the model at a variety of British short circuits.

Surtees had begun racing in 1950, acquiring his Grey Flash at the end of that year. As an apprentice at one of the Vincent factories in Stevenage, he was able to purchase an incomplete machine at a special price.

He rode the bike until 1952, then began preparing his own Manx Nortons, before becoming a works rider for Norton. Later, he joined the Italian MV Agusta firm as team leader, becoming a multi-world champion. His father, Jack, a well-known racer in his own right, also campaigned a Vincent V-twin sidecar outfit with considerable success.

The standard Grey Flash was capable of around 110mph, but the machines ridden by Surtees and Brown were both good for an extra 10mph.

Largely unknown to the general public at the time, the Vincent company went into liquidation during June 1949. However, it recovered, only to hit more trouble in 1955, this time terminal.

l. **1953 Vincent-HRD Black Shadow Series C**, 998cc, overhead-valve V-twin, 84 x 90mm bore and stroke, 55bhp at 5,700rpm, oncours condition.
£14,500–15,000 *CotC*

The Black Shadow Series C was built between 1948 and 1955.

1955 Vincent-HRD Black Knight, 998cc, overhead-valve V-twin.
£11,000–12,000 *BKS*

1955 Vincent-HRD Rapide Series D, 998cc, Shadow speedometer and brake drums, Lightning brake plates.
£14,000–16,000 *BLM*

Philip Vincent believed that ample weather protection, combined with an enclosed engine and gearbox, would make the Vincent Series D the ultimate 'gentleman's motorcycle'. However, delayed delivery of the fibreglass panels – plus continuing demand for traditionally-styled models – resulted in over half the production leaving the Stevenage factory in open form. The enclosed versions of the Rapide and Black Shadow were known as the Black Knight and Black Prince respectively. Other D-Series innovations included a new frame and rear suspension, a user-friendly centre stand and many improvements to the peerless V-twin engine. But by the time manufacture of Vincent's final range began in March 1955, the company was already in financial difficulty. When production ceased in December of that year, around 460 Series D V-twins had been built, 200 of which were enclosed models. This particular example of one of the rarest post-war Vincents is believed to be the machine exhibited at the Earl's Court Show when the model was introduced.

1998 Egli-Vincent Gode Replica, 998cc, Amal Concentric carburettors, aluminium tank, racing seat, fairing, Ceriani racing front forks, Fontana four-leading-shoe front brake.
£17,500+ *GODE*

YAMAHA (*Japanese 1954–*)

1977 Yamaha XS750, 747cc, double-overhead-camshaft 3 cylinder engine, 5-speed gearbox, shaft final drive, 68 x 68.6mm bore and stroke.
£1,400–1,500 *PC*

Built from 1977 until 1980, the XS750 triple was capable of 110mph and was one of the first of the company's multi-cylinder superbikes. Later, the engine's bore was increased by 3mm to give 826cc and create the XS850.

1982 Yamaha XT500, 499cc, overhead-camshaft single, 87 x 84mm bore and stroke, 33bhp at 6,500rpm.
£600–700 *VICO*

Yamaha saw the XT500 as a modern replacement for BSA's sadly missed Gold Star, but others said it did not come near the longstroke British single.

1986 Yamaha FZX, 749cc, double-overhead-camshaft four, 68 x 51.6mm bore and stroke, chain final drive.
£2,000–2,500 *PC*

The engine of the FZX was based on the FZ750 unit.

1980 Yamaha RD350LC, 347cc, 2-stroke twin, reed-valve induction, 6-speed gearbox, concours condition.
£1,600–1,700 *PC*

The RD350LC was introduced at the 1979 Paris show. With its 250cc brother, it was aimed primarily at the European market and displayed several major technological advances – including cantilever suspension and liquid cooling – to give street riders a new dimension in two-stroke performance.

1984 Yamaha RD350 YPVS,
347cc, concours condition.
£1,800–1,900 *PC*

In 1983, Yamaha became the first manufacturer to offer a production road-going two-stroke equipped with power valves. The Yamaha Power Valve System (YPVS) offered a high gas trapping capability at low engine speeds, and it also provided the necessary port area for peak power at high rpm.

ZENITH (*British 1904–50*)

1928 Zenith Model 750, 747cc, sidevalve JAP V-twin engine, 70 x 97mm bore and stroke, fully restored.
£4,000–5,000 *AT*

In the main, Zenith used JAP engines for their motorcycles, but also fitted Blackburne units. They were particularly successful in racing and record breaking, being first to achieve 100mph – by Bert Le Vack – at Brooklands in 1922, and breaking the absolute world speed record twice: in 1928 at over 124mph, and in 1930 at over 150mph.

AUTOCYCLES

1923 McKenzie Lady's Model, 200cc.
£950–1,050 *BKS*

Marketed by the London-based McKenzie concern, these machines were actually built by Hobart in Coventry, who had supplied the trade with frames, engines and ancillaries from the pioneer years until the 1920s, as well as marketing machines under their own name. The McKenzie utilised a two-stroke, single-cylinder engine, displacing 200cc, and was offered in both gentleman's and lady's guise from 1921 until 1925.

1937 Cyc-Auto Autocycle, 98cc, Scott engine, original, requires restoration.
£150–200 *BKS*

The Cyc-Auto, with its power unit mounted beneath the frame, was introduced at the British Industries Fair at Castle Bromwich in 1934. Later models were offered with a choice of Villiers or Scott 98cc engines.

1939 Sun Autocycle, 98cc.
£60–90 *BKS*

Sun entered motorcycle production in 1911, using Vitesse, Blackburne, JAP and Villiers engines until the outbreak of WWII. Post-war, their Autocycle was powered by a 98cc Villiers unit and was popular in a Britain yearning for economy and the chance to take to what was then the 'open road'.

1939 Rudge Autocycle, 98cc, 2-stroke, horizontal cylinder.
£150–180 *BKS*

Rudge introduced their 98cc Autocycle in 1938, at about the time they moved production to Hayes, Middlesex. Soon after, they sold the production rights and tooling for the model to Norman of Ashford, Kent.

1950 Cymota Cyclemotor, 45cc.
£460–500 *BKS*

Enclosed within a pressed-steel cowl, the 45cc two-stroke Cymota drove the front tyre through a carborundum-coated roller. The engine was rubber mounted to plates that were clamped to the front fork blades.

1950 Power Pak, 49cc.
£450–500 *BKS*

Mounted above the rear wheel of this tradesman's cycle, the engine of the 49cc two-stroke Power Pak had ball- and roller-bearings throughout, except for the small-end bearing, which took the form of a phosphor-bronze bush.

1952 Excelsior Autocycle, 98cc, single-cylinder 2-stroke, 2 speeds.
£60–90 *BKS*

The Excelsior was one of many lightweight autocycles that enjoyed enormous popularity in the austere post-war years.

1954 Cyclemaster, 32cc, 2-stroke, built in unit with single-plate countershaft cork clutch, chain primary and final drives.
£250–275 *PS*

The first Cyclemaster engine was of 25.7cc, but by 1954 this had risen to 32cc.

1955 Busy Bee Cyclemotor, 48cc.
£400–450 *BKS*

The extremely rare Busy Bee cyclemotor was hand-built during the 1950s from a set of plans published by The Model Engineer *magazine.*

1955 Bown Auto Roadster,
98cc, requires restoration.
£150–175 *BKS*

The Bown Cycle Co of Tonypandy, Glamorganshire, originally traded under the Aberdale name. From 1950 to 1958, they built a range of autocycles powered by 98cc Villiers two-stroke engines.

r. **c1956 BSA Winged Wheel,** 35cc.
£350–400 *AT*

Even the mighty BSA entered the cyclemotor scene during the 1950s, offering their Winged Wheel effort.

DIRT BIKES

c1928 Rudge Dirt Track, 499cc, overhead-valve twin-port single, 85 x 88mm bore and stroke.
£5,000+ *REC*

The Australians invented the sport of speedway, and it arrived in Britain in 1928, the first meeting being staged in Epping Forest, just north of London. This led to the establishment of tracks in several major cities, including London (White City), Edinburgh and Wolverhampton. Rudge listed their Dirt Track model until the 1931 season, and this particular machine is one of only two known to exist.

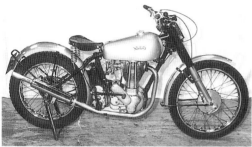

1953 Norton 500T, 490cc, overhead-valve single, telescopic forks, rigid frame.
£2,000–2,200 *BKS*

Norton listed their first trials model in 1949, production continuing under the designation 500T until 1954. The machine was based on the 16H frame, but the wheelbase was shortened by reducing the length of the rear stays and fitting new fork yokes that placed the fork legs in line with the steering head. The engine was a conventional pushrod unit fitted with a bi-metal alloy head and barrel. Camshafts and flywheels were stock ES2 components, and the compression ratio was set at 6:1. A 2½ gallon alloy fuel tank and other competition accessories were specified, the result being an attractive, if somewhat overweight, trials iron. However, the additional 'lard' did not stop the 500T from enjoying a long and successful career, one of its riders being none other than future world racing champion Geoff Duke.

1950s AJS 16MC Trials, 348cc, original, very good condition.
£4,500–5,000 *VER*

1953 DOT SCH3, 197cc, Villiers single-cylinder piston-port engine.
£1,000–1,200 *DOT*

This once-great Manchester-based marque, which had begun building motorcycles in 1903, became well-known for its off-road machines after WWII. The DOT trials story began in April 1951 with the 197cc Villiers-engined TD. Like most similar machines of the period, it employed what was basically a roadster frame. Alongside the 'feet-up' models came the scramblers, such as the SCH3, again using the venerable Villiers engine.

1953 AJS 16MC Trials, 348cc, overhead-valve pre-unit single, dismantled, some parts missing, requires restoration.
£460–500 *S*

The 16MC was the last of the true heavyweight, rigid-framed AMC trials models. All had mild-steel strengthening plates beneath the alloy mudguards, which were riveted to the frame and mudguard-stay mounting points.

l. **1954 AJS 7R Motocross,** 475cc.
£9,000+ *AMOC*

This particular machine was used by Bill Nilsson to win the 1957 European (World) 500cc Motocross Championship. Its engine is a road-racing 7R unit, suitably enlarged and modified, fitted in an off-road chassis.

1955 Matchless G3LC Trials, 348cc, overhead-valve single.
£2,100–2,300 *BKS*

By 1955, the production G3LC trials model had gained a swinging-arm frame which, together with reduced weight, made it a much more competitive machine. These developments were due, in part, to feedback from the factory's team riders.

1957 Ariel HT3 Trials, 346cc, overhead-valve all-alloy engine, 72 x 85mm bore and stroke, good condition.
£3,800–4,200 *BLM*

Smaller brother to the 500 HT5, the HT3 is very rare today. Only about 40 were built between 1957 and 1959.

1958 Royal Enfield Crusader Trials Replica, 248cc, overhead-valve unit-construction single, 70 x 64.5mm bore and stroke, dented alloy fuel tank, otherwise good condition.
£600–700 *BKS*

This replica machine was built from a road-going Crusader. The first pukka Crusader Trials model built by the factory did not appear until 1961.

1957 DMW Trials MkVII, 197cc, Villiers 9E semi-unit-construction 2-stroke single, fully restored.
£1,200–1,300 *PC*

From 1956, DMW offered their own make of Earles-type front fork. This, together with the swinging-arm rear suspension introduced a year earlier, helped the company produce an excellent trials iron.

1958 Triumph Tiger Cub Trials, 199cc, overhead-valve unit single.
£900–1,000 *BKS*

Triumph's adaptable little Cub turned its paw to most forms of motorcycle sport, but arguably it was most successful in one-day trials, where its light weight and short wheelbase gave it a competitive edge.

1958 Ariel HT5 Trials, 499cc, overhead-valve single, 81.8 x 95mm bore and stroke, modified with smaller alloy tank, smaller brake hubs and revised exhaust.
£3,000–3,250 *BKS*

The HT5 Trials was made famous by the likes of Sammy Miller and Ron Langston.

1959 Royal Enfield Bullet Trials, 346cc, overhead-valve single, original, requires restoration.
£1,500–1,700 *S*

Royal Enfield were well respected throughout the 1950s for their trials models, works rider Johnny Brittain twice winning the famous Scottish Six Day Trial for the Redditch marque. Enfield also produced small batches of works replicas for sale to the general public, this example being just such a machine.

1959 Greeves Hawkstone, 247cc, Villiers 2-stroke engine, completely rebuilt, concours condition.
£1,500–1,700 *BTS*

Men like Brian Stonebridge and Dave Bickers succeeded in putting Greeves on the European motocross map during the late 1950s and early 1960s.

1959 Royal Enfield Bullet Trials, 346cc, overhead-valve single.
£950–1,000 *BKS*

Royal Enfield introduced a revised trials Bullet in 1957, which benefited from developments made to the works machines ridden by such greats as Johnny Brittain. The new model had an alloy head and barrel, revised flywheels and a smaller carburettor to aid low-speed running. Various refinements were incorporated into the cycle parts to reduce weight, although the lightweight hubs used on the works machines were not present.

l. **1960 Greeves 14TS Scottish,** 246cc, Villiers 32A engine.
£2,000–2,200 *BKS*

The Greeves motorcycle factory was located at Thundersley in Essex. Their trials machines were very popular in the late 1950s and early 1960s, with a strong entry always being made in the Scottish Six Day Trial, Britain's premier event. In fact, an early works entry, in 1959, ridden by a young Billy Wilkinson, resulted in a win, which encouraged the factory to name their model the Scottish.

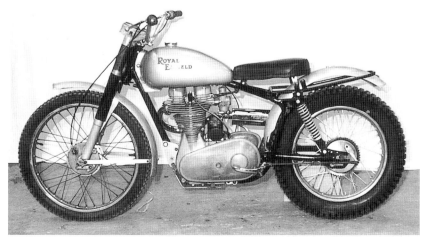

l. **1960 Royal Enfield Bullet Trials,** 346cc, overhead-valve all-alloy engine.
£750–850 *BKS*

1961 Greeves 20TC Scottish,
197cc, Villiers 9E engine.
£900–1,000 *PS*

1963 Triumph Tiger Cub Trials Replica, 199cc.
£1,050–1,250 *BKS*

*This machine was built from a standard roadster
using the correct trials gears.*

1963 Triumph T20 Trials, 199cc, overhead-valve
unit single.
£1,050–1,250 *BKS*

*Triumph offered the Tiger Cub as a sports model in
two versions: the high-performance T20S/L, and
the T20T trials with a low-compression engine and
wide-ratio gears. Many of the standard roadster
T20s were subsequently converted to trials
specification by privateers. This particular machine
was built by ex-Scottish trials champion Johnnie
Davies and won the pre-'65 Scottish Championship
during the early 1990s.*

l. **c1964 Triumph Tiger Cub Trials Replica,**
199cc, professional conversion.
£1,000–1,400 *BLM*

l. **1963 DOT/
Triumph Kyffin
Scrambler,** 490cc,
Triumph T100SS
unit engine, DOT
scrambler chassis.
£4,000+ *DOT*

*Special builder
Roger Kyffin created
this unique machine
in the early 1960s.*

1967 Cheetah Trials, 246cc, Villiers 37A engine, concours condition.
£2,500+ *DOT*

The Cheetah was made by Cheetah Engineering of Denmead, Hampshire, and today is extremely rare. Machines were also built with a variety of other engines, including the Triumph Cub and even a 350cc version of the Villiers unit.

c1970 Triumph Trackmaster Flat-Tracker, 649cc, 1969 Triumph Bonneville unit engine, 38mm Mikuni carburettors, TT pipes, ARD magneto ignition, lightened clutch, oil cooler, Trackmaster frame, Ceriani front forks, twin Airheart front disc brakes, single rear disc brake.
£5,300–5,500 *BKS*

By the mid-1960s, flat track machines had evolved into specialised mounts, the emphasis being placed on light weight and a short wheelbase. Welded frames from companies such as Trackmaster and Champion replaced the heavy, roadster-derived frames used previously, and British twins proved popular as the power source. This particular machine is believed to have been built in 1970 and raced at the Ascot Raceway until 1972, when it was registered for road use in California. It remained there until 1994.

l. **1967 Sprite Trials,** 246cc, Villiers 37A iron-barrel engine, Ceriani-type REH front fork assembly.
£425–475 *PS*

Frank Hipkin was the name behind the Sprite marque, which was based in Handsworth, Birmingham.

1971 Jawa Speedway, 499cc, 2 valve engine.
£820–900 *PS*
Originally designed by the ESO company, the Czech speedway machines were marketed in Britain under the Jawa name, that company having taken over ESO in the late 1960s.

1972 Bultaco Sherpa T350, 326cc, 83.2 x 60mm bore and stroke, 21bhp at 5,000rpm, good condition.
£500–600 *HCH*

r. **1975 Rickman Triumph Metisse,** 349cc, tuned Triumph 3TA unit engine, 22mm Amal Concentric carburettor, Boyer/Kirby Rowbotham electronic ignition, siamesed exhaust, Marzocchi front forks, Yamaha DT250 front brake, REH rear brake, Akront alloy rims.
£3,000–3,500 *BKS*

1972 Montesa Cota Trials, 247cc, 72.5 x 60mm bore and stroke.
£720–750 *BKS*

Founded in 1944, the Spanish Montesa concern introduced their first motorcycle, a 98cc two-stroke, to glowing reviews in 1945. This model was rapidly followed by competition success in road racing, establishing a link with motorcycle sport that was to characterise the company's activities for much of their history. By the late 1960s, the emphasis had shifted to off-road sport, particularly trials, which the firm came to dominate with their great rivals, Bultaco. The production Cota trials machines benefited from the experiences of the works riders, allowing Montesa to offer clubmen competitive mounts.

1975 Honda TL250, 248cc, overhead-camshaft single, 74 x 57.8mm bore and stroke, 16.5bhp at 7,000rpm.
£2,800–3,200 *BKS*

Produced with all the skill and expertise of Honda's racing department, the TL250 was designed to capitalise on the many victories being achieved in national and international trials by the factory riders. When launched in 1975, it looked like a certain winner. It was beautifully engineered and had a superb engine, while the build quality was years ahead of its Spanish rivals. It was also the best looking bike on the market. Unfortunately, it was heavier than the opposition and, as trials became an increasingly athletic sport, its weight and ground clearance proved too much of a handicap. As a result, Honda's magnificent four-stroke never sold in the numbers needed to ensure production beyond 1976. This particular example was built largely from brand-new parts in California and is one of the finest examples of this rare and beautiful off-road bike. The attention to detail is intense, even minor fixings being genuine Honda items. To build a bike to this standard today would cost tens of thousands of pounds – assuming the parts could be found.

MILITARY MOTORCYCLES

1939 Norton 16H, 490cc, sidevalve single.
£1,800–2,000 *MVT*

*Norton's managing director, Gilbert Smith, was
responsible for the company spending the months
prior to the outbreak of WWII not challenging
for racing honours, but building large numbers
of 16H models for the coming war. The result was
that 100,000 of the girder-forked, rigid-framed
sidevalve models were produced for military
use, making it a huge commercial success for
the company.*

c1940 Harley-Davidson WLA, 748cc.
£5,500–6,000 *LF*

*The WLA was the US-built model, while the WLC
was manufactured in Canada. Both were sidevalve
V-twins produced in large numbers for the
American and British armed forces.*

Don't Forget!

*If in doubt please refer to the 'How to Use'
section at the beginning of this book.*

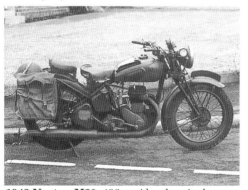

1943 Norton M20, 496cc, sidevalve single,
ex-WD despatch machine.
£1,500–1,750 *PM*

1943 Ariel W/NG, 346cc, overhead-valve single,
72 x 85mm bore and stroke, 17bhp at 5,800 rpm.
£2,200–2,400 *AT*

*The W/NG was one of the better-performing
wartime machines.*

1943 Indian 741B, 750cc, V-twin.
£4,500–5,500 *AT*

*The 741B – originally coded 640B – employed a low-compression version of the civilian Sports Scout engine
and was popular with the US forces.*

l. **1945 Moto Guzzi Alce,** 498.4cc, overhead-valve horizontal single, 88 x 82mm bore and stroke, fully restored. **£2,200–2,750** *MAY*

The main motorcycle model built for the Italian military during WWII was the Alce (Elk). It replaced the long-running and successful GT17, which had entered service in 1932. Over 8,000 Alce – and three-wheeled Trialce – models were produced between 1940 and 1944.

1969 BSA B40, 343cc, ex-MOD, restored.
£1,400–1,600 *BOC*

Miller's is a price GUIDE not a price LIST

1978 Cotton Military Prototype, 249cc, Rotax disc-valve 2-stroke engine, 5-speed gearbox, Grimeca front disc brake.
£4,000–£4,200 *COEC*

This bike is the sole prototype built by Cotton for evaluation by the British Army. It was well received by all involved, but the MoD placed the contract with Can Am and Armstrong, and Cotton ceased trading shortly after.

1979 Testi Militar, 49cc, fan-cooled 2-stroke, 8-speed gearbox.
£1,000–1,200 *MVT*

Testi motorcycles saw service with both the Italian and Norwegian armies, and were also available to civilian buyers. These machines were imported into the UK by Mick Walker of Wisbech during the late 1970s and early 1980s.

MONKEY BIKES

1967 Honda CZ100, 49cc, overhead-valve horizontal single.
£2,100–2,300 *S*

Honda's original Monkey Bike, the CZ100, ran from 1961 to 1967.

1970 Honda Z50K2, 49.5cc, overhead camshaft, 41.4 x 49.5mm bore and stroke, 2.5bhp at 6,000rpm.
£1,250–1,750 *RIM*

1977 Italjet Pack-A-Way, 49cc, single-horizontal-cylinder 2-stroke engine, automatic transmission.
£500–550 *MAY*

The Pack-A-Way could be folded up and transported in the boot of a car.

1980 Honda Z50R, 49cc, original, unused.
£2,000–2,200 *BKS*

The Z50R reflected the styling of Honda's competition machines at the time, while retaining the characteristics of a Monkey Bike. It was a popular choice as a child's machine because it could also accommodate an adult. It is one of the few Z50 models that cannot be registered for road use without making changes to the factory specification.

l. **1981 Honda Z50J Ltd,** 49.5cc, overhead-camshaft single.
£3,500–3,750 *BKS*

Produced in limited numbers, the Z50J Ltd had a special chrome and silver finish that set it apart from the standard model. Its teardrop petrol tank had a winged Honda badge on each chrome side panel, and a silver centre panel with black pinstriping. The saddle was covered in cream vinyl instead of the usual black.

1986 Honda Z50RD Ltd, original, unused condition.
£3,500–3,750 *BKS*

The Z50R Ltd was identical to the scrambler-styled Z50R in all but finish. It featured chrome plate to all surfaces that normally would have been finished in red paint. Other detail differences included a red – instead of black – saddle and red handlebar grips. This particular example is believed to be one of only 10 such machines in the UK.

1988 Honda ST DAX, 49cc.
£600+ *PC*

RACING BIKES

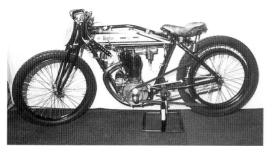

1912 Rudge Brooklands Racer, 499cc.
£10,000+ *REC*

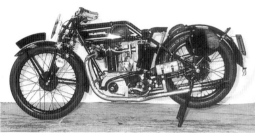

1928 Sunbeam Works TT90, 493cc.
£17,000+ *BKS*

The 1928 Senior TT had all the promise of a great race with a top-class entry, but it was dogged by rain, and many of the star riders retired. Marstons entered a cosmopolitan team of Arcangeli (Italian), Franconi (Swiss), Dodson (English) and Simcock (Australian) on TT90 models, fitted with the new 'bull nose' fuel tank. Despite a tumble at Keppel Gate on the sixth lap, Dodson clung to Graham Walker (on a Rudge) and, when he retired 10 miles from the finish, went on to win the wettest ever Senior by an eight minute margin. It was a glorious third victory for Sunbeam, who also secured the coveted Team Prize. This particular machine is thought to be one of the victorious works bikes from the 1928 event.

c1925 Moto Guzzi C4V, 498.7cc, overhead-camshaft 4 valve horizontal single, 88 x 82mm bore and stroke.
£30,000+ *AtMC*

During the early 1920s, the recently established Guzzi concern gained international fame by winning the European Championship at Monza, followed a few weeks later by the German Grand Prix. Both victories were gained by the latest racer, the C4V.

1935 New Imperial Grand Prix, 245cc, 4-speed foot-change gearbox, girder forks, rigid frame.
£6,000–6,500 *PM*

New Imperial won no less than six TTs, all in the 250cc class, except in 1924, when they did the double and took a 350cc win as well. Their last TT victory was in 1936.

 # Miller's Motorcycle Milestones

Velocette KTT MkVIII 349cc (*British 1939*)
Value £10,000–15,000
A Velocette won the first ever 350cc world road-racing championship series in 1949, and repeated that performance in the following year for good measure. So how could such a relatively small, family-owned marque have achieved such success? The answer was a very special motorcycle, the single-cylinder, overhead-camshaft KTT.

Velocette machines had been competing in the TT since 1913, and in 1926 Alec Bennett really put the name on the map when he won the Junior (350cc) TT on one of the company's new overhead-camshaft models. This design, the forerunner of the KTT, went on to achieve numerous Continental victories and win two more TTs, before being eclipsed by Rudge and Norton machinery.

A Velocette comeback began in 1934, when Walter Rusk finished third in the Senior (500cc) TT on a larger-capacity version of the 350 model.

On the production front, the first over-the-counter KTT racers had appeared in 1928, while in the following year, another TT victory had added impetus to their sales.

Design changes took place as the years passed, the first of any significance occurring in 1932,

when a redesigned cylinder head appeared. This was fitted with hairpin valve springs, which had been found necessary with engine revolutions rising above 6,000rpm. Other improvements included a 14mm spark plug, a more compact oil pump and a change in cylinder head material to a bi-metal aluminium-bronze. Finally, the frame was modified to carry a larger 3½ gallon fuel tank, and a new four-speed gearbox fitted. With all these changes, the KTT was sold as the MkIV. The MkV arrived for 1935, incorporating many improvements that had been developed on the works models.

During 1936 and 1937, the KTT was not offered, but in 1938 the MkVIII made its debut. Again, this featured many improvements gleaned from the factory racers (a swinging-arm frame had been used on works models from 1936 onwards). On the eve of WWII, Velocette decided to update the KTT, giving rise to the definitive MkVIII. Its most noticeable feature was the works-type swinging-arm rear suspension – a first on a production racer.

Employing a 10.9:1 compression ratio, the MkVIII was capable of over 110mph – a magnificent performance for its day. As proof of the machine's ability, Velocettes took 25 of the first 35 places in the 1939 Junior TT.

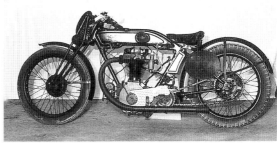

c1928 Norton Model 18, 490cc.
£4,725–5,000 *BKS*

Introduced for 1923, the Model 18 was Norton's first overhead-valve production machine.

1949 Triumph Grand Prix, 498cc, overhead-valve
pre-unit twin, 63 x 80mm, 40bhp at 7,200 rpm,
maximum speed 120mph, concours condition.
£12,000+ *PC*

*Built in small numbers between January 1948 and the
end of 1950, the Grand Prix was based on the 1946
Senior Manx Grand Prix winner, ridden by Irishman
Ernie Lyons. Unlike later Triumph twin-carburettor
models, such as the Bonneville, the GP had parallel-
mounted, rather than splayed, instruments.*

1949 Velocette KTT Racer,
348.3cc, double overhead camshafts,
74 x 81mm bore and stroke.
£14,000–15,000 *Vel*

*The final production KTTs were built in 1949,
the same year that Freddie Frith won the 350cc
World Championship for Velocette. Bob Foster
repeated the feat in 1950. The period
photograph shows Tommy Woods with his
works KTT after winning a race at Marseille,
France, in March 1950. In the process, he beat
riders such as Fergus Anderson, Enrico
Lorenzetti and Nello Pagani. This particular
machine is an ex-works racer, which would
have been ridden by riders such as Frith,
Foster and Woods.*

1956 BSA DB32 Racer, 348cc, overhead-valve
single, 26bhp at 7,500rpm, RRT2 gearbox, restored
1992–93, unused since, excellent condition.
£5,000+ *BKS*

*Introduced in 1954, the CB model Gold Star
adopted a new head and barrel featuring much
heavier finning than before. Other changes
included EN36 crankpin material and eccentric
rocker spindles to reduce the weight of the valve
train. An Amal GP carburettor replaced the TT
instrument on Clubman models, and a swept-back
exhaust was fitted. In 1955, the CB was superseded
by the DB model, the engine of which benefited
from improved lubrication and a change to the
cylinder liner. At the same time, clip-ons became
standard on the Clubman model, and the famous
'twittering' silencer became available. This marked
the final form for the 350, although the 500 would
see yet more changes to become the DBD.*

1956 Norton 30M Manx, 499cc, double-overhead-camshaft single, Amal GP carburettor, Lucas 2M TT racing magneto, Manx close-ratio 4-speed gearbox, clutch and forks, twin-leading-shoe front brake, conical rear hub, 19in wheel rims, Featherbed frame, mesh-type fly screen, modified with coil valve springs, otherwise original, excellent condition.
£21,000+ *S*

This particular machine was originally supplied to Slazenger of Horsbury, near Wakefield, who ran a racing team. It was a show model ridden by Jack Brett (the cam box is stamped 'JB') and later Alan Trow. Brett came into prominence as a member of the Norton works team in 1951, when he was placed fifth in the 350cc World Championship. By 1955, AMC owned Norton and AJS, and works entries were discouraged. However, production models continued to be made available to selected riders for certain races, and Slazenger, with assistance from Lord Montagu, provided support for a limited programme through 1955–56. The period photograph shows Alan Trow with Mrs Gwendoline Slazenger and the Slazenger Trophy at Brands Hatch in September 1956.

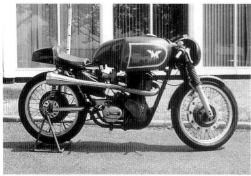

1961 Matchless G50, 496cc, single overhead camshaft, Amal GP carburettor, 4-speed close-ratio gearbox, largely original, modifications include high-level exhaust, seat and alloy muffs on front hub, unrestored.
£8,200–8,500 *S*

1957 BSA Gold Star Special, 499cc, overhead-valve single, Norton Featherbed frame, Marzocchi front forks, Yamaha TD2/TR2 brakes, alloy oil and fuel tanks.
£4,500–4,750 *PM*

1959 Ducati 125 Grand Prix, 124cc, double-overhead-camshaft single, 55.25 x 52mm bore and stroke, 17bhp at 12,500rpm 5- and 6-speed gear clusters, Amadora brakes, original.
£10,000+ *PC*

This machine is an ex-works Desmo racer with a factory-fitted valve-spring head. The exposed engine shows the shaft and gears that drive the camshafts, plus a Dell'Orto SS racing carburettor. The large pipe is part of an additional oil feed to the top end of the engine.

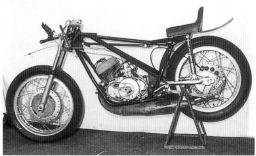

c1962 Yamaha TD1 Prototype, 246cc, early TD1 frame, later (1967) TD1C engine and rear brake, Robinson/Fahron front brake.
£2,500–3,000 *RIM*

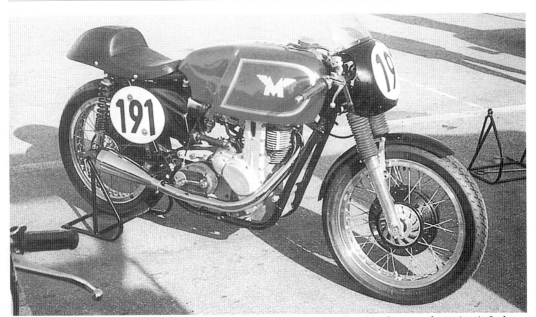

1962 Matchless G50 Racer, 496cc, restored to original condition, offered with spare short-circuit fuel tank, seat, exhaust system and top-half fairing.
£29,000+ *BKS*

The disappointing performance of the Matchless G45 twin-cylinder racer prompted AMC to develop an overbored version of the firm's successful AJS 7R 350 single as a contender for the 500 class. Using cycle parts that were virtually identical to the 7R, the prototype G50 first ran in 1958, production versions becoming available in the following year. With a claimed power output of over 50bhp, it should have been a winner, but it was not until after manufacture ceased in 1962 that tuner/entrants in Britain and the USA began to exploit the model's full potential. Frame and suspension developments – most notably by Tom Arter and Colin Seeley – kept the G50 competitive into the 'Japanese era', and it continues to be the mainstay of the 500 class in classic racing today. This particular machine, one of only 180 G50s built, was ridden in classic events during the 1980s by former Grand Prix racer New Zealander Hugh Anderson, four times World Champion for Suzuki.

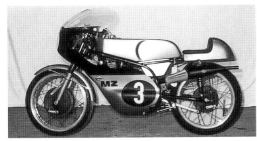

l. **1965 MZ Works RE125,** 124cc, disc-valve single-cylinder 2-stroke, water-cooled, 6-speed gearbox.
£16,000+ *BKS*

The Lancastrian rider Derek Woodman was signed by MZ in 1964, replacing Alan Shepherd who moved to Honda for 1965. This particular RE125 was one of the factory machines campaigned by Woodman during 1965. He finished third in the 125cc World Championships that year, his best placing being runner-up in the Czech round at Brno.

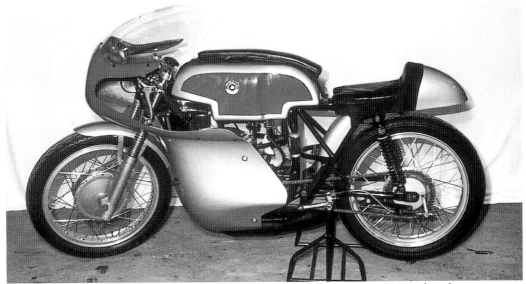

1966 Bultaco 250 TSS Racer, 244cc, piston-port 2-stroke single, 72 x 60mm bore and stroke, water-cooled, 38bhp (at crank) at 9,500rpm, 6-speed gearbox, original except for Boyer ignition.
£2,750–3,000 *BKS*

The 125 and 250 production TSS racers were offered with water-cooling from 1965 onwards.

l. **c1967 Aermacchi Ala d'Oro,** 344cc, external-flywheel engine, 5-speed gearbox, Ceriani forks, four-leading-shoe front brake, original. **£9,000+** *AtMC*

1969 Motobi Formula 3, 238cc, overhead-valve horizontal single, 5-speed gearbox, spine frame. **£2,000–2,200** *BKS*

Founded by Giovanni Benelli after he left the Pesaro factory, Motobi built machines that were characterised by the distinctive 'power egg' engine unit. Most Motobi racers were 175s, but a few 203cc and 238cc models were also constructed. They were successful in Italian junior racing events during the 1960s and early 1970s.

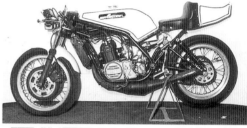

1977 Barton Sparton Three, 482cc, water-cooled 3 cylinder 2-stroke, 64 x 50mm bore and stroke, dry clutch. **£3,500–4,000** *RIM*

The Sparton was designed by Barry Hart. In original 458.3cc form, it was timed at 146mph in the 1975 Isle of Man TT, sharing 'fastest machine' honours with the works Kawasakis.

l. **1975 Yamaha TZ700,** 694cc, 4 cylinder water-cooled 2-stroke, 64 x 54mm bore and stroke, twin shock absorbers, wire wheels, triple disc brakes. **£6,500+** *RIM*

r. **1978 Yamaha TZ250E,** 247.3cc, water-cooled twin-cylinder 2-stroke, 54 x 54mm bore and stroke, 50bhp at 10,500rpm, 6-speed gearbox, fully restored. **£2,200–2,500** *BKS*

Yamaha introduced water-cooling to create the TZ series in 1973. This was followed by disc brakes instead of drums, then cantilever rear suspension on the 'E' model.

1979 MBA 125 Racer, 124.1cc, disc-valve twin-cylinder 2-stroke MBA engine, 43.9 x 41mm bore and stroke, 6-speed gearbox, Derby Racing Services square-section aluminium chassis, monoshock suspension unit between steering head and sub-frame, Campagnolo wheels, triple Brembo brakes.
£2,200–2,500 *RIM*

1979 Yamaha Spondon TZ750 Racer, 748cc, 4 cylinder water-cooled 2-stroke.
£2,900–3,200 *BKS*

Although Yamaha's four-cylinder TZ750 was endowed with more than enough power, its handling left a lot to be desired. In response, a number of specialist manufacturers attempted to improve on the Yamaha frame, one of the most successful being the Derby-based Spondon concern.

1980 Yamaha TZ500G, 499cc, water-cooled 4 cylinder engine, cantilever rear suspension with alloy swinging arm, triple disc brakes.
£10,000+ *VJMC*

Imported to the UK from Australia, this ex-Graeme Geddes machine was one of only 50 made by the factory.

1997 Matchless G50 Replica Rolling Chassis, by George Beale.
£13,000+ *GB*

SCOOTERS

1919 ABC Scootamota, 125cc, runs well.
£1,400–1,850 *AT*

The idea was simple – take a child's push scooter and add an engine. The first was the American-made Autoped of 1915–16, which was followed by the British Scootamota of 1919.

1954 Lambretta 150D, 148cc, single-cylinder 2-stroke, 57 x 58mm bore and stroke, 6bhp at 4,750rpm.
£1,700–2,000 *IVC*

1955 Zündapp R201 Bella, 198cc, single-cylinder 2-stroke, original condition.
£1,250–1,500 *VMSC*

Over 27,000 R201 scooters were built in 1955–56, the most of any Bella model.

Miller's
Motorcycle Milestones

Zündapp KS600 597cc (*German 1941*)
Value £4,000–5,000
On 17 September 1917, Zünderland
Apparatebau GmbH, better known as Zündapp,
was founded in Nuremberg. The new company,
which employed 1,800 workers, was a joint
venture between three established firms at the
height of WWI. The commercial stimulus was
war production, and the product came
under pressure to find a suitable peacetime
occupation. Then, it was bought by Dip Ing
Fritz Neumeyer in 1919.

Motorcycles began to be built in 1921. They
were the forerunners of more than three million
machines manufactured by the company during
the following 63 years.

The first model to enter series production was
powered by a 211cc, British-designed, Levis single-
cylinder, 2-stroke engine. By the end of 1924, other
models, powered by engines of Zündapp's own
design, had been added to the range. Four years
later, in 1928, the company constructed an entirely
new factory at Nuremberg-Schweinau. This
opened the following year and was hailed as the
most modern in the world.

Then came the Depression, but Zündapp
managed to come through this, and by 1933 the

German economy was making an impressive
recovery. This period saw the company's first
flat-twin four-stroke models, with capacities of
398 and 498cc, designed by Richard Küchen. All
were characterised by an unconventional, but
very successful, chain-and-sprocket gearbox.

On the very eve of WWII, Zündapp introduced
several new models, including the 597cc
(75 x 67.6mm) KS600 flat-twin. Although
retaining the chain-operated gearbox, the
newcomer sported overhead-valve rather than
sidevalve cylinder heads, and was clearly
developed from the KS500, sharing the same
pressed-steel frame with blade-type girder front
forks equipped with a central spring. Other
notable features included shaft final drive and a
four-speed gearbox with foot or hand operation.

From March 1940, all supplies to civilian
customers were discontinued until the end of
the conflict. Zündapp's 250,000th motorcycle,
a KS750, was built in March 1942.

Post-war, an improved version of the KS600,
the KS601, entered production. Nicknamed the
'Green Elephant', this remained available until
1959, as the last of the Zündapp flat-twin
series. Its memory is celebrated, however, by
Germany's famous winter motorcycle event,
the Elephant Rally.

1957 Maico Maicoletta M250, 247cc, 14bhp,
one owner from new.
£1,000–1,250 *MOC*

*The Maicoletta was designed by engineers Pohl
and Tetzlaff in secrecy, away from the eyes of all
but a few of the Maico management. Models with
175 and 277cc engines were also built.*

1957 Lambretta D150, 149cc.
£1,200–1,400 *MAY*

*The D150 was the same as the LD model, but minus
side panels; the 'L' designation stood for 'luxury'.*

1958 Lambretta LD150, 149cc, fitted with period accessories including screen, chrome trims, seat covers, spare wheel/cover, carrier and bag.
£1,700–2,000 *MAY*

1958 Lambretta Li150 Series 1, 148cc, horizontal single-cylinder 2-stroke, 57 x 58mm bore and stroke.
£1,000–1,500 *MAY*

The Li150 Series 1 was built from April 1958 until October 1959, and a total of 99,043 were made in that 18 month period. The Li (also in 125cc form) was based on the TV Series 1, which had been launched in September 1957.

1958 Maico Mobil, 197cc.
£2,000–2,500 *MOC*

The Mobil was launched in 1951 with a 148cc engine. In 1954, Maico updated the design with two new models in 173cc (61 x 59.5mm) and 197cc (65 x 59.5mm) capacities. The Mobil provided motorcycle handling and superb weather protection, but as one journalist put it, was styled 'like the Hindenberg Zeppelin on wheels.'

1959 Zündapp Bella, 198cc, original.
£850–900 *MAY*

From 1956, Zündapp used a swinging front fork in place of the original telescopics of the earlier Bella models.

1959 Lambretta Li150 Series 1, 149cc.
£1,200–1,500 *MAY*

The particular Li150 was one of the last Series 1 machines made.

1960 Lambretta TV Series 2, 174cc, restored, good condition.
£1,700–1,900 *MAY*

Innocenti moved quickly to replace the troublesome TV Series 1 with the Series 2, which appeared in January 1959, only 16 months after the former had been introduced. The Series 2 had a new engine with bore and stroke dimensions of 62 x 58mm. Mid-way through the Series 2 programme, its 23mm carburettor was replaced by a 21mm instrument to promote smoother running.

1960 DMW Bambi, 99cc, Villiers 4F 2-stroke engine, 2-speed gearbox.
£1,000–1,500 *DSCM*

The Bambi's chassis was made of steel pressings like the Vespa's, with a triangulated front fork controlled by a spring inside the steering column. The rear swinging arm was also constructed of steel pressings, as were the disc-type wheels.

1964 Lambretta TV175 Series 3 Slimline, 174cc.
£1,200–1,400 *MAY*

Although the 1957 Maserati motorcycle and the little-known, American-made Midget Motors Autocycle of 1961 got there first, Lambretta's TV175 Series 3 of 1962 was the first mass-produced powered two-wheeler in the world to be equipped with a disc front brake.

1964 Maico Maicoletta, 277cc.
£1,000–1,250 *MOC*

Many consider Maico's 277cc Maicoletta the finest scooter ever built. It certainly had one of the largest engines ever to be shoehorned into a production scooter.

r. **1966 Lambretta 150 Special X (SX150),** 149cc, good condition.
£1,250–1,500 *MAY*

The 150 Special X was a performance version of the basic Li series. A total of 31,238 were built between October 1966 and January 1969.

Miller's
Motorcycle Milestones

Vespa 98cc Scooter (*Italian 1946*)
Value £2,000–2,800
The Piaggio company was founded in 1884 in Genoa, where it made woodworking machinery for the local shipbuilding industry. In 1901, it turned to railway rolling stock, then aircraft. An aviation factory was built at Pisa before WWI, and a car manufacturing plant was acquired at Pontedera in 1924. The latter was extended for aero-engine and aircraft production to such an extent that, by 1939, Piaggio had 10,000 workers and had assumed a leading role in Italian aviation. Its most famous wartime type was the P108, the only Italian four-engined heavy bomber to see service during WWII.

By 1944, nothing was left of Piaggio's production facilities but bombed-out buildings and a work-force awaiting its next meal ticket. With the design of a small two-stroke auxiliary engine and hardly any machine tools, factory boss Enrico Piaggio called a management meeting. The result was the Vespa scooter which, together with the similar Lambretta, put Italy back on wheels. The Vespa embodied the very latest technology in motorcycle, automotive and aviation engineering. Production began in 1946, using a 98cc (50 x 50mm), single-cylinder, two-stroke engine. A mere 100 examples of the original Vespa were constructed before a refined version entered mass production later that year. In 1948, the first 125cc (56.5 x 49.8mm) Vespa arrived, effectively replacing the original 98cc model.

By the early 1950s, the Vespa was not only a familiar sight on the roads of Italy, but also around the world. Moreover, a number of manufacturing licences had been granted, notably to Douglas in Great Britain and Hoffman in Germany.

A new 150cc (57 x 57mm) Vespa made its debut in 1954. Then, on 28 April 1956, the millionth machine rolled off the production lines. At that point, the Italian plant was turning out 10,000 Vespas a month from a work-force of 4,000.

Throughout its first 20 years, the Vespa marque fought tooth and nail with its Lambretta rival (owned by Innocenti) for supremacy in the scooter sales war. As Piaggio are still churning out many thousands of Vespas a year in Italy (450,000 in 1980 for example), it can be said that they finally won the battle, even though Lambrettas (and Vespas, for that matter) are still being manufactured under licence in many countries.

l. **1966 Vespa Sprint 150,** 150cc, single-cylinder 2-stroke, 57 x 57mm bore and stroke, 7.1bhp at 5,000rpm, 4-speed gearbox, dual seat, fully restored.
£1,250–1,500 *MAY*

Piaggio replaced its 150GL with the 150 Sprint in 1965.

r. **1966 Lambretta 200 Special X (SX200),** 198cc, good condition.
£1,000–1,250 *MAY*

The 200 Special X was equipped with a revised version of the TV Series 3 mechanical front disc brake.

SIDECARS

1915 New Hudson with Mills & Fulford Sidecar, 499cc, sidevalve single.
£6,000–7,000 *BKS*

The origins of the New Hudson marque go back to 1890, when the Birmingham concern of Hudson & Edmunds made the Hudson bicycle. By 1911, having initially fitted Minerva clip-on engines to their own bicycle frames, they designed a 499cc sidevalve machine of their own. Examples of this machine soon appeared in competition, and their success ensured New Hudson a place in the UK market. This example was one of the last to be made for civilian use before the company turned to producing munitions during WWI. It has been fitted with a Mills & Fulford caster-wheel basket sidecar from about 1906.

1919 Quadrant with Sidecar, 499cc.
£4,000–4,500 *BKS*
The Birmingham-built Quadrant was made from 1901 until 1927, the firm being headed by W. L. Lloyd, one of the pioneers of motorcycle production.

1924 AJS Model G with Sidecar, 799cc, sidevalve V-twin, very good condition.
£5,500–5,750 *CotC*

1919 Matchless Model H with Sidecar, 998cc, Swiss inlet-over-exhaust MAG V-twin engine, side exhaust, parallelogram undamped rear suspension, spare wheel.
£7,500–9,000 *S*
Matchless machines built after WWI were renowned for their advanced specification.

l. **1922 James Model 7 with James Sidecar,** 750cc, sidevalve V-twin.
£6,500–7,500 *BKS*
Produced by The James Cycle Co Ltd of Greet, Birmingham, the James motorcycle was marketed as 'The King of Motorcycles'. The Model 7 was one of a comprehensive range of two- and four-stroke machines offered in 1922. It is equipped with an original James single-seater sidecar.

1950 BSA A7 with Swallow Sidecar, 495cc,
overhead-valve pre-unit twin, iron head,
alloy rocker box, plunger frame.
£2,000–2,500 *HCH*

r. **1951 Norton 633 Big 4 with
Swallow Sports Sidecar,** 596cc.
£2,500–2,850 *PM*

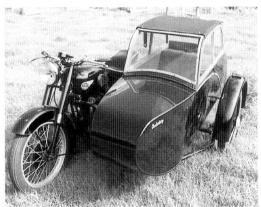

**1953 BSA A10 Golden Flash with Canterbury
Sidecar,** 646cc, overhead-valve pre-unit twin.
£3,000–3,200 *AT*

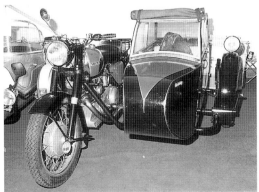

1961 Panther 120S with Canterbury Sidecar,
650cc, single cylinder, restored, excellent condition.
£2,500–2,750 *LSC*

SPECIALS

1995 Douglas TT Replica (c1931), 348cc, horizontally-opposed all-alloy twin-cylinder engine, 3-speed gearbox, TT-type frame and wheels, engine completely rebuilt and set up to run on dope, all original parts completely restored and overhauled, bills totalling £2,813.
£11,250–12,500 *BKS*

1952 BSA/Ariel Square 4 Special, 998cc, overhead-valve Ariel Square Four engine, BSA cycle parts, telescopic forks, swinging-arm rear suspension, non-standard frame, 'King and Queen' seat.
£2,500–3,000 *AOM*

l. **1950s Norton/Rudge 500 Special,** 499cc, 1930s overhead-valve twin-port single-cylinder Rudge engine, 4-speed BSA gearbox, mainly 1950s Norton cycle parts.
£3,000–3,500 *PM*

1960s Triton Café Racer, 649cc, pre-unit Triumph T120 motor, Amal Concentric carburettors, 5-speed gearbox, Norton wideline frame, Manx-style fuel tank, chrome-plated tool box and oil tank, swan-neck clip-ons, fork gaiters.
£3,500–4,000 *BLM*

1970s Triumph/BSA Special, 649cc, Triumph T120 Bonneville unit engine, pre-unit BSA frame, Triumph Trident 'ray-gun' silencers, alloy fuel tank, dual racing seat, alloy wheel rims, flat handlebars.
£1,500–2,000 *PC*

1970s Norton V-twin Special, 788cc, Norton AMC clutch and gearbox, Featherbed frame, Commando forks.
£4,000–5,000 *OxM*

1984 Harris/Ducati 900, 864cc, Ducati 900SS Desmo V-twin engine, Harris monoshock chassis, originally supplied by Sports Racing, concours condition.
£3,500–4,000 *PC*

MEMORABILIA
Books & Brochures

The Motor Cycle, No. 1, Vol 1,
Tuesday, March 31st 1903,
11 x 8in (28 x 20cm).
£12–15 LF

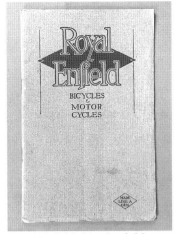

Royal Enfield, Bicycles & Motor
Cycles illustrated trade catalogue,
c1920, 8¾ x 5¾in (22 x 14.5cm).
£18–22 CGC

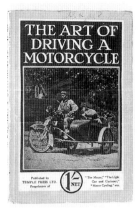

The Art of Driving a Motorcycle,
c1920, 7½ x 5in (19 x 12.5cm).
£15–20 DM

Omega Motor Cycles, brochure,
1927, 8½ x 5½in (21.5 x 14cm).
£20–25 DM

Levis Two Stroke
Motor Cycles
brochure, 1927,
9½ x 5½in (24 x 14cm).
£25–28 DM

r. Scott Motor
Cycles brochure,
1932, 10 x 5½in
(25.5 x 14cm).
£25–30 DM

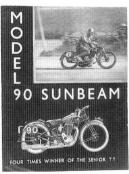

Sunbeam Model 90,
brochure, 1932,
11 x 9in (28 x 23cm).
£20–25 DM

l. Excelsior 1939
brochure, 9½ x 7in
(24 x 18cm).
£25–30 DM

A Marble Arch Motor
Supplies motor factor's
catalogue, c1936,
£15–20 LF

The Britax Scooterette brochure,
1955, 8½ x 5½in (21.5 x 14cm).
£2–3 *DM*

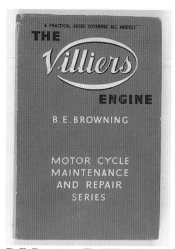

B. E. Browning, *The Villiers Engine*,
maintenance and repair manual,
1956, 7½ x 5in (19 x 12.5cm).
£5–8 *DM*

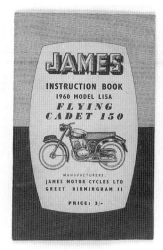

An instruction book for the 1960
James Model L15A Flying Cadet
150, 8½ x 5½in (21.5 x 14cm).
£4–6 *DM*

A workshop instruction manual
for 1945–55 Triumph twin-
cylinder models, c1960,
8½ x 5½in (21.5 x 14cm).
£12–15 *DM*

Philip H. Smith, *The Greatest of
all Trials*, a history of the classic
Scott motorcycle trials, 1963,
8½ x 5½in (21.5 x 14cm).
£12–15 *DM*

C. F. Caunter, *Motor Cycles, a
technical history*, 1970, 8½ x 5½in
(21.5 x 14cm).
£9–12 *LF*

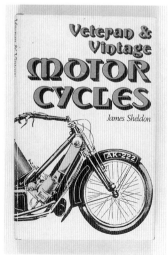

James Sheldon, *Veteran &
Vintage Motor Cycles*, 1971,
9 x 6in (23 x 15cm).
£15–20 *DM*

An owner's handbook for 1971
Triumph 500cc models, 1971,
8½ x 5in (21.5 x 12.5cm).
£4–6 *DM*

An instruction manual for
the BSA Model D10, 1971,
8½ x 5in (21.5 x 12.5cm).
£4–6 *DM*

Noel B. Pope, *Full Chat*,
1972, 9½ x 6in (24 x 15cm).
£10–15 *DM*

Luigi Rivola, *Illustrated Colour
Guide, Racing Motorcycles*,
1977, 8 x 5in (20.5 x 12.5cm).
£8–10 *DM*

Photographs & Posters

A photograph commemorating the
England vs Australia Speedway Test
Match, 16 June 1930, Nottingham,
13 x 15in (33 x 38cm).
£4–6 *DM*

A Motos Automoto advertising
poster, by M. Ponty, French,
1930s, linen backed,
47¼ x 31½in (120 x 80cm).
£650–700 *S*

A Lambretta advertising
poster, c1960.
£40–50 *MAY*

A poster advertising motorcycle racing
at Snetterton, Norfolk, 31 July 1958,
20½ x 15in (52 x 38cm).
£90–100 *LE*

Miscellaneous

A set of 50 Wills's cigarette
cards, depicting motorcycles,
New Zealand issue, 1926.
£125–150 *ATF*

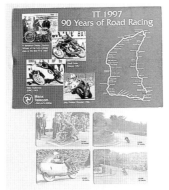

A set of 4 telephone cards, issued
for the 1997 Isle of Man TT and
commemorating 90 years of road
racing, 10th set.
£10–15 *JCa*

The Norwich Trophy.
£1,200–1,500 *COYS*

*The Norwich Trophy was
awarded to the rider who broke
an existing lap record by the
greatest margin at Snetterton. It
was presented to Mike Hailwood
in 1960, 1961 and 1962, also for
holding all four solo class lap
records at Snetterton in the 1958
season. That year, Hailwood
made his mark by winning
against all the established aces to
take ACU Star awards for
season-long excellence in the 125,
250 and 350cc classes.*

Locate the Source
*The source of each illustration in Miller's can be found by
checking the code letters below each caption with the Key
to Illustrations.*

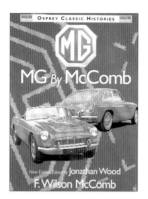
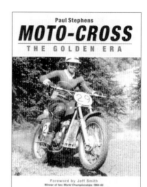

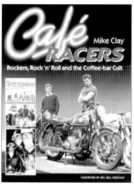
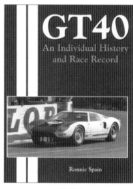

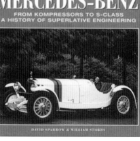

GLOSSARY

We have attempted to define some of the terms that you will come across in this book. If there are any other terms or technicalities you would like explained or you feel should be included in future editions, please let us know.

ACU – Auto Cycle Union, who control a large part of British motorcycle sport.

Advanced ignition – Ignition timing set causing firing before the piston reaches centre top, variation is now automatic.

Air-cooling – Most motorcycles rely on air-cooling to the atmosphere.

Air intake – The carburettor port admitting air to mix with fuel from the float chamber.

AMCA – Amateur Motor Cycle Association, promoters of English off-road events.

APMC – The Association of Pioneer Motor Cyclists.

Auto Cycle Club – Formed in 1903 it was the original governing body of motorcycle sport, in 1907 became the Auto Cycle Union.

Automatic inlet valve – Activated by the engine suction. Forerunner of the mechanically operated valve.

Balloon tyres – Wide section, low pressure, soft running tyres, used on tourers for comfort.

Beaded-edge tyres – Encased rubber beads in channel on wheel rim.

Belt drive – A leather or fabric belt from engine or gearbox to rear wheel.

BHP – A measure of engine output, eg to lift 33,000lb one foot in a minute requires one horsepower.

BMCRC – British Motor Cycle Racing Club, formed in 1909.

BMF – British Motorcycle Federation.

Bore/stroke ratio – Cylinder diameter ratio to stroke.

Caliper – Brake disc device with operating pistons.

Cam – Device for opening and closing a valve.

Camshaft – The mounting shaft for the cam, can be in low, high or overhead position.

Carburettor – Used to produce the air/fuel mixture.

Chain drive – Primary form of drive from engine to gearbox and secondary gearbox to rear wheel.

Combustion chamber – Area where the fuel/air mixture is compressed and fired, between piston and cylinder head.

Compression ratio – The fuel/air mixture compression degree.

Crankcase – The casing enclosing the crankshaft and its attachments.

Crankshaft – The shaft for converting the up-and down piston motion into rotary.

Cylinder – Containing the piston and capped by the cylinder head, is the site of the explosion which provides power.

Cylinder head – In a vertical engine caps off the top end of the cylinder. In a 4-stroke engine carries the valves.

Damper – Used for slowing down movement in suspension system or as crankshaft balance.

Displacement – The engine capacity or amount of volume displaced by the movement of the piston from bottom dead centre to top dead centre.

Distributor – A gear driven contact sending high tension current to spark plugs.

DOHC – Double overhead camshaft.

Dry sump – Two oil pumps, one supplying oil to the bearings from a tank, the other to return it to the tank.

Earles forks – An unusual front fork design. A long leading link and rigid pivot through both links behind the wheel.

Featherbed – A Norton frame, designed by Rex and Crommie McCandless, Belfast, used for racing machines from 1950, road machines from 1953.

FIM – Federation Internationale Motorcycliste, controls motorcycle sport worldwide.

Flat twin – An engine with 2 horizontally opposed cylinders, or 4 to make a Flat Four.

Float – A plastic or brass box which floats upon the fuel in a float chamber and operates the needle valve controlling the fuel.

Flywheel – Attached to the crankshaft this heavy wheel smooths intermittent firing impulses and helps slow running.

Friction drive – An early form of drive using discs in contact instead of chains and gears.

Gearbox – Cased trains of pinion wheels which can be moved to provide alternative ratios.

Gear ratios – Differential rates of speed between sets of pinions to provide higher or lower rotation of the rear wheel in relation to the engine.

GP – Grand Prix, an international race to a fixed formula.

High camshaft – Mounted high up on the engine to shorten the pushrods in an ohv formation.

IOE – Inlet over exhaust, a common arrangement with an overhead inlet and side exhaust.

Leaf spring – Metal blades clamped and bolted together, used in suspension many years ago.

Magneto – A high tension dynamo producing current for the ignition spark. Superseded by coil ignition.

Main bearings – Bearings in which the crankshaft runs.

Manifold – Collection of pipes supplying mixture or taking away fumes.

MCC – The Motor Cycling club which runs sporting events. Formed in 1902.

Moped – A light motorcycle of under 50cc with pedals attached.

OHC – Overhead camshaft, can be either single or double.

OHV – Overhead valve engine.

Overhead cam – An engine with overhead camshaft or camshafts operating its valves.

Overhead valve – A valve mounted in the cylinder head.

Pinking – A distinctive noise from an engine with over-advanced ignition or inferior fuel.

Piston – The component driven down the cylinder by expanding gases.

Post-vintage – A motorcycle made after December 31, 1930 and before January 1, 1945.

Pressure plate – The plate against which the clutch springs react to load the friction plates.

Pushrods – Operating rods for overhead valves, working from cams below the cylinder.

Rotary valve – A valve driven from the camshaft for inlet or exhaust and usually a disc or cylinder shape. For either 2-or 4-stroke engines.

SACU – Scottish Auto Cycle Union, which controls motorcyle sport in Scotland.

SAE – Society of Automotive Engineers. Used in a system of classifying engine oils such as SAE30, IOW/50 etc.

Shock absorber – A damper, used to control up-and-down movement of suspension or to cushion a drive train.

Silencer – Device fitted to the exhaust system of an engine whereby the pressure of the exhaust gases is considerably reduced before reaching the outer air.

Swinging arm – Rear suspension by radius arms carrying the wheel and attached to the frame at the other end.

Torque – Twisting rotational force in a shaft, can be measured to show at what point an engine develops most torque.

INDEX TO ADVERTISERS

BIBLIOGRAPHY

Bacon, Roy; British Motorcycles of the 1930s, Osprey, 1986
Bacon, Roy; Matchless & AJS Restoration, Osprey, 1993
Bacon, Roy; Norton Twin Restoration, Osprey, 1993
Bacon, Roy; Triumph Twins & Triples, Osprey, 1990
Birkitt, Malcolm; Harley-Davidson, Osprey, 1993
Champ, Robert Cordon; Sunbeam S7/S8 Super Profile, Haynes, 1983
Davis, Ivor; It's a Triumph, Haynes, 1980
Morley, Don; Classic Motorcycles, Triumph, Osprey, 1991
Stuart, Garry; and Carroll, John; Classic Motorcycles, Indian, Osprey, 1994
Tragatsch, Erwin, ed; The New Illustrated Encyclopedia of Motorcycles, Grange Books, 1993

Walker, Mick; Aermacchi, Transport Source Books, 1995
Walker, Mick; Benelli, Transport Source Books, 1996
Walker, Mick; British Racing Motorcycles, Redline Books, 1998
Walker, Mick; and Carrick, Rob; British Performance 2-strokes, Transport Source Books, 1998
Walker, Mick; Ducati Twins, Osprey, 1998
Walker, Mick; Hamlyn History of Motorcycling, Hamlyn, 1997
Walker, Mick; Italian Racing Motorcycles, Redline Books, 1998
Walker, Mick; Morini, Transport Source Books, 1996
Walker, Mick; MZ, Transport Source Books, 1996
Woollett, Mick; Norton, Osprey, 1992

DIRECTORY OF MUSEUMS

Battlesbridge Motorcycle Museum
Muggeridge Farm, Maltings Road, Battlesbridge, Essex
SS11 7RF Tel: 01268 769392/560866
An interesting collection of classic motorcycles & scooters
in a small informal 'museum'. Open Sundays 10.30am–4pm.
Adults £1, children free.

Birmingham Museum of Science & Industry
136 Newhall Street, Birmingham, B3 1RZ
Tel: 0121 303 1651
A small collection of motorcycles right in the heart of the
city. Open Monday to Saturday 9.30am–5pm. Sunday
2pm–5pm. Closed December 25–26, and January 1.
Admission free.

Bristol Industrial Museum
Princes Wharf, City Docks, Bristol, Avon BS1 4RN
Tel: 0117 925 1470
A small collection of Bristol-made Douglas machines,
including the only surviving V4 of 1908. There is also a
1972 Quasar. April–October open Saturday to Wednesday
10am–5pm. Closed Thursdays and Fridays.
November–March open weekends 10am–5pm, closed
December 25–27 and January 1. Adults £1.05, Over 60s
50p, under 16s and educational parties etc free.

Brooklands Museum
The Clubhouse, Brooklands Road, Weybridge, Surrey
KT13 0QN Tel: 01932 857381
The birthplace of British motorsport and aviation,
Brooklands has several motorcycles on display.
March–October open weekends 10am–5pm.
October–March open weekends 10am–4pm.
Guided tours at 10am and 4pm on Tuesdays, Wednesdays
and Thursdays. Adults £4, OAPs & students £3, children £2.

Craven Collection of Classic Motorcycles
Brockfield Villa, Stockton-on-the-Forest, Yorks YO3 9UE
Tel: 01904 488461/400493
A private collection of over 180 Vintage & Post-War
Classic Motorcycles. Open to the public on first Sunday of
every month and Bank Holidays, 10am–4pm. Club visits &
private parties arranged. Adults £2.60, children under ten
years free.

Foulkes-Halbard of Filching
Filching Manor, Jevington Road, Wannock, Polegate,
Sussex BN26 5QA Tel: 01323 487838
A collection of 30 motorcycles, including pre-1940s
American bikes ex-Steve McQueen, as well as
100 cars dating from 1893–1993. Open Easter to end
October Thurs, Fri, Sat & Sun 10.30–4.00pm.
Adults £3.50, OAPs and children over five £2.50.

Grampian Transport Museum
Main Street, Alford, Aberdeenshire, AB33 8AD
Tel: 019755 62292
A collection of 30–40 machines ranging from a 1902
Beeston Humber to a Norton F1 Mods and Rockers caff
display with Triton and Triumph Tina scooter.
Competition section includes 1913 Indian twin and 1976
Rob North replica Trident racer. Open March 28–October
31, 10am–5pm. Adults £3.00, children £1.25, OAPs £2.00,
family ticket £7.00.

Haynes Sparkford Motor Museum
Sparkford, Yeovil, Somerset BA22 7LH
Tel: 01963 440804
Collection of over 30 machines from a 1914 BSA onwards.
Video theatre. Bookshop. Open Monday to Sunday
9.30am–5.30pm. During school summer holiday open until
7.30pm. Closed December 25–26 and January 1. Adults
£4.95, OAPs £4.25, children £2.95, Family ticket £12.95.

Sammy Miller Museum
Gore Road, New Milton, Hampshire BH25 6TF
Tel: 01425 619696
Sammy Miller is a living legend in the world of motorcycle
racing, and what started out as a hobby 30 years ago has
become a collection of what is arguably the best selection
of competition motorcycles in the country. The museum
was opened in 1983 by John Surtees and is much more
than a static collection. All bikes are in working order and
wherever possible are run in classic bike events
throughout the year. Many of the racing bikes are still
fully competitive. At present there are 200 bikes in the
Museum, many of them extremely rare. New exhibits are
being sought all the time to add to the collection, with
much of the restoration work being carried out on the
premises by Sammy Miller himself. There are interesting
artefacts and items of memorabilia connected to the
motorcycling world on display, including many cups and
trophies won by Sammy over the years. A typical
motorcycle workshop of 1925 has been reconstructed,
showing a large display of the tools used at that time.

Open April–October 10.30am–4.30pm every day,
November–March 10.30am–4.30pm Sats and Suns.
The museum is situated 15 miles west of Southampton
and 10 miles east of Bournemouth at New Milton, Hants.

Mouldsworth Motor Museum
Smithy Lane, Mouldsworth, Chester, CH3 8AR
Tel: 01928 731781
Open February to end November Sundays & Bank
Holidays 12.00–5.00pm, Wednesdays in July & August
12.00–5pm.

Murray's Motorcycle Museum
Bungalow Corner, TT Course, Isle of Man
Tel: 01624 861719
Collection of 140 machines, including Hailwood's 250cc
Mondial and Honda 125cc and the amazing 500cc
4 cylinder roadster designed by John Wooler.
Open May to September 10am–5pm. Adults £3,
OAPs and children £2.

Museum of British Road Transport
St. Agnes Lane, Hales Street, Coventry, Warwickshire
CV1 1PN
Tel: 01203 832425
Collection includes 65 motorcycles, with local firms such
as Coventry Eagle, Coventry Victor, Francis-Barnett,
Triumph and Rudge well represented. Close to city centre.
Open every day except December 24–26, 10am–5pm.
Admission free.

Museum of Transport
Kelvin Hall, 1 Bunhouse Road, Glasgow, G3 8DP
Tel: 0141 357 3929
Small collection of motorcycles includes Automobile
Association BSA combination.
Open Monday to Saturday 10am–5pm. Sunday
11am–5pm. Closed December 25 and January 1.
Admission free.

Myreton Motor Museum
Aberlady, East Lothian, Scotland EH32 0PZ
Tel: 01875 870288
Small collection of motorcycles includes 1926 350cc
Chater-Lea racer and Egli Vincent.
Open Easter to October 10am–6pm and October to Easter
10am–5pm. Closed December 25 and January 1.
Adults £3, children £1.

National Motor Museum
Brockenhurst, Beaulieu, Hants SO42 7ZN
Tel: 01590 612123/612345
Important motorcycle collection. Reference and
photographic libraries. Open Easter to September
10am–6pm, October to Easter 10am–5pm.
Closed December 25. Adults £8.75, OAPs/students £7.50,
children 4–16 £6.75, Family ticket £28.50 (includes
museum, rides and drives, Monastic Life Exhibition and
entry to Palace House and grounds).

National Motorcycle Museum
Coventry Road, Bickenhill, Solihull, B92 0EJ
Tel: 0121 704 2784
Open 10.00am–6.00pm, closed December 25. Adults £4.50,
children aged 5–16 and OAPs £3.25.

Royal Museum of Scotland
Chambers Street, Edinburgh, EH1 1JF
Tel: 0131 225 7534
Small display of engines and complete machines includes
the world's first 4 cylinder motorcycle, an 1895 Holden.
Open Monday to Saturday 10am–5pm. Sunday 12.00–5pm,
Tuesdays open till 8pm. Closed December 25, January 1.
Admission free.

Science Museum
Exhibition Road, South Kensington, London SW7 2DD
Tel: 0171 589 3456
Interesting collection of engines and complete machines,
including cutaway BSA A10 and Yamaha XS1100.
Recent additions to displays include 1940 500cc BMW and
1969 Honda CB750. Open Monday to Saturday
10am–5.50pm. Sunday 11am–5.50pm. Closed December
24–26. Adults £6, OAPs and children 5 years and over
£3.00, disabled free. The bulk of the Science Museum's
motorcycle collection is stored at Wroughton Airfield
near Swindon, Wiltshire. Tel: 01793 814466

Stanford Hall Motorcycle Museum
Stanford Hall, Lutterworth, LE17 6DH
Tel: 01788 860250
The collection of older machines and racers.
Open Saturdays, Sundays, Bank Holiday Mondays and
following Tuesdays Easter to September, 2.30–5.30pm.
(Special events and Bank Holidays 12–6pm). Admission to
grounds: Adults £2.20, children £1.00
Motorcycle Museum: Adults £1.00, children 35p.

DIRECTORY OF MOTORCYCLE CLUBS

If you wish to be included in next year's directory or if you have a change of address or telephone number, please would you inform us by 30 April 1999. Entries will be repeated in subsequent editions unless we are requested otherwise.

ABC Owners' Club, D. A. Hales, The Hedgerows, Sutton St Nicholas, Hereford HR1 3BU Tel: 01432 880726

Aermacchi Harley-Davidson Motor Club, Tuninfluiter 74, 3906, NS Veenendaal, The Netherlands

Aircooled RD Club, Susan Gregory (Membership Secretary), 6 Baldwin Road, Burnage, Greater Manchester M19 1LY Tel: 0161 286 7539

AJS & Matchless Owners' Club, Northants Classic Bike Centre, 25 Victoria Street, Irthlingborough, Northamptonshire NN9 5RG Tel: 01933 652155

AMC Owners' Club, c/o Terry Corley, 12 Chilworth Gardens, Sutton, Surrey SM1 3SP

Android Classics, 70 Broadway, Frome, Somerset BA11 3HE Tel: 01373 471087

Ariel Owners' Club, Andy Hemingway, 80 Pasture Lane, Clayton, Bradford, Yorks BD14 6LN Tel: 01274 882141

Ariel Owners' Motor Cycle Club, Swindon Branch, 45 Wheeler Avenue, Swindon, Wiltshire SN2 6HQ

BMW Club, c/o John Lawes (Vintage Secretary), Bowbury House, Kirk Langley, Ashbourne, Derbyshire DE6 4NJ Tel: 01332 824334

Bantam Enthusiasts' Club, c/o Vic Salmon, 16 Oakhurst Close, Walderslade, Chatham, Kent ME5 9AN

Benelli Motobi Riders' Club, 43 Sherrington Road, Ipswich, Suffolk IP1 4HT Tel: 01473 461712

Best Feet Forward MCC, Ian Leslie, 14 Haredale Road, London SE24 0AF Tel: 0171 274 7526

BMW Owners' Club, c/o Mike Cox, 22 Combermere, Thornbury, Bristol, Gloucestershire BS12 2ET Tel & Fax: 01454 415358

Bristol & Avon Roadrunners' Motorcycle Club, 177 Speedwell Road, Speedwell, Bristol, Glos BS5 7SP

Bristol & District Sidecar Club, 158 Fairlyn Drive, Kingswood, Bristol, Gloucestershire BS15 4PZ

Bristol Genesis Motorcycle Club, Burrington, 1a Bampton Close, Headley Park, Bristol, Gloucestershire BS13 7QZ Tel: 0117 978 2584

British Motor Bike Owners' Club, c/o Ray Peacock, Crown Inn, Shelfanger, Diss, Norfolk IP22 2DL

British Motorcycle Club of Guernsey, c/o Ron Le Cras, East View, Village De Putron, St Peter Port, Guernsey, Channel Islands GY1

British Motorcycle Owners' Club, c/o Phil Coventry, 59 Mackenzie Street, Bolton, Lancashire BL1 6QP

British Motorcyclists' Federation, Jack Wiley House, 129 Seaforth Avenue, Motspur Park, New Malden, Surrey KT3 6JU

British Two-Stroke Club, 5 Madden Close, Swanscombe, Kent DA16 0DH

British Two-Stroke Club, Ralph Hynn, Membership Secretary, 32 Glebe Gardens, Harlington, Beds LU6 5PE

Brough Superior Club, c/o Piers Otley, 6 Canning Road, Felpham, Sussex PO22 7AD

BSA Owners' Club, Rob Jones, 44 Froxfield Road, West Leigh, Havant, Hampshire PO9 5PW

CBX Riders' Club (United Kingdom), 9 Trem y Mynydd, Abergele, Clwyd LL22 9YY Tel: 01745 827026

Chiltern Vehicle Preservation Society, Chiltern House, Aylesbury, Buckinghamshire HP17 8BY Tel: 01296 651283

Christian Motorcyclists' Association, PO Box 113, Wokingham, Berkshire RG11 5UB

Classic Kawasaki Club (Formerly The Kawasaki Triples Club), PO Box 235, Nottingham, Notts NG8 6DT

Classic Racing Motorcycle Club Ltd, Peter Haylock (Membership Sec), 19 Kenilworth Avenue, Harold Farm, Romford, Essex RM3 9ME

Cossack Owners' Club, Phil Hardcastle, 19 Elms Road, Bare, Morecambe, Lancashire LA4 6AP

Cotton Owners' & Enthusiasts' Club, Stan White, 62 Cook Street, Avonmouth, Bristol, Dorset BS11

Derbyshire and Staffordshire Classic Motorcycle Club, 51 Westwood Park Newhall, Swadlincote, Derbyshire DE11 0R5 Tel: 01283 214542

Dot Owners' Club, c/o Chris Black, 115 Lincoln Avenue, Clayton, Newcastle-upon-Tyne, Tyne & Wear ST5 3AR

Ducati Owners' Club, Martin Littlebury, 32 Lawrence Moorings, Sawbridgeworth, Hertfordshire CM21 9PE

Edge & District Vintage Motorcycle Club, 10 Long Lane Larkton, Malpas, Cheshire SY14 8LP

Exeter British Motorcycle Club, 7 Parkens Cross Lane, Pinhoe, Exeter, Devon EX1 3TA

Exeter Classic Motorcycle Club, c/o Martin Hatcher, 11 Newcombe Street, Heavitree, Exeter, Devon EX1 2TG

Federation of Sidecars, Barry Miller (Membership Sec), 1 Bartin Cottage, Sutton Cullompton EX15 1NF Tel: 01884 34533

Fellowship of Christian Motorcyclists, Janice Thomson, The Treehouse, 22 Charlotte Gardens, Collier Row, Romford, Essex RM5 2ED

FJ Owners' Club, Membership Sec Karen Everett, 13 Severn Close, Charfield, Wotton-under-Edge, Gloucestershire GL12 8TZ Tel: 01454 261737

Forgotten Racing Club, Mrs Chris Pinches, 73 High Street, Morton, Bourne, Lincolnshire PE10 0NR Tel: 01778 570535

Francis-Barnett Owners' Club, 58 Knowle Road, Totterdown, Bristol, Gloucestershire BS4 2ED

Gilera Network, Pete Fisher, 4 Orton Grove, Penn, Wolverhampton WV4 4JN Tel: 01902 337626

Gold Star Owners' Club, c/o George Chiswell, 43 Church Lane, Kitts Green, Birmingham, West Midlands B33 9EG

Goldwing Owners' Club, 82 Farley Close, Little Stoke, Bristol, Gloucestershire BS12 6HG

Greeves Owners' Club, c/o Dave McGregor, 4 Longshaw Close, North Wingfield, Chesterfield, Derbyshire S42 5QR

Greeves Riders' Association, Dave & Brenda McGregor, 4 Longshaw Close, North Wingfield, Chesterfield, Derbyshire S42 5QR Tel: 01246 853846

Guernsey Motorcycle & Car Club, c/o Graham Rumens, Glenesk, Sandy Hook, St Sampsons, Guernsey, Channel Islands GY2 4ER

Harley-Davidson Manufacturers' Club Tel: 01280 700101

Harley-Davidson Owners' Club, 1 St Johns Road, Clifton, Bristol, Gloucestershire BS8 2ET

Harley-Davidson Riders' Club of Great Britain, SAE to Membership Secretary, PO Box 62, Newton Abbott, Devon TQ12 2QE

Harley Owners' Group, HOG UK, The Bell Tower, High Street, Brackley, Northamptonshire NN13 7DT Tel: 01280 700101

Hedingham Sidecar Owners' Club, Membership Sec John Dean, Hollington Fields Cottage, Fole Lane, Stoke-on-Trent Tel: 01889 507389

Hesketh Owners' Club, Peter White, 1 Northfield Road, Soham, Cambridgeshire CB7 5UE

Historic Raleigh Motorcycle Club, c/o R Thomas, 22 Valley Road, Solihull, West Midlands B92 9AD

Honda Monkey Club, 28 Newdigate Road, off Red Lane, Coventry, Warwickshire CV6 5ES Tel: 01203 665141

Honda Owners' Club (GB), Membership Sec, 61 Vicarage Road, Ware, Hertfordshire SG12 7BE Tel: 01932 787111

Indian Motorcycle Club, c/o John Chatterton (Membership Secretary), 183 Buxton Road, Newtown, Disley, Stockport, Cheshire SK12 3RA Tel: 01663 747106 (after 6pm)

International CBX Owners' Association, 9 Trem y Mynydd, Abergele, Clwyd LL22 9YY Tel: 01745 827026

International Laverda Owners' Club, c/o Alan Cudipp, 29 Claypath Road, Hetton-le-Hole, Houghton-le-Spring, Tyne & Wear DH5 0EL

International Motorcyclists' Tour Club, James Clegg, 238 Methane Road, Netherton, Huddersfield, Yorkshire HD4 7HL Tel: 01484 664868

Italian Motorcycle Owners' Club, Membership Secretary, 14 Rufford Close, Barton Seagrave, Kettering, Northamptonshire NN15 6RF Tel: 01536 726385

Jawa-CZ Owners' Club, John Blackburn, 39 Bignor Road, Sheffield, Yorkshire S6 1JD

Kawasaki GT Club, D. Shucksmith, Club Sec, Flat K, Lichfield Court, Lichfield Road, Walsall, West Midlands WS4 2DX Tel: 01922 37441

Kawasaki Owners' Club, c/o John Dalton, 37 Hinton Road, Runcorn, Cheshire WA7 5PZ

Kawasaki Riders' Club, Gemma, Court 1, Concord House, Kirmington, Humberside DN39 6YP

Kickstart Club Torbay, c/o Eddie Hine, 12 Vale Road, Kingskerswell, Newton Abbot, Devon TQ12 5AE

L E Velo Club Ltd, Kevin Parsons, Chapel Mead, Blandford Hill, Winterbourne, Whitechurch, Blandford, Dorset DT11 0AB

Laverda Owners' Club, c/o Ray Sheepwash, 8 Maple Close, Swanley, Kent BR8 7YN

LE Velo Owners' Club, P. Walker, Grantley House, Warwicks Bench, Guildford, Surrey GU1 3SZ

London Douglas Motorcycle Club, c/o Reg Holmes (Membership Secretary), 48 Standish Avenue, Stoke Lodge, Patchway, Bristol, Gloucestershire BS12 6AG

London Sidecar Club Tel: 01923 229924

Macclesfield British Motorcycle Owners' Club, 47 Cooksmere Lane, Sandbach, Cheshire CW11 1BQ

Maico Owners' Club, c/o Phil Hingston, 'No Elms', Goosey, Faringdon, Oxon SN7 8PA Tel: 01367 710408
Marston Sunbeam Register, IMI Marston Ltd, Wobaston Road Fordhouses, Wolverhampton, West Midlands WV10 6QJ
Military Vehicle Trust, PO Box 6, Fleet, Hants GU13 9PE
Morgan Three-Wheeler Club Ltd, Dennis Plater, Membership Secretary, Holbrooks, Thoby Lane, Mountnessing, Brentwood, Essex CM15 0TA Tel: 01277 352867
Morini Owners' Club, c/o Richard Laughton, 20 Fairford Close, Church Hill, Redditch, Worcestershire, B98 9LU
Morini Riders' Club, c/o Kevin Bennett, 1 Glebe Farm Cottages, Sutton Veney, Warminster, Wiltshire BA12 7AS Tel: 01985 840055
Moto Guzzi Club GB, Andy Harris, (Membership Sec), 158 Vale Road, Windsor, Berkshire SL4 5JN
Motorcycle Action Group, PO Box 750, Kings Norton, Birmingham, West Midlands B30 3BA
MV Agusta Club GB, c/o Martyn Simpkins, 31 Baker Street, Stapenhill, Burton-on-Trent, Staffs DE15 9AF
MV Agusta Owners' Club, A. Elderton, 108 Thundersley Park Road, South Benfleet, Essex SS7 1ES
National Association for Bikers with a Disability (NABD), Rick Hulse, 39 Lownorth Road, Wythenshaw, Greater Manchester M22 0JU
National Autocycle & Cyclemotor Club, 92 Waveney Road, Ipswich, Suffolk IP1 5DG
National Hill Climb Association, 43 Tyler Close, Hanham, Bristol, Gloucestershire BS15 3RG Tel: 0117 944 3569
National Scooter Riders' Association, PO Box 32, Mansfield, Nottinghamshire NG19
National Sprint Association, Judith Sykes (Secretary), 10 Compton Street, Clifton, York, Yorkshire YO3 6LE
National Trailers Owners' Club (NaTo), 47c Uplands Avenue, Rowley, Regis Warley, West Midlands B65 9PU
New Imperial Owners' Association, Lyndhurst House Victoria Road, Hayling Island, Hampshire PO11 0LU Tel: 01705 469098
North Devon British Motorcycle Owners' Club, 47 Old Town, Bideford, Devon EX39 3BH Tel: 01237 472237
Norton Owners' Club, c/o Dave Fenner, Beeches, Durley Brook Road, Durley, Southhampton, Hants SO32 2AR
Norton Owners' Club, Cambridge Branch, William Riches (Secretary), 8 Coombelands Rd, Royston, Hertfordshire SG8 7DW Tel: 01763 245131
Norton Rotary Enthusiasts' Club, Alan Jones, 112 Fairfield Crescent, Newhall, Swadlingcote DE11 0TB
Panther Owners' Club, Graham & Julie Dibbins, Oakdene, 22 Oak Street, Netherton, W Midlands DY2 9LJ
Professional and Executive Motorcyclists' Club, Paul Morris, Stonecroft, 43 Finedon Road, Irthlingborough, Northamptonshire NN9 5TY
Raleigh Safety Seven and Early Reliant Owners' Club, c/o Mick Sleap, Membership Secretary, 17 Courtland Avenue, Chingford, London E4 6DU Tel: 0181 524 6310
Riders for Health, The Old Vicarage, Norton, Daventry, Northamptonshire NN11 5ND Tel: 44 (0) 1327 300047
Rotary Owners' Club, c/o David Cameron, Dunbar, Ingatestone Road, Highwood, Chelmsford, Essex CM1 3QU
Royal Enfield Owners' Club, c/o John Cherry (REOC Secretary), Diments Cottage, 50 Dorchester Road, Stratton, Dorchester, Avon DT2 9RZ
Rudge Enthusiasts' Club Ltd, c/o Colin Kirkwood, 41 Rectory Green, Beckenham, Kent BR3 4HX Tel: 0181 658 0494
Scott Owners' Club, Brian Marshall, Walnut Cottage, Abbey Lane, Aslockton, Nottingham, Nottinghamshire NG13 9AE Tel: 01949 851027
Shrivenham Motorcycle Club, 12-14 Townsend Road, Shrivenham, Swindon, Wiltshire SN6 8AS
Sidecar Register, c/o John Proctor, 112 Briarlyn Road, Birchencliffe, Huddersfield, Yorkshire HD3 3NW
Street Specials Motorcycle Club inc Rickman O/C, Harris O/C & Featherbed O/C, c/o Dominic Dawson, 12 St Mark's Close, Gosport, Hampshire PO12 2DB Tel: 01705 501321
Sunbeam MCC, 18 Chieveley Drive, Tunbridge Wells, Kent TN2 5HQ Tel: 01892 535671
Sunbeam Owners' Club, David Jordan (Membership Sec), 72 Chart Lane, Reigate, Surrey RH2 7EA
Sunbeam Owners' Club, Stewart Engineering, Church Terrace, Harbury, Leamington Spa, Warwickshire CV33 9HL
Sunbeam Owners' Fellowship, PO Box 7, Market Harborough, Leicestershire LE16
Surrey Vintage Scooter Club, 8 Amesbury Close, Worcester Park, Surrey KT4 8PW Tel: 0181 337 2534
Suzuki Kettle Club, 66 Provene Gardens, Waltham Chase, Southampton, Hampshire SO32 2LE
Suzuki Owners' Club, PO Box 7, Egremont, Cumbria CA22 2GE
Tamworth & District Classic Motorcycle Club Tel: Tamworth 281244

The Vmax Club, 87 Honiton Road, Wyken, Coventry, Warwickshire CV2 3EF Tel: 01203 442054
Trail Riders' Fellowship, Tony Stuart, 'Cambrea', Trebetherick, Wadebridge, Cornwall PL27 6SG Tel: 01208 862960
Trident and Rocket 3 Owners' Club, John Atkins (Club Secretary), 47 Underhill Road, Benfleet, Essex SS7 1EP
Triumph Motorcycle Club, 6 Hortham Lane, Almondsbury, Bristol, Gloucestershire BS12 4JH
Triumph Owners' Club, 101 Great Knightleys, Basildon, Essex SS15 5AN
Triumph Triples Club, H. J. Allen, 50 Sylmond Gardens, Rushden, Northamptonshire NN10 9EJ
Velocette Owners' Club, Stuart Smith, 18 Hazel Road, Rubery, Birmingham, West Midlands B45 9DX
Velocette Owners' Club, Vic Blackman (Secretary), 1 Mayfair, Tilehurst, Reading, Berkshire RG3 4RA
Veteran Grass Track Riders' Association (VGTRA) Tel: 01622 204745
Vincent HRD Owners' Club, c/o John Wilding (Information Officer), Little Wildings, Fairhazel, Piltdown, Uckfield, Sussex TN22 3XB Tel: 01825 763529
Vincent Owners' Club, Andy Davenport, Ashley Cottage, 133 Bath Road, Atworth, Wiltshire SN12 8LB
Vintage Japanese Motorcycle Club, PO Box 515, Dartford, Kent DA1 3RE
Vintage Motor Cycle Club, Allen House, Wetmore Road, Burton-on-Trent, Staffs DE14 1TR Tel: 01283 540557
Vintage Motor Cycle Club, (Peterborough Branch), Jeremy Boycott Thurston (Sec), 34 Heath Road, Helpston, Peterborough, Cambridgeshire PE6 7EG
Vintage Motor Scooter Club, c/o Ian Harrop, 11 Ivanhoe Avenue, Lowton St Lukes, Nr Warrington, Cheshire WA3 2HX
Vintage Motorcycle Club of Ulster, c/o Mrs M Burns, 20 Coach Road, Comber, Newtownards, Co Down, Ireland BT23 5QX
Virago Owners' Club, John Bryning, River Green House, Great Sampford, Saffron Walden, Essex CB10 2RS Tel: 01799 586578
Woman's International Motorcycle Association, PO Box 612, Bristol, Gloucestershire BS99 5UQ
Yamaha Riders' Club, Alan Cheney, 11 Lodden Road, Farnborough, Hampshire GU14 9NR
ZI Owners' Club, c/o Sam Holt, 54 Hawthorne Close, Congleton, Cheshire CW12 4UF

INDEX

Italic page numbers denote colour pages; **bold** numbers refer to information and pointer boxes

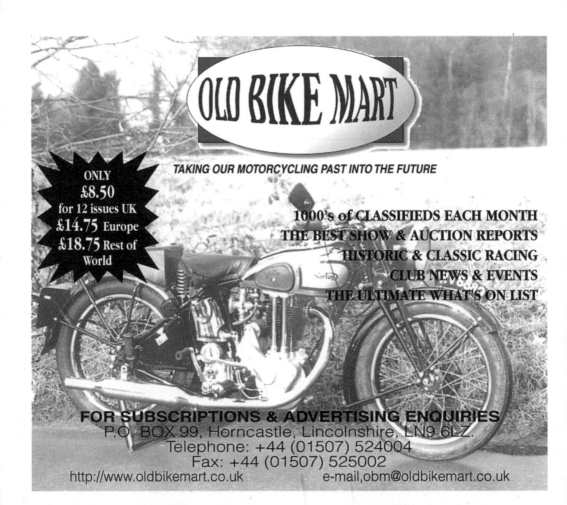